The Internationalization of Banks

Palgrave Macmillan Studies in Banking and Financial Institutions

Series Editor: Professor Philip Molyneux

The Palgrave Macmillan Studies in Banking and Financial Institutions will be international in orientation and include studies of banking within particular countries or regions, and studies of particular themes such as Corporate Banking, Risk Management, Mergers and Acquisitions, etc. The books will be focused upon research and practice, and include up-to-date and innovative studies on contemporary topics in banking that will have global impact and influence.

Titles in the series include:

Yener Altunbas, Blaise Gadanecz and Alper Kara
SYNDICATED LOANS
A Hybrid of Relationship Lending and Publicly Traded Debt

Santiago Carbó, Edward P.M. Gardener and Philip Molyneux
FINANCIAL EXCLUSION

Franco Fiordelisi and Philip Molyneux
SHAREHOLDER VALUE IN BANKING

Munawar Iqbal and Philip Molyneux
THIRTY YEARS OF ISLAMIC BANKING
History, Performance and Prospects

Philip Molyneux and Munawar Iqbal
BANKING AND FINANCIAL SYSTEMS IN THE ARAB WORLD

Andrea Shertler
THE VENTURE CAPITAL INDUSTRY IN EUROPE

Alfred Slager
THE INTERNATIONALIZATION OF BANKS
Patterns, Strategies and Performance

Palgrave Macmillan Studies in Banking and Financial Institutions
Series Standing Order ISBN 1–4039–4872–0

You can receive future titles in this series as they are published by placing a standing order. Please contact your bookseller or, in case of difficulty, write to us at the address below with your name and address, the title of the series and the ISBN quoted above.

Customer Services Department, Macmillan Distribution Ltd, Houndmills, Basingstoke, Hampshire RG21 6XS, England

The Internationalization of Banks

Patterns, Strategies and Performance

Alfred Slager

palgrave
macmillan

First published 2006 by
PALGRAVE MACMILLAN
Houndmills, Basingstoke, Hampshire RG21 6XS and
175 Fifth Avenue, New York, N.Y. 10010
Companies and representatives throughout the world

PALGRAVE MACMILLAN is the global academic imprint of the Palgrave Macmillan division of St. Martin's Press, LLC and of Palgrave Macmillan Ltd. Macmillan® is a registered trademark in the United States, United Kingdom and other countries. Palgrave is a registered trademark in the European Union and other countries.

ISBN 13: 978–1–4039–9874–3   hardback
ISBN 10: 1–4039–9874–4   hardback

This book is printed on paper suitable for recycling and made from fully managed and sustained forest sources.

A catalogue record for this book is available from the British Library.

Library of Congress Cataloging-in-Publication Data

Slager, Alfred, 1967–
    The internationalization of banks : patterns, strategies and performance / by Alfred Slager.
        p. cm. – (Palgrave Macmillan studies in banking and financial institutions)
    Includes bibliographical references and index.
    ISBN 1–4039–9874–4 (cloth)
    1. Banks and banking, International. I. Title. II. Series.

    HG3881.S539 2006
    332.1′5–dc22   2006041783

10   9   8   7   6   5   4   3   2   1
15   14   13   12   11   10   09   08   07   06

Printed and bound in Great Britain by
Antony Rowe Ltd, Chippenham and Eastbourne

Contents

List of Tables

List of Figures

List of Abbreviations

ATM	Automatic Teller Machine
BCCI	Bank of Credit and Commerce International
BIS	Bank for International Settlements
CI	Cost-Income ratio
DOI	Degree of Internationalization
EBIC	European Banks International Company
EC	European Community
EEC	European Economic Community
EMS	European Monetary System
EMU	European Monetary Union
EU	European Union
FDI	Foreign Direct Investment
FDIC	Federal Deposit Insurance Corporation
G-7	Forum of the world's largest seven industrial economies
IBA	International Banking Act
IMF	International Monetary Fund
IT	Information Technology
LDC	Less Developed Countries
LIBOR	London Interbank Offered Rate
LTCM	Long Term Capital Management
M&A	Mergers and Acquisitions
NAFTA	North American Free Trade Agreement
OECD	Organization for Economic Cooperation and Development
TMT	Telecoms, Media and Technology
UNTNC	United Nations Centre on Transnational Corporations

Name Conventions

Banks' names have changed frequently over time. Whenever possible the most recent name of the bank has been used, unless this does not match with the period of analysis. For example, the 1980s clearly refer to Lloyds Bank, and not to Lloyds TSB, the name used since the 1995 acquisition.

Preface

Preoccupation with the international or "global" dimension has become one of the outstanding features for the banking industry in the past decades. Bank managers regularly invoke the globalization mantra to substantiate bold expansion strategies abroad. While a fair number of these international mergers and acquisitions succeed, many do not. Major changes are indeed occurring; this book however takes a more balanced view of the internationalization process that has transformed the banking industry worldwide.

The approach of this book is to ask three simple questions. First, what are the international strategic patterns pursued by the world's largest banks? Second, to which extent have these strategies benefited bank profitability, stability and shareholder performance? Third, what are key themes for banks with successful or struggling internationalization strategies in the near future? A robust combination of fact finding, analyses and case studies form the ingredients for this book.

The book is roughly divided in three parts. Readers who want a quick overview of this book should read the first chapter; Chapter 1 describes the structure of the book with more explanation than the table of contents, and summarizes the main arguments of the chapters. Chapters 2 to 4 lay down the groundwork for analyzing internationalization strategies of banks. Chapter 2 discusses the main challenges that the world's largest banks have faced since the 1980s. Chapter 3 discusses the theoretical framework of international banking – why do banks internationalize and what are their expectations? Chapter 4 focuses on the world's largest banks, the object of my study – what are their key indicators and how do they differ from the other banks in the world.

Chapters 5 to 7 form the second part of this book and focus on patterns of internationalization, and the effect on performance. Chapter 5 discusses internationalization developments of the world's largest banks, while Chapter 6 unearths the international strategy development process. Chapter 7 analyses the performance of internationalized banks from different perspectives.

Chapter 8 focuses on future strategic directions. Which banks have successful internationalization strategies? What banks are least likely to succeed in international banking and what strategic changes could they pursue to alter this? Which international banks are best equipped for the challenges of regionalization, European integration and can achieve sustainable profitability?

The book is intended for two or more audiences. The first comprises banking and finance professionals, interested in a helicopter view of one of the major developments affecting the future of their industry, aiming to understand the strategic implications of the internationalization for banks. Also, the book provides insights for banking analysts, interested in key drivers for performance and valuation of banks. The second audience comprises university courses, either at the advanced undergraduate or graduate level, and executive development programs in international banking and financial markets. Participants in these courses may find it helpful to understand the structure and dynamics of the international banking industry, as background or in preparation for their careers in the banking and securities industry.

I owe great intellectual debt to Dick van Wensveen from the RSM/Erasmus University who supervised my PhD thesis which forms the basis for this book. He provided valuable feedback on various chapters of this book. I am also grateful to my father, who helped immeasurably in shaping the content of the book. Of course, none of them is to blame for the inevitable weaknesses and errors that remain.

Alfred Slager

1
Introduction

This book is concerned with the growing importance of the internationalization of banks. Banking strategy increasingly evolves into international banking strategy with geographic and regulatory borders receding, and information technologies rapidly expanding. For bank managers, future prospects are increasingly determined by their banking activities outside the home country. Nine of the 25 largest banks in the world now have more foreign than domestic activities; something only the British Standard Chartered Bank could claim ten years earlier. The interdependency between banks and foreign banking markets has also increased dramatically; cross border mergers and acquisitions are on the rise.

Outside their home countries the 25 largest banks in the world held over 10.2 trillion US dollars in assets, employed 916,000 staff and generated 36% of their total banking income in 2004. Recent international landmarks in the banking industry are the Spanish bank Santander acquiring the British savings bank Abbey National, or ABN AMRO expanding in Italy with the purchase of Banca Antonveneta. UniCredito acquired the ailing Hypovereinsbank, eyeing its coveted Eastern and Central European branch network.

The largest banks bask in a long tradition of international banking: many great historic periods are intertwined with banks. Famous landmarks were the Fuggers in the 15th century as banker to the European royal courts; Bank Mees & Hope, a predecessor of Fortis, helped finance the Louisiana Land purchase. The predecessor of JPMorganChase financed in 1860 the Civil War in the United States. In the late 19th century, European banks followed in the slipstream of the colonial expansion ambitions of their governments and created vast international branch networks.

But what do we know about the effects of internationalization: what international strategic patterns do the world's largest banks pursue, and to which extent have these strategies benefited bank profitability, stability and shareholder performance? Also, what internationalization strategies might prove successful for the future? These are the main themes of this book.

Foreign banking has compelling arguments going for it. A loan issued in the United States is similar to that in Europe, so is securities trading, financial advice or back office activities. Trying to take advantage of economies of scale is then an obvious incentive. Serving a domestic client wherever he is deepens the relationship (and long term profitability). Communication technologies provide the means and resources. When a Dutch client enters the Milan office of his domestic bank, his relationship manager has client information, banking products and other services at his fingertips, giving the client a true sense of global relationship. Foreign banking should also help weather the ups and downs of economic cycles. The banking market in the United States may have a different credit cycle than the banking market in Germany; combining these two could smooth earnings, lower reserves needed for bad loans and ultimately improve the bank's market value.

Operating in several markets allows the bank to grow, introduce new products to the foreign market or offer foreign banking products to their clients. Regulators have also regularly spurred the growth of international banking although not always intentionally. The Bank of England intentionally promoted London as a financial center, allowing the offshore market to grow there. The Federal Reserve restrained funding activities by imposing interest rate limits and unintentionally pushed American banks to London, laying the foundations for their sizable investment banking activities and skills there.

Banks in foreign countries sometimes touch upon a raw nerve with clients, regulators and critics of globalization. During the Asian crisis in 1997/98 foreign banks were considered instrumental in deepening and worsening the impact of the crisis. The mistrust is not entirely unfounded. International banking came at times close to a "global" meltdown in the last decades. The misfortunes of banks throughout the 1980s were dominated by the emergence and lack of resolve of the Less Developed Countries (LDC) crises, hitting American and English banks especially hard. The 1990s were marked by the fall of Barings in 1995, the British bank which defaulted because of its uncontrolled derivatives activities in Singapore. This was probably the most spectacular downfall of a bank since the Austrian CreditAnstalt had to close down in 1931. Infamously rising to the challenge of using foreign banking as an asset seeking strategy, Crédit Lyonnais raked up huge losses because of its ill managed international expansion strategy. Restructuring the bank cost the taxpayer 100 billion French francs, or 1.2% of the French GDP in 1999.

International banking and international firms have also become more intertwined. During the accountancy frauds, the largest banks played a dubious role at times. With the demise of Italian Parmalat several of the world's largest banks were involved, providing loans and setting up special finance vehicles.

On the other hand regulators, concerned about systemic risks, crafted one of the few successfully adapted international regulation frameworks: the Basle framework. Also, the "on regular basis" occurring financial crises aside, international banking goes a long way to stabilize foreign banking markets, especially in emerging countries. Banks like ABN AMRO, HSBC or BNP Paribas tend to stay in these markets for the long run, introduce new financial products and other financial innovations that help customers better with their financial needs, besides spurring competition and therefore help make the banking sector more efficient. Overall, research suggests that they stimulate economic growth.

Finally, internationalization poses great competitive challenges for banks, simultaneously competing with each other in different regions and services. HSBC competes in the north east region of the United States with Royal Bank of Scotland for retail clients. In the United Kingdom, competition is at a different level: with Barclays for capital markets and asset management. Then again, HSBC competes head on in Brazil with ABN AMRO and also in France with BNP Paribas. Walter (1988) aptly describes these competitive challenges as a three dimensional matrix where each box is a specific client-product-arena combination. Positioning the bank with the right combinations to gain competitive advantage is a daunting task for any bank manager. The number of "sub" markets to compete in increases substantially, demanding a focused management. Anecdotal evidence in this study suggests that internationally active banks tend to restructure their organization more often than domestic ones.

1.1. A perspective on internationalization

Internationalization of banks is not a new phenomenon. In 1913 there were approximately 2,600 branches of foreign banks worldwide.

The dominating factor at that time was colonization, over 80% of those branches belonged to British banks. The share of foreign banks accounted for one-third of banking assets in Latin America and over one-half in countries like South Africa, Turkey or China (Goldsmith, 1969). The financial empire of J.P. Morgan started out as a partnership financing American civil war loans from England (Chernow, 1990). Over time, innovations in financial instruments, telecommunication, information technology, organization innovation and the growing sophistication of customers have meant a dramatic transformation in the conduct of banking business and client relationships in international banking.

What sets the current internationalization of banks apart, and why does it merit a study? The major reason is that the sheer size of international involvement of banks has increased dramatically (cf. De Nicoló, Bartholomew, Zaman & Zephirin, 2004). Foreign assets of the 30 largest banks as a percentage of total assets have changed from 35% in 1980 to over 41% in 2004. However, the absolute size of foreign assets of the 30 largest banks has risen 16 fold from 650 billion US dollars in 1990 to 10,200 billion US dollars in 2004. The increasing importance of foreign activities has affected the profitability and stability of internationalizing banks in their home country; it can also have serious effects – positive as well as negative – on the host economies.

The vehemence with which banks have pursued internationalization strategies over a longer period also warrants an investigation. The dissolution of the British Empire after 1945 meant that British banks represented the "old" internationalization of banking. American banks on the other hand have been on the rise since the Second World War. American financial aid, exports of American firms and the export of American ideology such as freeing of competition or creation of uniform markets were feeding ground for the internationalization activities of American banks, usually using London as a springboard for activities in Europe and reversing the decline of London as a financial center as a side effect. From the 1960s onwards income in Western economies rose and banks developed more financial products to cater to households and businesses as an increasing scale of firms raised transaction volumes in corporate finance. American banks formed an apparent threat, seeking out the more profitable activities in investment banking in Europe, being equipped with better staff, more financial resources and more experience.

The creation of offshore markets to circumvent (American) regulation and the political potential of seizure of capital belonging to communist states induced the first series of international activities, later propelled by the inflation of capital markets when oil producing countries forced serious wealth transfers. European banks either tried to work together in consortium banks to participate in these activities (Roberts & Arnander, 2001) which in the beginning was a cost saving and knowledge rewarding construction, or set up foreign activities themselves. Redistribution of the surpluses of oil producing countries found their way to emerging markets, with American banks leading the way. The growing volume of loans masked growing economic imbalances, brought to light from 1981 onwards when Latin American countries defaulted in their loans. Internationalization of banks became a worldwide event (United Nations Centre on Transnational Corporations, 1991). Institutions like the IMF aided governments with restructuring loans, dealing with severed banks and capital markets in distress. Governments of the lender banks, especially the United States, faced potential crises at home when the losses in emerging markets were transferred by the large banks to their home country.

A consequence of this restructuring period was that in the 1980s capital strength and adequate supervision of internationally operating banks became major issues for bank regulators. A major coordination initiative took place in the Basle Accord of 1988, creating more transparency and uniformity among regulatory policies for internationally active banks. Among others the Basle Accord became one of the drivers for the Japanese banks to retreat from the international arena. Japanese banks increased international activities sharply from the early 1980s fuelled by strong domestic economic growth, a fast pace of deregulation and large flows of foreign direct investment by Japanese industrial firms. The Japanese stock market decline from 1989 showed that (international) banking strategies had not been based on sound banking practices, affecting bank capital and loan quality at the same time (Canals, 1997). Japanese banks found ways to stave off restructuring of their bad loans for almost a decade, contributing substantially to the prolongation of the domestic economic recession while steadily losing ground in international banking.

A general trend fuelling international activities was the ongoing process of disintermediation from mid-1960: large firms found it more profitable to arrange loans directly with institutional investors, thereby bypassing the role of banks as financial intermediaries. Additionally a structural increase of competition and decrease of interest rates, especially in the 1990s, consequently lowered interest income from the core business of banks. These trends forced banks to reconsider their strategic business portfolios. Non-interest income, especially the high margins of fees and commissions in investment banking, became a promising route. The liberalization of British securities markets in 1984 was followed by an unprecedented acquisition wave where notably American, German and Dutch banks bought British investment banks. By the end of the 1990s British owned investment banks or securities houses in London were few in number; London as an important financial center had become a manifest of internationalization activities of banks.

Internationalization of banks was also a strategic response to further regional integration and deregulation (cf. Group of Ten, 2001, January). In Europe especially, banks were aware that the competition for larger clients extended over the geographic borders, but the competition for retail clients remained a domestic issue. In the mid-1980s European integration created momentum for internationalization in Europe, redefining markets for banking activities on a multinational scale. Mergers and acquisitions became an important strategic tool for banks. They generally took place in two phases: domestic consolidation and then, international expansion; the creation of higher domestic concentration in order to more effectively compete internationally. Opportunity was provided by the capital markets (lower interest rates and higher stock market prices) and the regulators, privatizing banks or not opposing the takeovers.

The close of the decade shows the financial might of just a handful of banks: the top 25 banks in 1980 had total assets of 1,858 billion US dollars, equal to 30% of Gross Domestic Product (GDP). In 2000 this had risen to 64% of GDP, a combined total of 12,781 billion US dollars. Of this amount, 41% are assets outside the home country. In fact, foreign banks practically control the banking sectors in many Eastern European countries; for some observers the "single global banking space is almost a reality" (Mullineux & Murinde, 2003). The foreign owned assets of the largest banks exhibit uneven geographic patterns, "regions and/or countries of the developed world currently represent the most interconnected cluster of national banking systems" (De Nicoló, Bartholomew, Zaman, & Zephirin, 2004).

1.2.   Aims, objectives and main results

For most clients and bank products there is no such thing as a "global banking strategy", a favorite phrase of bank managers in the 1990s. I argue that internationalization should be considered as a separate strategic decision. Understanding the development of internationalization, the strategies chosen and developing a sense of what the most successful strategies in the near future might be is therefore a useful research area for bank management. To make this a broad and encompassing study, the international strategies of 45 banks are examined between 1980 and 2004, covering the vast majority of international banking activities in eight countries. For each bank, its internationalization pattern is established, using self constructed internationalization measures. Five strategies emerge. The next question is whether internationalization has been effective, for the whole group and for the identified strategies. Has the bank increased profitability, improved stability of earnings, created enhanced performance, and have shareholders gained by it? The long period offers additional (as well as sobering) insights into the development of banks' strategies and their results.

As a sideline, this book also touches upon the internationalization (or globalization) debate of banks from a comprehensive bottom up approach: what have banks actually done? Here too we find insights that were previously not published.

The contribution that the book seeks to add might seem new, the line of research is not. The 1990s saw the publication of several standard publications on banks and their strategic challenges. Authors like Canals (1993, 1997), Walter (1988), Smith and Walter (1990, 1997) have published extensively on banking strategies. The challenges of disintermediation, European integration and formulating the right strategic responses are important themes.

It first of all builds on the research of Canals (1993) on European banking strategies, updating it with developments over the last ten years, and extending the comparative analysis with banks in the United States and Japan. Second, it aims at a systematic description and analysis of internationalization strategies. This study adds a broad and comprehensive analysis to this line of research. Third, the study contributes to the research field by extending the time period of analysis to 25 years, quantifying the extent of internationalization by measuring the degree of internationalization and addressing the question of effectiveness of the banks' strategies.

Our main emphasis is therefore on the issues of formulation, implementation and evaluation of the internationalization strategies of banks. Which strategies have succeeded because they have ultimately shown to be competitive in foreign banking? Are the strategies still applicable for the near future? There is no single strategy that will work for all. My effort in this book is aimed at making clear the process of strategic decisions, and how banks should rethink their role within international banking. Six major findings resonate throughout the book.

1. Internationalization of banking has increased dramatically in absolute terms. The relative growth – that is foreign compared to domestic activities – is however far more subdued. I construct an internationalization index and find that internationalization has increased dramatically in value terms between 1980 and 2004. The relative degree of internationalization has only risen substantially since 1995. On average, more than 36% of income is generated outside the home country.

2. Individual international patterns diverge widely. The study identifies five strategies:

   - *Accelerating*: strong increase in internationalization activities; the bank holds more foreign than domestic activities. Drivers are the small or regulated home market, and ambitions to position oneself between the world's major banks.
   - *Moderate*: domestic activities make up the largest part of the bank. International activities are based on a) wholesale banking activities to support domestic clients, b) extension of successful domestic niche activities, and c) extension of the domestic market to a regional home market: targeting banking activities in neighboring countries.
   - *Retreating*: a financial crisis forces management to recover financially and refocus, selling of foreign assets and expanding domestically if possible. Foreign activities are reduced to supporting wholesale banking activities.
   - *Established*: the bank has found the right organizational fit between international and domestic banking activities. The bank is committed to its international activities, building on a long history.
   - *Imploding*: the bank set on a substantial foreign expansion course to catch up in market position. The acquisitions are however mismanaged or a bad fit in the bank's overall strategy and the bank has to restructure heavily, divesting its international activities after a short period.

3. For most banks, internationalization is seldom the preferred strategy. Given the opportunity, domestic growth activities are seized in favor of foreign activities. Banks that pursue consistent internationalization strategies tend to be located in home markets that are either highly regulated or small, offering limited growth opportunities.

4. Internationalization for banks as a group produces doubtful results for bank profitability and shareholders. Foreign profitability is on average lower than domestic; an increase in internationalization therefore lowers total profitability. Also, foreign banking activities do not improve stability of earnings. Geographical diversification benefits were not observed for the total banking organization. A small group of banks succeeds though.
5. Successful strategies are banks that are fully and long term committed to internationalization (*Established*), having a long internationalization track record to show for it. Successful banks are also banks that fully commit themselves to domestic expansion (*Retreating*). Over a period of 25 years *Established* and *Retreating* banks delivered five times more shareholder return than *Accelerating*, an additional 7% return per year.
6. Banks, especially *Accelerating* and *Moderate*, have restructured since 2000. Successful long term future internationalization strategies rewarding the shareholder will presumably be:

- Banks with *Accelerating* Strategies. These banks will have to decide whether they are able to develop their internationalization strategies into activities with relatively stable sources of income (emulating *Established* banks) or if they have to retreat, either because domestic growth opportunities become available or because management is unable to create durable profitability from the sizeable foreign activities, eventually selling them off. In the past shareholders rewarded both scenarios.
- Banks with *Established* strategies. These banks have found the right organizational fit and stable development strategies between international and domestic banking activities. They are committed to their international activities, building on a long history. Their extensive learning curve probably allows them to reap first mover advantages in new markets or products.

Future internationalization strategies with likely negative long term shareholder implications will be:

- Banks with *Retreating* internationalization have two strategic alternatives: either to maintain or further decrease internationalization activities, or to increase them again. Barclays has reentered European and South African retail banking, Lloyds TSB has publicly speculated about a similar move in Europe. The reinternationalization of these banks is not a repetition of the internationalization activities in the 1980s. Compared to earlier periods, the banks have shown a strong focus on domestic banking activities and efficiency. However, these organizations have to rebuild their learning curves in these arenas, potentially depressing total profitability.

- Finally, question marks surround the future shareholder returns of *Moderate* banks: they have the widest range of strategic options available to them, and are probably the most diverse bank group of realized strategies. However, most of the *Moderate* banks have as yet sought to increase their degree of internationalization.

1.3.　Contents

The book is divided into two parts. Chapters 2 to 4 lay down the groundwork for analyzing internationalization strategies of banks. Chapter 2 discusses the main challenges that the world's largest banks have faced since the 1980s. Chapter 3 discusses the theoretical framework of international banking – why do banks internationalize and what are their expectations. What impact does internationalization have on the foreign and domestic banking markets? Chapter 4 focuses on the world's largest banks, the object of our study – what are the key indicators and how have they developed over time?

Chapters 5 to 8 form the core argument of this book and focus on patterns of internationalization and its performance. Chapter 5 discusses internationalization developments and the international strategy development process. How banks set up these international activities is the main theme in Chapter 6; Chapter 7 analyzes the performance of internationalized banks.

Chapter 8 is directed at future directions. Which banks have successful internationalization strategies and can achieve sustainable profitability? What banks are least likely to succeed in international banking and what changes could they pursue to alter this?

2
Banking since the 1980s: Challenges and Issues

ING Direct seems a small coffee shop in New York, not caring too much about attracting customers walking by. Looks deceive however. The billboard promoting coffee is accompanied by the current checking account interest rate. ING Direct is an internet bank, active in nine countries with 145 billion US dollars or 40% of ING total entrusted funds. Making the most of deregulation, advances in information technology and changing customer preferences, ING Direct has developed a successful business model to take full advantage of these changes.

This chapter surveys trends that affected the internationalization of banks between 1980 and 2000. Four areas have influenced the internationalization activities of banks (cf. Mullineux & Murinde, 2003, Smith & Walter, 1997):

- Changing international role of banks: disintermediation, the increasing role of securities markets
- Transformation of the banking industry worldwide: deregulation, financial crises and changing new monetary paradigms
- Emerging economic structures in the European Union
- Evolution of financial services and products.

These trends have shaped international banking since the 1970s when banks started to substantially increase their foreign activities and innovations of capital markets also took a flight. The main innovations revolved around securitization, involving both disintermediation, the growth of direct finance (bypassing banks), and making loans tradable on securities markets (Mullineux & Murinde, 2003). In the 1990s, progressive relaxation of capital controls took place, while some countries moved earlier than others. Relaxation of capital controls stimulated the rapid growth in overseas portfolio investments by institutional investors where banks captured the brokerage function by investing in investment banking that took off in the major financial centers. The furthest integration took place in Europe, culminating in the European Union, an integrated financial zone that should lead to cross border activity. This has not yet materialized but in anticipation banks consolidated domestically.

2.1. Changing role of banks

The increase in international banking from the 1970s onwards was spurred by a process involving disintermediation, securitization and the increasing role of securities markets. The growing role of securities markets and the eagerness of banks to capture a permanent market share in that business was driven by fear of disintermediation, potentially reducing the role of banks. Banks also operated in different financial structures, with different consequences for disintermediation. Deutsche Bank had limited opportunities to increase its securities activities in a bank based system, where capital markets play a more subdued role. How has disintermediation changed between 1980 and 2000, and did changes or differences in financial structure have consequences for international activities? Differences in financial development, not financial systems may have influenced international activities.

2.1.1. Disintermediation process

Disintermediation and securitization imply an increasing role of non-bank competitors. Investment funds, mutual funds, insurance companies and financing companies have increasingly absorbed the capital flows redirected from banks.[1] Three claims with regard to disintermediation can be made:

- The importance of banks and other institutional investors have increased in importance between 1980 and 2000.
- The role of banks compared to direct competitors has declined between 1980 and 2000.
- The role of banks compared to other sources of funding has declined.

Disintermediation is the development of markets for a variety of negotiable securities, *replacing* loans as a means of borrowing.[2] Investors and borrowers bypass banks and transact business directly

(Davis, 1995). The replacement of loans can be substitution of loans at banks or, prior to the funding origination, the replacement of loans as one of the alternatives to fulfill the financing need, bypassing the bank altogether.

Securitization is an important element in the process of disintermediation: debt instruments (loans and mortgages) are converted into negotiable securities that individual or institutional market participants purchase (Davis, 1995). Securitization occurs when an asset holder restructures its activities, to increase profitability, reduce mismatch between assets and/or liabilities or to adjust the overall size and capacities of its balance sheet. Securitization has mainly grown dramatically in the United States since the 1980s (Smith & Walter, 1997):

- A general decline in long term interest rates after 1981 and the return of a positively sloped yield curve increased the attractiveness of debt instruments with fixed interest rates in general.
- The credit quality of bank certificates of deposits had deteriorated in the early 1980s after the banks coped with large exposures to loans in problem sectors and LDC debt. This meant that high grade companies could attract funding at lower rates than banks, making banking financing a high cost source of funds.
- The LDC debt burden led to a restriction of growth in assets to protect deteriorating capital ratios. The banks' answer was to sell existing loans already on their books, and attract new funds. The issue of new capital strengthened the capital base, while issuance of new debt led to an overall lower cost of funds, due to better capital market conditions.
- The growth in volume, depth, and turnover in capital markets, combined with a widening variety of financial instruments, drew more loan activity away from banks because of lower rates, more suitable maturity structures and other special features.

Overall, banks defended their financial intermediation role by internalizing the competitive threats of disintermediation (European Central Bank, 2000a):

- Securitization has not bypassed the banking system; banks increasingly managed the securitization process, thus creating non-interest income.
- Banks have increased their product range.

- The role of provider of loans has remained intact over the years. For households, the majority of debt consists of mortgages and credit card financing, which is channeled to the banks. The growth of capital markets between 1980 and 2000 has not created more alternatives for financing to smaller and medium sized companies.
- For larger corporations, the major change for banks had already taken place in the 1970s with the introduction of commercial paper, and the issuance of corporate bonds. The direct access to the capital market has not meant that the role of banks has been bypassed as shown earlier.

The effect on the income structure of banks has been twofold. The off-balance sheet activities (such as a letter of credit, a swap or loan commitments) have increased as banks diversified their product range. The other effect has been in the development of non-interest income; from 1980 onwards the increase in non-interest income offset the decrease in interest income to a large extent. Diversification into non-interest generating activities shifts the balance towards non-interest income; banks accelerate such a change in income structure by securitizing assets on the bank's balance sheet (Llewellyn, 1999). For the EU countries, the European Central Bank investigated the changes in income structure for banks between 1993 and 1998. A finding was that non-interest income has increased in importance,[3] owing as much to the increase in non-interest income as to the decrease in interest income. On average, the rise in non-interest income did not completely compensate the fall in interest income during the period investigated. Non-interest income has been especially vital as a "cushion", either reducing or compensating the fall in interest income to a large extent.[4]

2.1.2.   Growth of securities and derivatives markets

Significantly expanding securities markets generated high margins over longer periods, induced banks to increase their market share in these activities and establish or buy operations in the main financial centers. Most internationalization strategies are "layered": the first major international activities took place in investment banking activities in New York or London. For the equities markets alone, market capitalization worldwide increased from 4,667 billion US dollars in December 1985 to 31,212 billion US dollars in June 2005, roughly doubling in size every six years. This has been the result of a combination of several factors:

- Firms increasingly sought the securities markets as a source of funding.
- Institutional investors became larger and adapted a more active approach, increasing the turnover of shares, enhancing liquidity and increasing its attractiveness as a source of funding.
- The market for corporate control mergers and acquisitions (M&As) increasingly funded its activities through the securities markets; shifting from capital transactions in cash to capital transactions in securities.
- Privatization also created additional supply of new publicly traded shares. Walter and Smith calculate that from 1990 to 1998, the amounts raised by privatization worldwide increased from 29.9 billion US dollars to 114.5 billion US dollars, an average annual growth rate of 18%. More than half of these amounts raised originated from the European Union, whereas the share of privatizations in the United States was negligible (Walter & Smith, 2000).

After the liberalization of the New York Stock Exchange in 1975, abolishing fixed commissions (Dicken, 1998), other countries with major financial centers aimed to at least replicate the following growth. Other major stock exchange liberalizations took place in Paris (1984) and London (1986). Over time a hierarchical structure was created with New York, London and Tokyo as the first tier stock markets to establish a presence (Dicken, 1998), the major European countries, Hong Kong and Singapore as second tier, and finally the other countries. Banks aiming to develop securities activities replicated this pattern with their presence, and sought to establish presences in at least the first tier major centers, being more selective about the second and third tiers, depending on their strategy.

In the 1990s securities activities moved towards fully electronic trading. Physical presence at the exchange became less necessary. Deregulation and electronic trading stimulated lower margins; combined with a high rate of information technology investments and increasing volumes of transactions these trends stimulated a concentration in the banks active in global investment banking.

2.1.3. Consolidation

The banking industry has consolidated on an unprecedented scale since the 1980s. American mergers in the early 1990s led to the rise of Chase Manhattan and Bank of America, while a decade later regional banks were acquired by Bank of America and JPMorganChase.

In Europe mergers also have been prominent. Cross border mergers were relatively infrequent in the 1990s; most mergers typically involved unions between large domestic universal banks: ABN and AMRO in 1990, SBC and UBS in 1997. In Japan Tokyo and Mitsubishi merged in 1996 but consolidation took off after the three-way merger of IBJ, Dai Ichi Kangyo and Fuji Bank forming Mizuho in 1999. Cross border mergers were a relatively Northern European phenomenon: ING and BBL (1997), or the formation of Nordea in Scandinavia. In the report published in 2001 the Group of Ten, studying financial consolidation patterns in the G10 countries, found that:

- The level of M&A activity increased over time creating a significant number of large, and in some cases complex, financial institutions.
- Most M&As involved firms competing in the same segment of the financial services industry and the same country.
- During the 1990s acquisitions of banks accounted for 60% of all financial mergers and 70% of the value of those mergers.
- The number of banks decreased in almost every studied country in the 1990s. The concentration of the banking industry, as measured by the percentage of a country's deposits controlled by the largest banks, tended to increase.
- Consolidation patterns differed across countries.

Table 2.1   National consolidation in the European banking sector as of 2004

Country	Consolidation phase
Germany	Consolidation started; obstructive tax legislation and public sector banking system are being tackled
Italy	Consolidation gaining speed; reforms in the banking sector and foreign acquisitions
France	Consolidation to be finalized
Spain	Consolidation of saving banks
United Kingdom	Consolidation almost complete
Portugal, Ireland, Greece, Austria, Switzerland, Netherlands, Belgium, Nordic countries	Substantially completed

Source: Based on Van Dijcke (2002).

The Group of Ten identified two major causes for consolidation. First, interviewed practitioners found cost savings and income growth primary motives for M&As. Also, the Group of Ten found that consolidation was encouraged by improvements in information technology, financial deregulation, globalization of financial and real markets, and increasing shareholder pressure for financial performance.

While small bank M&As are mostly being carried out for cost saving reasons and to achieve a size that allows survival, larger bank M&As often have an element of strategic repositioning besides the cost motive (European Central Bank, 2000b).

2.1.4. Financial structure

There has been a great deal of research aiming to classify the different financial systems, usually amounting into an Anglo-American versus Continental European/Japanese classification. Each financial system has its unique traits, evolved over time to deal with country specific issues; a classification of financial systems might be interpreted broader than the scope of finance due to its socio-economic characteristics (Scholtens, 1996). Demirgüç-Kunt and Levine (Demirgüç-Kunt & Levine, 2001) examined the financial structure for a large set of countries over several decades. Classifying financial systems as underdeveloped, market based or bank based, they found that:

- Banks and securities markets are larger, more active and more efficient in richer countries. Financial systems are on average more developed in richer countries.
- In high-income countries, stock markets become more active and efficient relative to banks. There is some tendency for financial systems to become more market oriented as they become richer.
- Legal and regulatory measures matter: countries with a common law tradition, strong protection of shareholder rights, good accounting regulations, low levels of corruption and no explicit insurance tend to be more market oriented. The opposite is true for French civil law tradition, where countries with poor protections of shareholder and creditor rights, high levels of corruption, poor accounting standards, restrictive regulation, and high inflation tend to have underdeveloped financial systems (Demirgüç-Kunt & Levine, 2001).

Beck et al. (2001) studied the relationship between measures of economic development and the degree to which a financial system is market or bank based, for 34 countries between 1980 and 1995. They conclude that financial structure is not useful to distinguish among financial systems: "countries do not grow faster, financial dependent industries do not expand at higher rates, new firms are not created more easily, firms' access to external finance is not easier, and firms do not grow faster in either market- or bank-based financial systems" (Beck, Demirgüç-Kunt, Levine & Maksimovic, 2001). The overall development of the financial sector and legal system does however matter. Also, similar results were found by Levine (2002) for a sample of 48 countries for the 1980–95 period.

Schmidt et al. (1998) investigated whether the financial systems of Germany, France and the United Kingdom changed between 1980 and 1994. They found neither a general trend towards disintermediation, nor a transformation from bank based to market based, nor a loss of importance of banks in the financial system for Germany and the United Kingdom. For France, a declining role of banks was observed. In other words, convergence to a market based financial system is not a general assumption.

For determining bank profitability, the difference between bank and market based systems might also not be useful (Demirgüç-Kunt & Huizinga, 2001). Here too, financial development matters. The analysis suggests that banks have higher profits and margins in underdeveloped financial systems. Greater bank development lowers bank profits and margins (Demirgüç-Kunt & Huizinga, 2001). The implications for the internationalization of banks might have been the following:

- Since most Western economies have highly developed financial systems, shifts within the financial structure between 1980 and 2000 probably have not created significant differences in bank profitability or economic growth within this group of countries.
- Differences in financial development might have been an incentive for banks to internationalize to developing countries, but not to developed countries.

Elements specifically attributed to bank based or market based systems – such as long term versus short term relationships or equity participations – do not present specific additional internalization advantages which might be exploited through internationalization. What might be exploited, are new products, resulting from differences in financial development.

2.2.   Transformation of the banking industry

The 1980s can be characterized by the controlling of inflation through changes in monetary regimes, and the ongoing efforts to stabilize exchange rate fluctuations, either through concerted actions of central banks or the further development of exchange rate regimes. This affected the structure and income of the international activities of banks in several ways. Other notable achievements were the international regulation and reregulation of the financial services markets. Within a relatively short period, financial regulators have removed many barriers for banks to undertake new activities, albeit for different reasons. Reregulation also took place for international banks, formed by the internationally applied rules for capital adequacy. Regulation is a reaction to, or anticipation of financial instability. Banking crises have occurred from time to time. The LDC debt crisis is singled out for discussion, marking the reorientation of (American) bank's international strategies, and the increasing role of international organizations.

2.2.1.   Monetary and exchange rate regimes

Exchange rate movements have influenced the timing and attractiveness of foreign acquisitions. For example, acquisition of US assets for European banks became more attractive between 1984 and 1988 when the US dollar depreciated against major European currencies. For Japanese banks, the appreciation of the Japanese yen against the US dollar lasted until 1994, marking nearly a decade where Japanese banks could buy cheaper US banking assets. However, a falling US dollar might have speeded investment decisions of British banks in the United States, but not necessarily the decision itself to invest in the United States (Jones, 1993).

Two major events transformed the international monetary environment at the end of the 1970s for the next decades: coordinated policies to stabilize exchange rates, and the shift in monetary regimes to effectively control inflation.

A major shift in monetary regime occurred in 1979, when prices were rising again after a second oil price hike in a decade, triggered by the invasion of Iran by Iraq. Governments were, compared to a decade earlier, prepared to apply different economic policies. In the years before, price controls were used as a mechanism to keep inflation down, which turned out to be ineffective. To effectively combat inflation, monetary growth had to be rigorously restrained. Paul Volcker, chairman of the Federal Reserve bank, was determined not to witness a repetition of high inflation rates, and raised short term interest rates above 12% from

October 1979 onwards, reaching 20% by the end of March the following year, to be repeated again in the third quarter of 1980. This policy was also applied in the United Kingdom and (for a longer period) in West Germany, "accentuated by the election of right wing governments" (Channon, 1988). For most countries, inflation subsequently fell and stayed on a relatively low level compared to the 1970s.

The changing monetary regime and the economic slowdown had several long term consequences. The first was that oil prices and other commodity prices fell dramatically. Compared to the earlier oil price

Table 2.2 Major monetary and exchange rate events

Year	Exchange rate event	Monetary event	Event	Effect on internationalization of banks
1979		•	Start EMS	
1979	•		Tighter monetary policy by Federal Reserve	Credit crunch for US banks, repatriation of foreign loans, start of LDC loan crisis
1985		•	G-5 central bank interventionto devalue the US dollar ("Plaza Accord")	Relative attractiveness of bank acquisitions in the United States increased
1987		•	G-7 finance ministers' agreement to stabilize the US dollar exchange rate	
1992		•	EMS crisis/realignment of currencies	Increased value of international activities
1996	•		Zero rate policy of Bank of Japan	
1996	•		Independence of Bank of England	
1998	•		Establishment of European central bank	
1999		•	Irrevocable pegging of eurocurrencies	Loss of foreign exchange business
2003	•	•	Conversion to eurocurrency in 12 countries	

Source: Adapted from Eichengreen (1996) and Braithwaite and Drahos (2000).

hike, economies had readjusted themselves, decreasing their dependence on oil, by then mainly in use for transportation purposes. Lower economic growth reduced the need for oil products strongly, negatively affecting the income of oil producing countries. On the same note, commodity prices were hurt badly. This meant that the main source of income of developing countries, using this income as collateral for loans and interest payments, dried up. Banks and supranational agencies such as the IMF and World Bank would spend considerable amounts of capital in the 1980s to resolve the financial crisis stemming from this development. The crisis marked the withdrawal of banks like Citicorp, Bank of America and Lloyds from South America.

Later currency crises were not to have the same impact on internationalization, and even created entry opportunities. Strong devaluations in 1997–98 forced Asian governments to open their banking markets to foreign banks, seeking external capital to stabilize the banking sector. Thailand, Korea and Taiwan became buying opportunities for European and American banks, afraid to miss the expected Asian economic recovery boom.

2.2.2. Regulation

Financial regulation after 1945 differs for each country but the national regulatory frameworks of the countries share three elements (Canals, 1997): separation of activities between commercial banks and investment banks, a deposit guarantee to protect the depositor should the bank fail and control over interest rates of the bank's lending and deposit taking activities. This regulatory structure was applied by countries until the late 1970s, and has at least brought financial stability in most Western countries. Canals lists five motives for the regulatory frameworks to change since the late 1970s. First, liberalization of capital movements between countries exposed banks to competition from international capital markets and also increased the limits to foreign investments in the financial sector.

Second, the disintermediation process, making it possible for companies to turn directly to the capital markets for financing, decreased the (perceived) financial intermediation role of banks. The separation between commercial banks, specialized in funding and lending, and investment banks, specialized in financial consultancy and capital market operations, favored the investment banks at the expense of commercial banks as a result of this process. The liberalization of capital flows also affected the disintermediation process on the funding side of banks, where investors became more active in finding better returns for their deposits.

Table 2.3   Major regulatory events

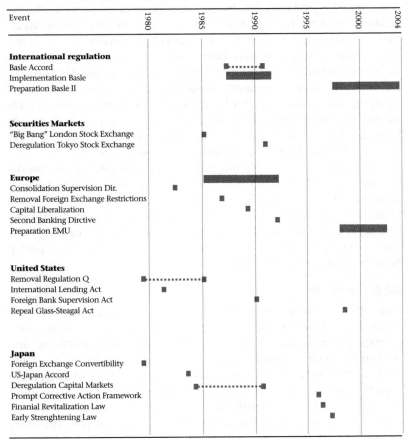

Event	1980	1985	1990	1995	2000	2004
International regulation						
Basle Accord						
Implementation Basle						
Preparation Basle II						
Securities Markets						
"Big Bang" London Stock Exchange						
Deregulation Tokyo Stock Exchange						
Europe						
Consolidation Supervision Dir.						
Removal Foreign Exchange Restrictions						
Capital Liberalization						
Second Banking Dirctive						
Preparation EMU						
United States						
Removal Regulation Q						
International Lending Act						
Foreign Bank Supervision Act						
Repeal Glass-Steagal Act						
Japan						
Foreign Exchange Convertibility						
US-Japan Accord						
Deregulation Capital Markets						
Prompt Corrective Action Framework						
Finanial Revitalization Law						
Early Strenghtening Law						

Third, financial innovation affected regulation. Initially, financial innovation was motivated by the need to cope with the high inflation rates of the 1970s and to sidestep the restrictions on certain operations imposed by the central banks. During the 1980s financial innovation received another growth incentive through the increasing application of information technologies. Fourth, information technologies have changed the way banking business is performed. This has not only affected the organization of activities but also the geographic and time span, challenging the boundaries of regulation.

The fifth development has been increased competition. The number of financial organizations competing for the same clients has grown, caused by deregulation itself, the liberalization of capital flows, the lifting of the price controls, financial disintermediation and the entry of new competitors in the market.

Historically, the central banks have played an important role as regulators, their interest being the control of monetary policy and financial stability. Domestically, various regulators have been established, for banks and/or securities. From 1974 onwards, on a supranational level the Bank for International Settlements acted as a neutral international banking club on regulatory matters, whereas the EU Commission prepared and monitored banking policy under the Single Market Act, to be enforced by domestic regulators.[5]

Table 2.3 lists major regulatory developments between 1980 and 2000, clustered per region and country. The table indicates that relatively many regulatory events were shaped in a short period: from the mid-1980s until the early 1990s. The capital adequacy regulation codified in the Basle Accord is regulation specifically designed for international active banks, as the subsequent discussion will show the implementation has especially influenced internationalization of Japanese banks, hastening their retreat from international banking. The following issues will be discussed in some more detail: capital adequacy regulation, regulation in the European Union, the United States and Japan.

Capital Adequacy Regulation

Supranational regulation is difficult to enforce, especially if enforcement is on a voluntary basis. The implementation of the Basle Accord has been a notable success in that area. Internationalization of banks confronted central banks in the 1970s with a capacity problem and an information problem: regulators did not have powers over the international banking system, and with increasing complexity of cross border activities regulators had to base their oversight on poor information. Added to this, the problem of spillover, transmitting financial crises from one country to another through higher integrated capital markets became greater, demonstrated by the collapse of Herstatt Bank because of foreign exchange dealings and the failure of US wholesale bank Franklin. The central bankers from the ten largest economies formed in response to these crises the Basle Committee.[6] The initiative came from English regulators where foreign banks, especially US banks, formed an important part of the domestic financial system. Two objectives had to be achieved: the maintenance of London as a major financial center, as well as the reduction of systemic risk (Braithwaite & Drahos, 2000).

After first coordinating supervisory responsibilities for international banks in the 1975 Basle concordat, central banks devised the Basle ratios to solve two problems. The level of capital relative to loans had been falling steadily prior to 1988. That was worrying because capital is the cushion that protects depositors by absorbing losses when loans default (*The Economist*, 1992). An ulterior problem to be solved was to eliminate the funding cost advantage of Japanese banks because they put up inadequate amounts of capital to back up their loans, seizing more than one-third of international lending in the 1980s (Wagster, 1996).

In 1988, the Committee decided to introduce a capital measurement system commonly referred to as the Basle Capital Accord. The Accord obliged banks to maintain a minimum capital standard, measured as a ratio of equity and quasi-equity funding to risk-weighted assets, of 8% by end 1988. The regulators' intentions were to reinforce financial stability, establish a level playing field for banks from different countries, and third, in the case of some countries, to reduce explicit or implicit costs of government-provided deposit guarantees (Ediz, Michael & Perraudin, 1998).

Since 1988, this framework has been progressively introduced not only in member countries but also in virtually all other countries with active international banks. As a result banks increasingly became better capitalized. An undesirable side effect was the shift from high risk-weighted assets to low risk-weighted assets.[7] Banks adopted more conservative (and perhaps less diversified) lending policies, for example when US banks shifted from corporate lending to investments in government securities in the early 1990s. Ediz et al. (1998) review research that suggests a change in lending behavior caused by the Basle Accord system. Their own research for UK banks between 1989 and 1995 suggest another impact of the Basle Accord: rather than substituting assets on the balance sheets banks appear to have adjusted their capital requirements upwards primarily by directly attracting capital.

The establishment of an international level playing field was especially hard felt in Japan[8] when the central bank of Japan adopted the Basle Accord guidelines, where an exception was made to include capital gains from investing in the (Japanese) stock market. Japanese banks invested more strongly than British or German banks in securities, generating large capital gains during the strong growth period of the Japanese stock market in the 1980s (Canals, 1993). Japanese accounting rules allowed unrealized capital gains in securities to be posted as profit generating resources that could be transferred to reserves, increasing the bank's net worth. When the Japanese stock market moved downward from 1990 onwards, due to tightening monetary policy triggering an economic recession, Japanese banks had to confront capital losses shrinking the net worth of the banks. This forced the banks to contract their lending activity and among others concentrate on the domestic market, withdrawing from international markets.

The combination of economic recession and capital losses posed further problems for achieving minimum capital requirements. First, Japanese banks already showed internationally the lowest capital ratios, their ratio being around 3% which was below the minimum required. The regulation however did not allow for the unrealized capital gains to be considered net worth. As a temporary measure, the Bank of Japan allowed up to 45% to be included as reserves, with the clear intention of reducing this percentage to zero. This too added to the cutback of lending activity.

Implementation of the capital adequacy rules in accordance with the Basle Accord meant that banks had to restructure their activities: "unable to increase the capital numerator, bankers have slashed the asset denominator", resulting in efforts to securitize and sell off loans, and divest loss making subsidiaries. The Institutional Investor reported in 1991 that many banks subsequently intended to refocus on their domestic markets, rationalizing their less profitable foreign operations. In the process, more than 20 US banks had withdrawn from Europe, while foreign banks also reduced their presence in the United States.

The Basle Accord became counterproductive to some extent over time. The requirement to reserve 8% capital against all loans provided an incentive to make loans to risky institutions and not to high grade companies where margins were already thin. This created a gap between real economic risk, as perceived by banks, and regulatory risk, as perceived by regulators. US banks in particular had been running greater risks in the 1990s to remain competitive in their on- and off-balance sheet activities. The crises in 1997–98 (Asia, Russia, LTCM) created a sense of urgency to change the capital adequacy framework (Fleming, 1999). In June 1999, the Committee issued a proposal for a New Capital Adequacy Framework to replace the 1988 Accord, aiming to implement the new framework in 2004.[9]

Basically, its aim was to improve the existing 1988 Accord on a number of issues: the weighting approach of risk gave banks an incentive to shift from high quality to low quality loans, and internally, the more sophisticated risk systems of banks deviated from the capital adequacy framework. The proposed capital framework consisted of three pillars: minimum capital requirements, which seek to refine the standardized rules set forth in the 1988 Accord; supervisory review of an institution's internal assessment process and capital adequacy; and effective use of disclosure to strengthen market discipline as a complement to supervisory efforts.[10]

European regulation

The work of the Committee on Banking Regulations and Supervisory Practices of the BIS consisted of proposals which need not be followed by national authorities. On the other hand, directives in the European Union form part of EU law and should be implemented in the national legislations of the EU member states (Burgers, 1991). The major directives of the 1992 program for financial services in the European Union can be divided into four categories: banking, investment services, collective investments and insurance. For banking, there had already been harmonization activities in several stages such as the First Banking Directive in 1977, requiring member states to establish systems for authorizing and supervising credit institutions (Burgers, 1991; Chrystal & Coughlin, 1992). The 1983 Consolidation Supervision required that credit institutions be supervised on a consolidated basis; another provision mandated the exchange of information between supervising authorities while the 1986 Bank Accounts Directive assisted this by harmonizing accounting rules for credit institutions.

The Second Banking Coordinating Banking Directive was the main directive for the 1992 program. The directive established "home country control and host country rules": jurisdiction over the supervision of the bank's solvency and liquidity was given to the bank's country of origin, regulation regarding the execution of monetary policy and other operation norms were transferred to country of destination (Canals, 1993). Credit institutions authorized in one member country could establish branches and provide banking services elsewhere in the EC. This common passport allowed home country authorization, but the credit institution must conform to all local laws.

Finally, the directive is supported by the Own Funds Directive, establishing common definitions for the bank's capital base, and the Solvency Ratio Directive, where these definitions are used to establish minimum asset ratios for all credit institutions.

Regulation in Japan

At the beginning of the 1980s, the Japanese financial system was essentially a closed financial system.[11] Strict regulatory controls discouraged financial transactions and internationalization of financial markets did not grow substantially relative to economic growth (Arora, 1995). An important step towards liberalization was the revision of the Foreign Exchange Law in December 1980, practically allowing full convertibility of the yen into foreign currencies and the abolishment of prior notification of cross border portfolio investment, both inward and outward. The new freedom, coupled with an attractive interest rate differential between the United States and Japan, led to a substantial increase in long term capital outflows in the 1980s (Arora, 1995).

By 1984, Western governments realized that the Japanese economy maintained high barriers to entry and pressured the Japanese for greater access to the domestic financial markets. The US government especially pressured the Japanese government for these measures, arguing that liberalization would address the strong dollar problem by stimulating demand for yen denominated instruments and would help American banks to enter the Japanese market (Kanaya & Woo, 2000). Financial liberalization in Japan was acknowledged in the US–Japan Accord of May 1984, where Japan agreed to open its financial markets and promote the internationalization of the yen (Arora, 1995). The mid-1980s therefore witnessed acceleration in the pace of financial deregulation, consisting of (Kanaya & Woo, 2000):

- Relaxation of interest rate controls, starting with the liberalization of term deposit rates in 1985.
- Capital market deregulation, including the lifting of the prohibition on short term euroyen loans in 1984, the removal of restrictions on access to the corporate bond market, and the creation of the commercial paper market in 1987, enabling corporations to borrow directly from the market.
- Relaxation of restrictions on activities of previously segregated institutions, including the raising of different types of lending ceilings.

The liberalization and the increased importance of the yen worldwide provided a platform for Japanese banks' internationalization. Banks like IBJ, Mitsubishi, and Tokyo expanded in the major financial centers, dominating loan issuance. Although barriers were gradually dismantled, foreign banks were only able to open representative offices. From 1998, with the worsening of the Japanese banking crisis, they were able to significantly expand their activities.

Japanese regulatory developments in the 1990s centered on the implementation of the Basle Accord, and regulation to cope with the banking crisis emerging from 1990 onwards. The Basle Accord was fully implemented in 1993. Japanese authorities required only banks with international operations to comply with the 8% capital adequacy requirement, but many domestic banks also chose to comply to 8% even though they had to comply with the domestic 4% requirement. Kanaya and Woo observe that "even though regulations permitted banks to use only 45% of these unrealised gains (amounting to 22 trillion yen) towards their tier 2 capital, these nevertheless accounted for about 25% of total bank capital [in 1993]" (Kanaya & Woo, 2000)

From 1998 onwards, foreign banks began to play a role in the restructuring of the Japanese banking sector, taking over loan financing from Japanese banks. Foreign banks had played a small and decreasing role in the first half of the 1990s when credit by foreign banks fell from 2.7% in 1991 to 1.6% in 1995 of total credit in Japan. From 1995 onwards this increased to 2.3% in 1998, while the total amounts of credit roughly remained the same.[12] Blue chip firms migrated loans from Japanese banks to foreign banks, especially for euroyen loans (Kanaya & Woo, 2000). Another development caused by the banking crisis and the resulting changing regulatory environment was that foreign banks were allowed to acquire banks in Japan, previously prohibited. Merrill Lynch bought Yamaichi Securities in 1998, and the American investment firm Ripplewood acquired the nationalized Long Term Credit Bank.

Regulation in the United States

Regulation and foreign bank activity have traditionally been intertwined in the US. Prior to 1980 US regulation stimulated American banks to undertake foreign activities. Regulation Q introduced interest rate caps, helping to ensure the growth of the eurodollar market outside of New York, as multinational corporations and others preferred to place funds earned overseas in London, rather than return them to New York. The US government also imposed controls on the flow of capital overseas, effectuated from the early 1960s through the interest equalization tax, the Voluntary Foreign Credit Restraint Program and restrictions on direct foreign investment (Channon, 1977). This period laid the foundation for the substantial and successful presence of American investment banking in London.

The activities of foreign banks in the United States attracted the attention of Congress in the late 1970s, perceiving that foreign banks enjoyed a competitive advantage over the domestic banks. Foreign banks could undertake activities in more than one state, while this was denied to domestic banks, and could offer a full range of services, also denied to domestic banks. Also, domestic banks had to maintain reserves at the Federal Reserve System, while foreign banks did not have to. After four years, the International Banking Act (IBA) was approved in 1978, creating a regulatory structure for agencies and branches, with the aim of eliminating the competitive advantages of foreign banks (State of New York Banking Department, 1999).

From 1980 onwards regulators had to deal with a number of issues (Federal Deposit Insurance Corporation, 1997). For one, the trend towards deregulation placed more importance on capital adequacy. Prior to 1988, different guidelines were set for groups of banks based on their asset size. The 17 largest banks, mostly internationally active, were monitored individually and had no mandated capital requirements, in the expectation that their capital adequacy ratios would improve in time. The LDC debt crisis from 1981 onwards created great anxiety about the condition of the largest banks. Although regulators at first did not respond to this pressure, the International Lending Act of 1983 stipulated that all banking institutions maintain adequate capital levels, and failure to do so was made an unsound and unsafe practice for different types of domestic banks. The adoption of the Basle ratios led to further convergence of capital standards in 1991 (Federal Deposit Insurance Corporation, 1997)

Foreign banks were in 1991 again the subject of regulation with the passage of the Foreign Bank Supervision Enhancement Act (FBSEA). Direct reaction for drafting this regulation was the fraud scandals of two banks, the Bank of Credit and Commerce International (BCCI), a Middle East bank chartered in Luxembourg, and Banca Nazionale Del Lavoro, an Italian bank. The FBSEA gave the Federal Reserve Board a more direct role in the supervision of foreign banks, mandating annual on-site examinations of all foreign branches. Also, the FBSEA imposed that the Federal Reserve Board approve the establishment of any new organizational activity by a foreign bank (State of New York Banking Department, 1999).

A major influence in the consolidation in the US banking industry was the April 1998 acquisition of Citicorp by insurer Travelers for 82.5 billion US dollars, driven by the prospect of cross selling retail financial services. The newly formed company was acclaimed to be the world's largest financial services firm and received regulatory approval for the merger, provided that the US Congress drop its restrictions against the banking and insurance combination, shaped by the Glass Steagal Act. This was achieved in the Gramm-Leach-Bliley

Act in 1999. The Act also had far-reaching consequences for foreign banks operating in the United States. Prior to the Act in 1999, a consequence of the separation of investment, banking and insurance activities was that entrants (from Europe) had to choose which activity the bank would undertake. This theoretically limited the application of the universal banking model, and its potential profitability in one of the largest banking markets. Domestic M&As could have far-reaching consequences for foreign bank activities in the US. When ING, a Dutch bank and insurance company, was formed, it had both insurance and banking activities in the United States. ING was given leeway to operate with a banking licence in the United States until the group decided itself to give up its banking licence (Wolffe & Waters, 1998). The opposite was also true, domestic mergers were influenced by United States regulation. Merger talks between Dutch insurer Nationale Nederlanden (forerunner of ING) and ABN (forerunner of ABN AMRO) were discontinued because if the merger had taken place, substantial activities of either insurance or banking in the United States would have to be divested which neither party agreed to.

In the end, the insurance-banking combination did not work well in the United States. Citigroup dissolved and sold off most of its insurance activities in 2004, returning to its banking operations.

2.2.3.   Financial crises

Financial crises have been a recurring theme as well as a major influence on the internationalization activities of banks. Major crises in the 1980s and the 1990s were the international debt crisis (1981–1989), the currency crisis in Europe (1992–1993), the "Tequila" crisis in Latin America (1994–1995) and the crisis in South East Asian countries (1997–1998). The IMF (1998) identifies four types of financial crises: foreign debt crisis, currency crisis, bank crisis and systemic crisis. A foreign debt crisis arises when a country cannot service its (corporate of sovereign) foreign debt. A currency crisis occurs when a speculative attack on the currency results in a devaluation of the currency or forces authorities to defend its currency by increasing international reserves or raising interest rates. A banking crisis refers to a situation where actual or potential bank runs or defaults force banks to suspend internal convertibility of their liabilities; to prevent this the government may intervene by providing assistance on a large scale (International Monetary Fund, 1998). A banking crisis can grow into a systemic crisis, spilling over to other sectors in the economy, because banks play a key role in payment and settlement

Table 2.4   International monetary, securities and banking crises and their effect on internationalization

Year	Monetary and securities crises	Banking crises	Individual failures	Crises	Effect on internationalization of banks
1981	•			Polish crisis	Withdrawal of emerging market loans by European banks
1982–89	•	•		International debt crisis (LDC)	Withdrawal of emerging market loans for most major banks, increasing role of international monetary institutions, creation of Basle Accord in 1988
1983			•	Failure of Continental Illinois Bank, Banco Ambrosiano	
1987	•			Stock market crash, LDC crisis	Large provisioning
1987–92		•		Banking crises in Finland, Norway and Sweden	Regional effect
1989	•			Stock market crash	Large provisioning
1989		•		Savings and loans crisis	Consolidation and liberalization of US banking market, refocusing of large US banks on home market
1990	•	•		Japanese banking crisis	Withdrawal of Japanese banks from internationalization activities
1991			•	Failure BCCI	Increased international regulation
1994–95	•			Mexican crisis	Large provisioning
1994	•			Bond market crisis	
1995			•	Failure of Barings	Expansion in internationalization by ING group
1996	•			Brazilian crisis	
1996			•	Failure of Sumitomo Bank	
1997–98	•	•		Asian banking crisis	
1998	•			Long Term Capital Management	Speeding up proposal for Basle II
1998	•			Russian crisis	Withdrawal of derivates/investment banking activities
2000–03	•			TMT stock market crash	Decrease of capital market activities (IPOs)

Source: Adapted from Van Eerden (forthcoming).

systems where a failure to meet obligations could trigger domino effects. Most financial contracts the bank intermediates in are intertemporal; when uncertainty arises about the credibility of the financial commitment of the bank market expectations may shift substantially leading to large asset price fluctuations (De Bandt & Hartmann, 2000).

The IMF study (1998) counted between 1975 and 1997, 158 currency crises and 54 banking crises for 50 countries. Currency crises had a relatively higher occurrence in the first period (1975–1986) than in the second period (1987–1997) while for banks an opposite result was found.

The longevity or severity of financial crises since 1973 has not been different, but the frequency of crises has doubled. An important reason for this higher frequency has been that crises increasingly occurred in pairs, combining banking crises as well as currency crises (*twin crises*). For 1975–97 the IMF study estimated that the combination of currency and banking crises were the most persistent and have the largest average recovery time, also being responsible for the largest cumulative losses. The average cumulative loss relative to trend is between 4% and 7% of GDP for currency crises, increasing to 12% for banking crises and 15% for twin crises (International Monetary Fund, 1998; Kaminsky & Reinhardt, 1998). Table 2.4 shows the monetary, securities and banking crises between 1980 and 2003 with international consequences.

The crises had a major impact on the internationalization of banks, and the international regulatory design. Crises present both risks and opportunities. For internationally active banks, a risk might be that deteriorating economic conditions cause an increase in bad loans and provisioning. The devaluation of foreign currencies changes balance sheet and income statement, and can worsen earnings and risk profile. Worse, counter-parties of the internationally active bank may default, creating losses. This might lead banks active in foreign countries with crises to retreat from foreign activities, selling off activities, to restore domestic financial health (if losses are incurred there). Finally, crises might also lead to nationalization or capital restrictions of banking activities in foreign countries. ABN AMRO lost its branch in 1979 after the regime switch in Iran; the Argentine government froze foreign banks' assets during the currency crisis in 2002.

Crises also present opportunities. Foreign banks are put up for sale after a crisis, creating entry opportunities in previously closed financial markets. After the Asian financial crisis in 1997, several Korean and Japanese banks were privatized and sold to foreign investors. Also, the retreat of other foreign banks increases the market share of incumbent banks. NMB Bank became a market leader in emerging debt loans after American and English banks effectively retreated from this activity. Importantly, customers in countries with crises can move their activities to (foreign) "blue chip" banks with high reputation. Fearing the collapse of domestic banks, Japanese customers strongly increased their deposits with foreign banks in Japan in 1998 (OECD, 1998).

An important case study is the LDC debt crisis in the 1980s, (re)shaping the internationalization strategies of banks for almost a decade, and clearly demonstrating the risks of international banking and the importance of controlling it. The crisis not only forced restructuring of American and European banks, it was also an impetus for the creation of a capital adequacy framework. The LDC debt crisis surfaced in 1982 when the Mexican government announced that it was unable to service an 80 billion US dollar debt. The situation worsened and by the end of 1983, 27 countries owing 239 billion US dollars had rescheduled or were in the process of doing so.

American banks had been active in Latin America since the 1950s, attracted by higher growth rates in the LDC countries, generating corporate investments and financial services. The sharp rise in crude oil price with the oil crisis 1973–74 marked the beginning of almost a decade of inflation and serious balance of payments problems for developing countries, coping with higher costs of oil and imported goods. These deficits were financed through loans from the international capital market, where the eurodollar market increased strongly through the expanding deposit base of oil producing countries. These loans were usually dollar denominated and had interest payments tied to the LIBOR rate.

In reaction of the undesired inflation hike during the second oil crisis of 1979–80 the Federal Reserve raised interest rates. Debt service cost for LDC countries grew progressively because the LIBOR rate was closely tied to US interest rates, and also because the US dollar began to appreciate against other currencies, raising costs for dollar denominated debt further. A slowdown in economic growth and drop in commodity prices left exports stagnant and service commitments hard to meet. The announcement by the Mexican and other Latin American governments to defer payments and the following rescheduling of debt forced American banks' provisions up from 25% to 34% of net income in 1982. Starting in 1987 banks began to realize that a large portion of the LDC loans were not to be repaid. Loan provisions in the United Kingdom and the United States soared to respectively 84% and 120% of net income.

The United Nations Center on Transnational Corporations (UNTNC) examined in 1991 the role internationally active banks played during the lending and the following debt restructuring process, organizing and participating in syndicated loans. The UNTNC study categorized banks in three groups: leaders (five large US banks that dominated the loan syndications), challengers (ten relatively smaller banks, mainly non-US, which actively competed with the leaders in the organization of loan syndication), and followers (ten large non-US banks which, though active in organizing loan syndication, where less active than the challengers).[13]

Banks overlent to major debtors during the lending boom for different reasons. Increased competition meant that banks tended to forgo a risk premium and assume excessive exposure, a form of disaster myopia.[14] Short term profit orientation led banks to shift from more creditworthy clients to riskier clients such as non-guaranteed private sector clients, where "those borrowers suddenly found [the leading banks] to persuade them to take on huge credits which they had not necessarily contemplated borrowing or, at least, not in such large volumes. The [banks] thus tended to depend on income more from special deals with riskier clients..." (UNTNC, 1991, p. 3). Although applicable to a situation ten years later, *The Economist* commented on the state of world banking that "[for a while] lending outstripped economic growth in many countries because banks assumed that loan growth was synonymous with high profits" (*The Economist*, 1992).

During the resulting debt restructuring process, banks exercised much control and influence over the process, forming a cohesive bloc at the beginning. The much higher exposure of US banks than other banks, and the natural concern of US officials to safeguard the domestic financial system, also meant a similar interest of the US government as the banks in the restructuring process.

While provisions might help banks, the austerity policies introduced by the United States and the IMF in exchange for financial assistance did little to reduce the outstanding LDC debt problem for the Latin American countries between 1983 and 1989.[15] Restructuring plans combined the requirement for domestic restructuring with financial assistance, expecting that the resulting economic growth would help cover the debt and interest owed. The creation of a plan by Nicholas Brady, US Secretary of the Treasury, in 1989 finally solved the debt problem by acknowledging that troubled debtors could not fully service their debt and restore growth at the same time. Approximately 32% of the 191 billion US dollars in outstanding loans was written off while the remaining debt was rescheduled converting loans in other financial instruments. In exchange developing countries had to agree to introduce economic reforms. The resolve of the LDC debt crisis forced provisions once again up in 1989.

2.3. Emerging economic structures in the European Union

The emergence of trading blocs has played an important role for banks to internationalize. Trading blocs are essentially discriminatory in nature: they attempt to gain scale advantages in trade by creating large markets for firms, while offering protection from outside the bloc. The creation of trading blocs helped redefine bank management's perception of home markets: the European Union, not Germany or France, became the home market to base the bank's strategy on, triggering further internationalization within the trading bloc.

From all existing regional economic blocs, the European Union is the furthest developed economic bloc.[16] The European Economic Community (EEC) was created by the Treaty of Rome in 1957 with the intention to create an integrated Common Market within which goods, services, labor and capital would move freely. The implementation first focused on the elimination of tariff barriers between member countries, while barriers affecting labor mobility were greatly reduced. 1985 marked the initiative to eliminate all remaining barriers to intra-EC trade, referred to as the Single Market Program or "1992".

A complex interplay between existing commitments to coordinate exchange rates and rigidities in the labor market accelerated the European integration process in the mid-1980s (Eichengreen, 1996). After readjustments in the European Monetary System (EMS) between 1979 and 1983, governments were committed to pegging their exchange rate to the EMS low inflation anchor. This reduced the freedom of European countries to use independent macroeconomic policies to pursue their domestic objectives. Their alternative to realize income distributional objectives and social goals was to turn to micro economic policies of wage moderation, enhanced job security, and increasingly generous unemployment compensation. This in turn hampered the flexibility and efficiency of the labor market, leading to high and rising unemployment.

High unemployment provided the impetus for the Single Market Program in 1986. This program sought to bring down unemployment and create economic growth by less regulatory structures, intensified competition and facilitation of European firms' scale and scope. Prior to removing restrictions on cross border trade of financial services, exchange controls were removed by the Capital Liberalization Directive of June 24, 1988.

A further step to integration was taken in December 1991, when member states of the European Union agreed to create a single currency. At that time, 12 currencies coexisted within the EC, tied together by exchange rate target zones of the EMS. A measure of coordination of European exchange rate was first created in 1972 when the European exchange rate "Snake" agreement was formed, followed by the EMS in 1979 creating the Exchange Rate Mechanism and the European Currency Unit.

Banks were early in recognizing and formulating a strategic response for the developments leading to European integration. In the 1960s and 1970s various forms of cooperation between European banks were initiated. While some were more research or information exchange oriented, others pursued cooperation through intensified correspondent relationships and joint ventures (Roberts & Arnander, 2001). Besides the intention to operate together, these clubs also limited participating banks to expand in the home country of a partner bank. Their legacy played a minor role in the 1990s, when cross shareholdings became important in the increasing number of cross border M&As. For example, ING seemed to prefer acquiring former banking group members,[17] probably due to an intimate knowledge of their operations built up over the years.

Banks were as most market participants caught up in the belief that (European) market share mattered and staged a number of acquisitions, aided by raising stock market prices and falling equity risk premiums. Although European banks greatly increased in size between 1990 and 2000, the relative market position for most of the largest European banks did not materially change over the period. A single market in financial services does not necessarily imply a homogenous market for all services; "retail customers will continue to do business with their familiar institutions in their countries, while wholesale market arbitrage and potential competition ensure that product prices are brought closely into line throughout the EC" (Chrystal & Coughlin, 1992). Or as *The Economist* observed in 1992, "the merger wave is a preemptive strike at competition that has not materialized" and "as merged banks [in the European Union] reduce local competition, they raise the level of competition on a European scale" (*The Economist*, 1992).

Subsequent research pointed in a similar direction: additional concentration without clear signs of efficiency effect through increased competition within Europe, and a segmentation of products and clients in local versus regional markets. Between 1992 and 1996 European integration had low positive effect on banking efficiency, with decreasing scale efficiency and increasing technology efficiency, suggesting that any productivity increase was mainly due to technical progress (Dietsch & Weill, 1998). Davis and Salo (1998) support this for the 1989–95 periodfinding excess banking capacity in the European Union and concluding that the EMU increases the importance of an orderly removal of banking capacity.

The introduction of the Euro in 2002 presaged renewed speculation about an integrated European banking market, and further consolidation. The deterioration of the securities and loan market however forced banks to restructure their activities; the acquisitions of JPMorganChase and Bank of America were probably more instrumental in revitalizing the European banking market discussion.

2.4. Evolution of financial services and products

Changing needs of clients and (de)regulation increasing financial sophistication have caused a large growth in financial products to cater for the clients' needs. Technology has been an important enabler in this process: new distribution channels were created, and process oriented activities were heavily automated. Production of services has become less location bound. The new distribution channel increasingly allowed banking to be "footloose".

2.4.1. Financial innovation, products

Technology is an important enabler for product innovation. Banks produce services: their financial products are mostly transparent, cannot be patented and are easily imitated. The main core products of the banks, deposit taking and extending loans, became mature products, especially in the Western economies after the 1970s. The floating exchange rates environment that existed after the suspension of the US dollar convertibility in the Bretton Wood system presented banks with further opportunities in the foreign exchange markets. More opportunities led to more risk. Banks began to devise hedging instruments, developing markets for future contracts, swaps and currency options (Braithwaite & Drahos, 2000).

The foreign exchange markets grew dramatically; by 1991 the daily net turnover in foreign exchange (including derivate products like futures, options and swaps) was estimated at 900 billion US dollars, close to the total foreign currency reserves of all IMF members. Almost 25% of the foreign exchange business was done in London, New York 16% and Tokyo 11%, with most of the rest spread among Frankfurt, Singapore, Hong Kong, Zurich and Paris. Less than 5% related to underlying trade flows, the demands of companies and individuals that sell or buy in foreign currency. Another 10–15% represented capital movements from institutional investors. The remaining share consisted of dealing that (investment) banks did among themselves (*The Economist*, 1992).

The market changed during the 1990s, reducing the number of participants in the foreign exchange market. The already thin margins, increasing sophistication of corporate clients increasingly managing foreign exchange deals themselves and the prospect of the EMU reducing currencies reduced the number of players further. In 2000 the three biggest foreign exchange banks – Citigroup, Chase Manhattan and Deutsche Bank – commanded 28.9% of overall revenues, while a further 13 banks such as JPMorgan, Bank of America, HSBC, Credit Suisse and UBS, had a market share of 31.4% (Swann, 2000).

Other opportunities occurred through the growth of the offshore currency markets. The Eurocurrency market grew into the world's largest capital market. International banks became key operators, both as lenders and as borrowers. The markets became a crucial source for multinationals, and governments. The combination of floating currencies and the sheer size of the markets brought new risk. Currency speculators had found a new source to fund their activities. Participants trading tangible goods realized that their trade could be wiped out by currency fluctuations. Their desires for risk protection fuelled a new form of service, that of risk protection through the creation of derivative financial instruments. Some forms of these derivates became tradable on the exchanges, creating derivatives markets (Braithwaite & Drahos, 2000)

2.4.2.   Technology/distribution channels

In 1997, Carrington et al. studying the role of technology with British banks, stated that "technology is transforming retail banking and creating value in the economy but [...] it is benefiting consumers rather than the providers. By increasing market efficiency, technology is [...] reducing industry profit and shareholder return" (Carrington, Langguth

& Steiner, 1997). Of the service industries, banks use technology most intensively (Morris, 1987) because of the labor intensive nature of the industry. Technology is a change process: "it makes possible new structures, new and organizational and geographical arrangement of economic activities, new products and new processes, while not making particular outcomes inevitable" (Dicken, 1998). Two technologies have helped overcome the frictions of space and time relevant to the internationalization of firms: transport systems, transferring materials and people from place to place, and communication systems, transmitting information from place to place in different forms (Dicken, 1998). A catalyst enhancing worldwide communication was the development of satellite technology, in essence making communication costs increasingly insensitive to distance.

Information technology emerged from the late 1950s, converging communications technology and computers (Dicken, 1998). From the outset, a main goal was rationalization of existing processes. In the United Kingdom, banks began to invest heavily in computers in the late 1950s and the early 1960s as a response to a projected increase in workload. This was anticipated to follow from an increase in wage payments from retail clients. Growth in demand for bank services led initially to a rapid rise in bank personnel which were becoming increasingly costly. Computers were then implemented to handle routine transactions and increase the capacity of the branches. In the mid-1970s, most branches were connected to a central computer (Channon, 1977). The first automatic teller machine (ATM) was

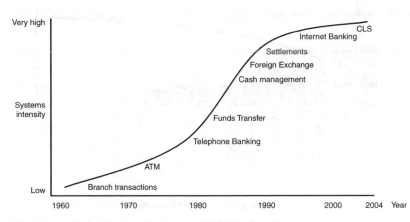

Figure 2.1 Technological developments within banking
Source: Adapted from Carrington et al., 1997, p. 80

installed by Barclays in 1968, and in 1969 Chemical Bank installed the first ATM in the United States.

Between 1980 and 2000, information technology (IT) had changed most banking markets. It enabled outsourcing, especially in high volume and low margin activities. A clear example of this is the custody activities of banks. The increase in securities and transactions raised the IT costs of maintaining custodial activities, while margins fell. Banks increasingly retained the fund management itself but outsourced the administering and settlement of securities to other banks. The establishment of settlement protocols (SWIFT) aided this process of concentration.

Also, an increase of scale and of operations took place in the securities markets. The amount of transactions handled increased dramatically. Information systems also allowed the frequency of quotations of publicly traded shares to increase to real time, increasing liquidity. The speed of securities activities rose dramatically. On the one hand information technology did help reduce the settlement risk,[18] on the other hand it did help increase the volume of transactions dramatically.

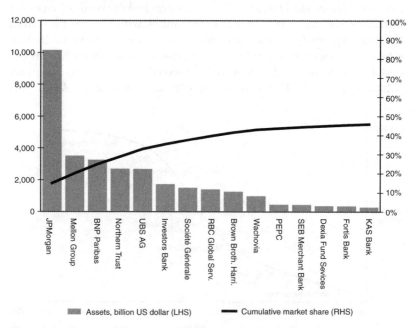

Figure 2.2   Concentration in worldwide custodial activities
Source: www.globalcustody.net

Another major development has been insourcing. What home banking, cash management and internet banking have in common is that the bank provides the client with technology to perform parts of the production process of the bank which were previously proprietary. In the case of cash management, firms increasingly managed without the help of a bank. The main advantage for firms were cost savings; banks on the other hand sought to generate new cash management activities to keep or retain fee income.

From the mid-1990s onwards, internet was added as an additional distribution channel. It basically provided a cheaper distribution channel, with the potential to reduce barriers to entry into the banking industry. By 2000, internet proved successful in providing trading platforms for securities, and the offering of commoditized financial services. It is also an enabling technology for insourcing and outsourcing of activities.

Due to the high interrelatedness of banks through payments and settlements as one of their core activities, the creation of common technology standards or cost sharing were important issues to consider. Sometimes new organizations were set up to handle specific activities.[19]

The effect of information technology on internationalization activities has been twofold. First, it enabled as well as forced the restructuring of activities of banks. Processing and transaction related activities could be centralized. For administration purposes, banks would have to focus on finding skilled personnel as one of the main location decisions. Ireland attracted a number of back office activities in the 1990s, although its significance as a financial center or banking market is minor. Smaller branches and representative offices, especially those located in dense banking regions, could be closed and clients served from regional centers. For example, Dutch clients could also be served from Brussels or London. Also, the activities could simply be closed and trading activities could be conducted electronically elsewhere, still represented in the foreign country by for example an electronic chair at the stock exchange.

The higher degree of information and communication technology also allowed a greater degree of control of foreign activities. Country specific differences aside, banks could in theory monitor and consolidate their foreign activities with higher frequency. This would suggest that monitoring costs were lowered, raising internalization advantages of international activities. Viewed from this angle, information technology might have been an enabler for asset seeking strategies.

3
International Banking, a Theoretical Framework

What are the specific characteristics of internationally active banks? This is the research subject of international financial intermediation, the theoretical foundation for banks. Financial intermediation exists because risks and costs related to financial intermediation functions are expected to be lower when organized by a bank. A review of the literature is presented. Subsequently, what incentives can a bank have to pursue internationalization? Incentives to internationalize are reviewed and clustered, and their relative importance as drivers to internationalize assessed.

A separate section discusses the interaction between financial systems and internationalization. The role financial intermediation plays within the economy is considered, leading to a stylized description of different financial systems, each with distinct consequences for the internationalization motives of banks.

3.1.   The theoretical groundwork for internationalization

In contrast to the growing body of financial intermediation literature, international financial intermediation has been relatively underexposed. A common denominator of international financial intermediation theories is that they incorporate a spatial dimension within mainstream economic analysis. The spatial dimension becomes visible when considering an applicable definition for an international operating bank which has the following characteristics:

1. Assets and/or liabilities other than in the home country and/or home country currency,

2. rights and/or claims other than in the home country and/or home country currency, part of which is
3. issued and collected outside the home country.

This definition agrees with the one the Bank of International Settlements (BIS) uses for international banking statistics (Bank for International Settlements, 2000) and is a slight expansion to the one given by Bryant (1987) and a broadening of Scholtens' definition (1991): any financial transformation that has a cross currency and/or cross country dimension. A pragmatic definition stems from Casson who defined a multinational bank as a bank that owns and controls banking activities in two or more countries (Casson, 1990). Robinson defined multinational banking as "operating a bank in, and conducting banking operations that derive from, many different countries and national systems" (Robinson, 1972). With each of these definitions off balance sheet activities as well as balance sheet activities are covered. Gray and Gray (1981) limited their definition to a financial corporation which acquires deposits and initiates loans from offices located in more than one country, excluding non-interest income.

In theory, international banking activities might be conducted in the home country when the financial intermediary only trades with other financial intermediaries who are active internationally. To exclude the possibility of a narrow interpretation of international financial intermediation a third condition has been added to the definition: there has to be actual cross border activity implying real changes within the organization. With regard to the internationalization part of the definition, no restrictions are formulated with regard to the number of countries or the type of activities. It extends to the whole range of activities of a financial intermediary and international implies simply one or more foreign countries. This is more extensive than for example Cho (1985) who defined a multinational bank as specifically having branches in one or more foreign countries, since more organizational forms than branches can be identified.

3.2.   Incentives to internationalize

A relatively small group of authors has explained the incentives to undertake international financial intermediation. Table 3.1 summarizes the incentives for banks to internationalize forwarded by several authors. Pecchioli (1983) investigated the incentives within the OECD countries, addressing the recent surge of international banking activity

Table 3.1 Incentives to internationalize

Incentive	Description	Relevancy
1. Net interest margin	• Differences in spreads sign of more efficient banking, incentive to exploit outside home country • Related to economies of scale • Related to countries with differing degrees of financial innovation	• Relevant for countries with different spreads, not relevant for countries with same spread • Difference in spreads may not be exploited due to regulatory barriers
2. New markets • New market, similar demand	• Exploit internalization advantages with existing internationalizing clients • Exploit economies of scale/scope	• Relevant if characteristics of financial service can be easily replicated outside home country
• New market, new demand	• Provide financial service that cannot be generated at home, for example in offshore markets or large financial centers	• Relevant for countries without large financial centers
• Rescaling home boundaries	• Enlarging concept of "domestic market", depending on political/societal framework	• Relevant if banks are located in the European Union or NAFTA
3. Differences in economic structure • Different characteristics	• Differences in wealth causes different intensity demand: might be exploited	• Relevant if entry takes place in developing countries such as Eastern Europe where financial services and sophistication has scope to grow • Countries with different social security and/or financial systems: different wealth accumulating structures and different needs for financial services
• Difference in economic cycles	• Incentive based on risk/return diversification	• Not relevant if countries are financially and economically converging, like the European Union
• Demographics	• Aging population versus young population • Shift from interest to fee income (diversification)	• Relevant if for example European banks expand into Latin America or Asia, not if European banks expand within their own region

Table 3.1 Incentives to internationalize – *continued*

Incentive	Description	Relevancy
	• Uphold rate of return	• Not relevant if internalization in major western economies (similar demographics)
4. Herding	• Rational reaction to potential opportunity loss caused by action of first mover bank	• Relevant if disproportional high investment allocation in certain activities/areas; not relevant if explaining why the first mover is the first mover
5. Regulation		
• Incentive to internationalize	• Limited growth opportunities in home country	• Relevant for relatively highly regulated countries
• International regulation	• Upward regulation to achieve stable international financial system	• Relevant for banks with higher quality standards: signaling advantage is incentive • Not relevant for banks with low solvency: compliance with international regulation serves as barrier to entry
6. Market power and concentration		
• Concentration as incentive to internationalize	• Efficiency leads to market concentration, incentive to exploit abroad	• Relevant for highly concentrated domestic banking markets
• Concentration as pull factor	• Concentration suggests higher margins to be earned	• Relevant if there are low barriers of entry in the foreign banking markets • Not relevant if concentration is stimulated by foreign regulatory authorities; accompanied with high barriers of entry
7. Clients		
• Follow client	• Fear of losing client (negative impulse) or capitalize on existing internalization advantage (positive impulse)	• Relevant if foreign banking market has higher degree financial innovation and/or lower cost structure

Table 3.1 Incentives to internationalize – *continued*

Incentive	Description	Relevancy
• Lead client	• Enhancing self-image of organization: identifying growth opportunities for its domestic clients and helping them to exploit these • Anticipate FDI and export flows	• Relevant if banks set up activities in countries expecting financial liberalization
8. Economies of scale and scope	• Marginal costs lower and/or revenues increase with each additional unit (per client) sold outside the home country • Defence for existence of universal banks and financial conglomerates	• Relevant if economies can only be achieved outside home country • Relevant if banks' home markets are small • Relevant for investment banking, asset management and other corporate finance activities. Less relevant if economies are aimed in areas such as retail banking, unless common processes, technology or information platforms are shared between foreign and domestic retail branch networks
9. Cost of capital	• International activities are undertaken to lower current cost of capital and/or to uphold current rate of return • Combination of financial leverage and risk/return diversification	• Relevant if relative stock market valuation in home country is higher than bank valuation in foreign countries • Not relevant if countries share same cost of capital, or no major differences in stock market valuation exists
10. Risk/return diversification	• Adding new activities in different countries lowers correlation between activities. This should stabilize earnings, and increase market value	• Not relevant if activities are set up in countries with same economic structure/cycle
11. Historical and cultural determinants	• Common language, administrative system knowledge of country lowers hurdle to undertake activities in foreign country	• Relevant if foreign country is former colony • Relevant if foreign country shares perceived cultural or legal characteristics

in the 1970s. Aliber (1984) reviewed empirical literature published on international financial intermediation. Bryant (1987) presented an overview of reasons for financial intermediaries to internationalize. Walter (1988) examined the internationalization process of banking while Scholtens (1991) identified building stones needed for an integrated theory of international financial intermediation.

Scholtens (1991) classified explanatory theories for international financial intermediation into five categories: trade and foreign direct investment; industrial organization; internalization; portfolio; and eclectic explanations. The application of a multinational enterprise framework by Dunning (1992) combines three types of competition advantage that are a prerequisite to undertake foreign activities: Organization, Location and Internalization advantages. Canals (1997) investigated internationalization strategies of banks and presented an internationalization model which is based on three groups of incentives. A combination of scale, customer service and resource transfer are the main motives for international activity.

The major incentives to internationalize are considered here.

3.2.1. Client

Banks go abroad to serve their domestic customers who have gone abroad, described by Metais as a gravitational *pull effect* (Metais, 1979, quoted in Aliber, 1984). The pull effect traces its roots to three explanations. The first is that domestic banks in foreign countries are poorly equipped to serve the branches set up by the entering firms. Thus, clients setting up activities in foreign countries only trigger an incentive for banks to internationalize if the financial innovation and sophistication in the foreign country lags behind that of the home country.

A second rationale is that banks follow their domestic customer abroad to reduce the likelihood that they might lose their business to host-country banks. Ceteris paribus this likelihood increases if the financial sophistication of the host country is greater than that of the home country. If so, one would expect the services and organization of the foreign activity of the bank to be similar to that of the home country, since it merely serves as an extension.

A third approach is that banks follow their customer abroad to further exploit the internalization advantages built up in the home country, providing mutual added benefits for both bank and firm. "Having a presence [...] cements a relationship that already exists at home" (Walter, 1988).

The *pull effect* can also change into a *push effect*: with a presence in a host country a bank can lead or even coax its domestic customers into foreign activities. A bank that is well established abroad can provide the services needed to facilitate the decision of a firm to enter a host market (Walter, 1988). Bryant observed that "bankers talking about location decisions for foreign banks and subsidiaries often portray their organization behaving in a anticipatory way, seeking new customers and profit opportunities in advance of the current service requirements of existing customers" (Bryant, 1987).

3.2.2.   Perception of market

Entering new geographical markets when a bank feels the boundaries in the home market are stretched or has limited further opportunities is an intuitive incentive, especially for banks with a small home market. The perception of what constitutes a market changes when banking customers from the home market demand certain products, part of which cannot be generated in the home market. A good example of this is the Euromarket (Roberts & Arnander, 2001). Eurocurrencies are deposits of major currencies with banks physically situated outside the home market of the currency. At the outset the eurodollar market, i.e. deposits of US dollars with banks outside the United States, was located in European financial centers.

Economic and political integration effectively change boundaries of a market too. After the Second World War, banks in Europe engaged in international activities but their main focus stayed the home country. This began to change when advanced plans for a common economic union finally took off from 1991 onwards. This also shifted the strategic framework in which financial intermediaries had to think. The groups of buyers were not only domestic but could be found throughout Europe.

3.2.3.   Spreads

For most banks the net interest income earned on loans (spread) is the main source of income. Profiting from higher spreads elsewhere is then a powerful motive. Differences in spreads might be a location-specific advantage that reflects the relative factor endowments of a country rather than a firm-specific advantage owned by a group of firms (Aliber, 1984). Spreads can also be interpreted as cost differentials, and relative cost differentials can be exploited by trade benefiting both domestic and foreign banking market. The law of comparative advantage has been a traditional explanation why international trade of goods and services take place and a convincing statement how trade can be welfare enhancing. The Hekscher-Ohlin-Samuelson framework can straightforward be applied to financial services (Scholtens, 1991). Countries that are endowed with different comparative costs for the production of goods and services have a potential comparative advantage in a number of goods and services which they can exploit by trade.

For financial intermediaries this advantage is visible through the loan-deposit spread. A lower spread would suggest more efficient financial intermediaries. Banks in countries with relatively low spreads have an incentive to establish foreign activities because they have developed low cost technologies for intermediation (Aliber, 1984). Thus spreads can serve as a push factor on the cost side (exploitation of low cost technology) but simultaneously as a pull factor on the earnings side, earning higher spreads elsewhere.

Several distorting factors can be identified. These differences in spreads can also be the result of regulation combined with different local financing habits. Differences in financing structure of firms and households between countries could also cause distorting signals for the use of spreads as a motive to internationalize. For example the term structure of the United Kingdom has shown a flat or even negative sloping term structure during the 1980s and 1990s. In contrast to other European countries British households tend to finance their mortgages with short term loans, which ultimately results in a negative spread in contrast to other European countries which usually exhibit a positive spread. These differences cannot be exploited by international financial intermediation.

3.2.4. Differences in economic structure

The structure, and growth rate of the domestic economy compared to foreign economies is hypothetically an incentive to internationalize. Differences in economic structure and financial systems can be exploited, the existence of different economic cycles, as well as different demographics. Differences in economic growth are a driver for internationalization activities; higher economic growth in foreign countries implies theoretically a lower level of provisioning for bad loans, an increase in loans and a stronger capitalization of the balance sheet. On average, economic growth and GDP per capita are positive drivers for bank profitability (Demirgüç-Kunt & Huizinga, 2001).

For the internationalization activities of banks being in the right geographical market at the right time might make a difference. The effect of geographical diversification has decreased over time though. Dalsgaard et al. (2002) found that for the business cycles of OECD countries the divergence in output gaps decreased between 1980 and 2000, caused by a reduced importance of stock building and more stable private consumption. Also, divergence in output gaps across OECD economies diminished since the 1960s, especially since the 1990s. Regional integration and financial integration could explain this tendency (Dalsgaard, Elmeskov & Park, 2002).

Structural changes in economic and financial structure can also be an important incentive to internationalize (Dalsgaard, Elmeskov & Park, 2002). The transition from an industrial society to a service oriented society implies a shift in the structural composition of the financial savings and investments patterns. Emerging countries for example tend to focus in an earlier stage on the build up of industry which is capital intensive, creating larger borrowing needs for longer periods of time. On the other hand, economies which become more service oriented also become less capital intensive, creating larger saving surpluses. Demographic factors magnify the incentive to internationalize: service oriented economies tend to have an aging population, who have had the opportunity to build up savings over a longer period of time. In an aging population the demand for mortgages will be reduced, shifting both the balance sheet composition of a bank and its product mix. Also, an aging population will eventually decline in size and limit the growth rate of financial services. One of the incentives for Spanish banks to internationalize to Latin America is the (aging) population of Spain compared to the growing population of Latin America (Sebastian & Hernansanz, 2000).

3.2.5. Regulation

(De)regulation, domestic or foreign, has always been a strong incentive to internationalize. Four groups of incentives can be identified: 1) domestic regulation as an incentive for banks to internationalize, 2) regulation controlling the entry and conduct of foreign banks in the country, 3) international regulation and 4) deregulation and privatization.

- *Domestic country regulation as incentive for banks to internationalize*

  Regulatory biases between countries can provide an incentive to conduct business through activities in foreign countries offering greater freedom from supervision than in the home country. The most relevant regulatory provisions relate to exchange controls, taxation, monetary policy, entry in the market and the relationship between different financial activities (Dicken, 1998, Pecchioli, 1983). Regulation as an incentive can be viewed as a push incentive, also known as escape motive, or as a pull incentive.

The differential fiscal treatment and double taxation conventions have always been an important factor to promote financial activities abroad. Banks in highly taxed countries may have an incentive to set up subsidiaries in countries with lower taxes, and channel business through there. Strict implementation of limiting the scope for business expansion, application of a reserve requirement, ceilings on interest rates, and other quantitative controls in domestic bank credit expansion can promote offshore growth of business.

- *Regulation controlling the entry and conduct of new foreign banks in host country*

The regulator of the foreign country has also some instruments to control entry and conduct of foreign banks (Dicken, 1998), such as regulation to govern the entry of firms: a barrier to entry in the market, or regulation to govern relationships between different financial activities: the influencing of market conduct.

The regulation to govern the entry of banks can result in a generic or specific regulation as a barrier to entry in the market. The generic one is through its macroeconomic policy, combining exchange controls, monetary policy and differential tax treatments. It concerns all firms wanting to do business in the foreign country but hits financial intermediaries especially.

A financial intermediary might have a strong incentive to overcome these regulations in the following situations when part of the financial intermediary's customer base has dealing in that country. This was the case with expanding US banking presence in Europe after the Second World War. Alternatively, the bank might have a long term strategy in mind. There exists an expectation of above average returns as a long term investor which will materialize when reforms take place and capital can be converted. This explains banking presence in China or other countries in South East Asia.

A special case of generic regulation is entry of foreign banks as a by-result of domestic regulation. When the American Franklin National Bank failed, there were few potential banks in the United States able to buy the bank because of interstate banking laws. In another case, when transport company GATX was required to sell LaSalle National Bank of Chicago, US banks could not acquire

LaSalle because of Illinois and federal banking laws and restrictions (Walter & Gray, 1983).

Finally, regulatory authorities can use regulation as a competitive weapon, easing regulation controlling the entry and conduct of banks compared to other countries. Countries with a competitive advantage in the production of banking services are more likely to prefer open banking systems (Walter & Gray, 1983). Buch and DeLong (2001) find that in general, regulation has had a negative effect on foreign bank mergers and acquisitions between 1978 and 2001.

3.2.6.   Historical and cultural determinants

Geographic proximity, a former colonial period or immigration are important factors to explain why a bank decides to undertake activities in a foreign country. A shared common language, administrative system and culture are an enormous help for banks wishing to enter these markets (Sebastian & Hernansanz, 2000). The expansion of American banks setting up offices in London in the 1950s and 1960s had been advanced by the fact that both countries share a common language (Roberts & Arnander, 2001). The presence of British banks in the 1970s in Africa can be explained by the former presence of British colonies there, with a similar case for French banks in Central Africa and South East Asia or Spanish banks in South America. Australian banks sought markets where similar products and services could be offered as supplied through their domestic branches, leading the banks to internationalize to countries such as New Zealand and the Pacific islands, sharing a common British heritage (Merrett, 2002).

These cultural and historical determinants offer several advantages when banks are internationalizing. First, banks can commercialize the same products with similar marketing techniques, lowering entry and sales costs of new banking services. The use of the same language facilitates the transfer of know how and could help the process of integration within the organization, when foreign expansion is achieved by acquiring local banks.

3.2.7.   Herding

Herding takes place when a bank imitates the actions of other banks; the bank must be aware of and be influenced by other banks' actions. The bank can be said to herd when knowledge that others are investing changes its decision from not investing to making the investment (Bikhchandani & Sharma, 2000). Herding can be embedded in Vernon's and Hymes' framework of oligopolistic behavior of transnational corporations (Dicken, 1998). Vernon found that the development sequence consists of three phases, innovation based oligopolies, mature oligopolies and senescent oligopolies. Whereas the innovation based phase is still located in the home country, in the mature phase firms will try to react to match the actions of their major competitors. Location patterns tend to show a follow-the-leader strategy whereby a move of a firm to undertake activities in a certain country is likely to be followed by the other major competitors, leading to a clustering in time and space.

For the formation of financial centers, a long term exhibition of herding, the spatial combinations of trade, political power and minimization of transportation and communication costs between banks have been instrumental in the nurturing of such financial centers (Kindleberger, 1974).

When payments require a physical relationship of either wealth transfer or administrative papers, the efficiency of a single center with intermediaries specializing in clearing is paramount. The rise of a number of financial centers is intertwined with the rise of trade activities in those cities. Also, political and administrative concentration of functions in one city might help. The formation and growing duties of central banks have been an important thrust for many financial centers.

After the initial founding, the financial center creates its own momentum for structural herding over time: communication costs are structurally lowered, lags in communication time lowered (of crucial importance before the invention of the telegraph), pools of human resources for financial intermediation created and other infrastructure or tax related advantages. When the securities markets were deregulated in the 1980s, European, American and Japanese banks acquired or set up investment banking activities in London because the city had a well developed banking structure, and enjoyed attractive features[1] which helped it offset the disadvantage of not having a large domestic currency base like the financial centers of New York or Tokyo.

3.2.8. Market power and concentration

Market power and concentration within banking markets can provide incentives for international activities. First, an increase in concentration of banking activities can limit expected earnings growth a bank can achieve. An increase in domestic market share might be difficult to achieve because of the high(er) market shares of other banks; earnings growth is then more easily achieved outside the home country in markets where domestic limitations do not apply. Dutch and Swiss banks operated from a small home market with high concentration, German banks operated from a large home market with limited growth opportunities due to regulation. Second, because some banks are more efficient or successful than others, they tend to gain more market share leading to a higher concentration ratio. Thus higher concentration is a sign that a number of banks are very efficient. Banks then could have an incentive to exploit this efficiency further outside the home country.

Efficiency gains may also be the result of merger and acquisition activity. Most commonly mentioned are the benefits which can be derived from lower costs if economies of scale and scope can be achieved (Pilloff & Santomero, 1998). Cost efficiency may also be improved if the management of the acquiring institution is more skilled at achieving lower expenses for any given activity than that of the acquired firm. Third, analogous to the cost efficiency argument, additional revenues can be achieved as a result of larger market power. This argument can only serve as an incentive if the cross border M&A concerns a specialized and global financial service where the number of competitors is limited, such as custody or investment banking.

Fourth, the bank can diversify its activities through mergers or acquisitions. Diversification in itself does not enhance efficiency; it broadens the geographic reach of a bank or increases the breadth of products. In theory this could lead to less variability in earnings raising the market value of the bank, although the nature of the diversification itself can also have negative repercussions for the market value of the bank. It may lead to a discount in market value reflecting agency problems between shareholders and management (Lins & Servaes, 1999).

Markets are imperfect; the greater the imperfection the greater will be the incentive for a bank to perform the function of the market itself by *internalizing* market transactions (Dicken, 1998): it is more efficient or profitable for the firm to create an internal market within the firm and do the transaction than to do the transaction in the open (capital) market. Specific advantages result from internalizing a long term relationship with the client. A bank following its client can adequately be explained with internalization (cf. Casson, 1990). Internalization can be generated by economies, cost of capital or risk/return diversification.

3.2.9. Economies

The internationally active bank can rationalize or base this decision on two major types of potential cost advantages: economies of scale and economies of scope. Existence of economies of scale in this area is doubtful (Canals, 1993). Llewellyn (1999) found that the results on research of bank economies were "at best, inconclusive and ambiguous".

However, he pointed out that many studies on scale efficiencies in the late 1980s and early 1990s used US data from the 1980s, finding in general a flat U-shaped cost curve with slightly more efficiency benefits for smaller than for larger banks. Also, more recent research using different econometric techniques suggests that there might be more substantial gains from consolidation. Another area which has increased in importance in relation to economies of scale is investments in information technology.

If it has been difficult to obtain a clear picture of economies of scale as an incentive to internationalize, economies of scope is in some respect even more complex. A cost reduction with economies of scope results through cross selling. Relationships between client and financial intermediary can be built through interactions over multiple products. The bank can spread any fixed costs of producing information about the client over multiple products, increasing the precision of the borrower's information (De Bondt, 1998). Here too, similar reservations as with economies of scale apply. "The alleged case for financial conglomerates is based ultimately on economies of scope which in practice often fails to materialize" (Llewellyn, 1999). Few cost savings have been found in research studies, most studies are inconclusive, and existing reports suggest modest gains that have been achieved.[2] Data availability and complexity of the research methodology to analyze this does not help either (Berger & Mester, 1999).

As incentives for internationalization, economies can be an incentive to internationalize if it cannot be achieved domestically, or if it can be achieved more easily outside the home country:

- Economies as an incentive to internationalize are relevant if they cannot be achieved in the home market: the absolute growth potential in the home market is limited in size and/or market share.
- Economies are more easily achieved in the foreign country than in the home country: structural difference in costs may originate because the bank has to politically commit itself to the country of origination.

The first argument relates to physical or competitive boundaries. The market share of the financial intermediary is such that either government can prohibit further expansion in the home country, or that there are no further opportunities to expand. Even so, the opportunities to expand can result in diseconomies of scale when the market is overbanked. The marginal cost of acquiring market share may be larger than the marginal cost reductions achieved by the larger market share. Small countries tend to exhibit high concentration ratios, and also a strong incentive to internationalize (Netherlands, Switzerland).

Tschoegl (2002) found that size correlates with foreign expansion of banks; linking it to the client incentive. Large banks tend to have enough domestic multinational companies and clients engaged in foreign trade to justify going abroad. This suggests that banks have a hurdle rate for return on investments, income or number of clients in mind when considering internationalization to a country.

3.2.10.   Cost of capital

Capital markets in different countries can impose very different capital costs on banks. In the 1980s, banks with high capital costs found it difficult to compete in the US wholesale market with low margins and lost market share, while banks with low capital costs gained market share (Zimmer & McCauley, 1991). An incentive for internationalization is that financial intermediaries strive to achieve a minimal acceptable return, for their total banking activities. If domestic returns start to fall, and there are no alternatives available in the home country, then foreign activities are sought after to supplement the return. An example of this was provided by a study of the Spanish banks' strategy in Latin America (Sebastian & Hernansanz, 2000). Here, the success of these strategies is measured (among other factors) by the degree that the increase of income from Latin America has compensated for the fall of income in Spain.

Aliber (1984) cited a number of authors who found that foreign banks expanded in the United States because American bank stocks were relatively low compared to bank stocks in other major stock markets. A depressed equity value could be interpreted as an indication that the cost of capital is relatively high. This opportunity can be grasped by foreign banks setting up activities in the United States with comparable or lower cost of capital as in the home country, an unlikely proposition according to research by Nolle (1995) or Peek et al. (1999). Another alternative route to profit is by acquiring the depressed stocks and creating subsidiaries. The combination of balance sheet and earning figures of the home country and foreign subsidiary then provides a more favorable leverage, increasing market value at home. Cost of capital linked to stock market value can also be an argument why domestic consolidation takes precedence over international expansion for certain periods. In the Netherlands the upsurge of international activities in the 1990s was preceded by a domestic consolidation wave. One of the main reasons for the consolidation was the relatively low share price valuation of Dutch banks compared to other foreign banks, making it more worthwhile for management to merge with another domestic partner than a foreign one.

3.2.11. Risk/return diversification

Another approach to explain – more to rationalize – international financial intermediation stems from investment theory. The financial intermediary could be modeled as a portfolio manager in accordance with the modern portfolio theory, taking advantage of the low correlation between withdrawals by depositors and the loans extended (Pyle, 1971). Since loans correlate less than perfect with deposits, the bank could construct a mean-variance efficient portfolio as a combination of loans and deposits. As a result the risks and costs of organizing financial intermediation activities through the bank are expected to be lower than if these are achieved through open markets and economies of scope.

This argument can be geographically extended. Available empirical research suggests that some types of geographically diversified organizations are likely to improve their risk-expected return trade off. An early adaptation of modern portfolio theory is made by Rugman (1976), finding that a higher ratio of foreign to total operations is positively related to a lower variability of earnings to book value. He concludes that internationalization is risk reducing. Literature on commercial banks in the United States generally finds that larger, more geographically diversified institutions tend to have better risk-return trade off (Berger, DeYoung, Genay & Udell, 2000).

This argument has limited validation if geographical diversification takes place in countries which share similar economic structures resulting in market characteristics with high correlations (cf. Dalsgaard, Elmeskov & Park, 2002). However it can be a validation for diversification between different economic regions: the larger the geographical and cultural distance, the more chance a financial intermediary has that it is not properly valued. Furthermore, risk diversification can also be achieved by acquiring foreign activities not related to financial intermediation or by acquiring activities as purely financial investments. Portfolio theory as an incentive is therefore a more ex post reasoning.

Also, geographical diversification of activities tends to be associated with economies of scale. Goldberg (2001) investigated determinants for American bank loan exposure in Latin America and emerging Asian countries for American banks between 1984 and 2000, and found that large American banks maintain claims on a larger number of countries than smaller banks. Finally, potential risk/return diversification benefits must be weighed against the introduction of currency risk and geographical diversification against the introduction of country risk in the overall portfolio (Shapiro, 1985).

Banks do not fully exploit risk/return diversifications. Stulz (2005) compared outstanding claims of a country with that of banks; and found that banks underallocate their foreign weightings; Buch et al. (2004) constructed mean-variance efficient bank portfolios with aggregated data and argued that in an optimal setting, banks should increase their weighting.

3.2.12.   Shareholder return and market value

A fundamental assumption in investment literature over the last decades is that the share price is determined in a more or less efficient manner: all information is reflected in the price of equity (Reilly & Brown, 2000). A change in equity price implies that new information has been assessed by the participants on the stock market and has been incorporated. This also implies that shareholder return can be influenced by an overwhelming number of variables. Over the years several valuation techniques have been developed to provide a basis for decision-making and control purposes, identifying drivers for management to increase shareholder value, which in turn should positively influence shareholder return. Typical drivers for banks are cost of capital, capital employed, (residual or free) cash flow, gross income and operating expenses (Davies, Arnold, Cornelius & Walmsley, 2000). The relationship between shareholder return and the valuation drivers has yet to be empirically determined. Davies et al. (2000) cite research by consultancy firms determining the extent to which valuation models explain the change in shareholder return, however warning that little independent research support such findings.

In a stylized world shareholders provide the funding for the bank's capital and are as stakeholders interested in propositions to internationalize if this leads to an increase of the bank's capital and reserves, and an appreciation of the shareholder return during the process. Table 3.2 presents a possible relationship between factors driving shareholder return and how internationalization strategies might influence

Table 3.2 Shareholder return drivers and internationalization

Description	Drivers	Internationalization activities to influence factors
Shareholder value drivers	Cash flow generation	• Higher income host country
	Loan quality	• Activities in host countries with higher economic growth
	Cost-to-income ratio	• Activities in host countries with lower costs • Similar activities in host countries for economies of scale
	Return on equity	• Generate higher income with relatively same amount of capital outside home country
	Ratio of non-interest income to gross income	• Activities in countries with higher non-interest market
Investor relations drivers	Stability in earnings	• Lower variability through geographic diversification
	Earnings surprises	• Lower variability through geographic diversification
	Risk management	• Improve loan provisions through geographic diversification of bad loans
	Peer group performance	• Improve earnings • Lower variability of earnings • Herding
	Beta bank compared to peer group	• Improve earnings, • Lower variability of earnings • Herding
Stock market characteristics	Characteristics of stock market: relative valuation	• Mergers and acquisitions in host country to improve earnings if the relative valuation (for example, price-earnings ratio) in the home country is higher than in the host country.
	Characteristics of stock market: relative valuation: size, liquidity	• Funding bank capital outside the home country

these factors. For example, if cash flow generation is a driver that management can influence to increase shareholder return, and higher cash flow generation cannot be achieved at home, then it might be a driver to internationalize. By setting up or acquiring foreign activities, a higher expected cash flow might be achieved.

Table 3.2 shows drivers for shareholder return that can be (partly) influenced by internationalization. When implementing these drivers, bank management has to balance the negative and positive effects of internationalization activities on shareholder return. For example, management might decide that an increase in the non-interest income to gross income ratio is best achieved with banking activities in a foreign country. While this counts as a positive stimulus for shareholder value drivers which management can control, it can also be assessed by shareholders as a negative sign: variability of earnings might rise, increasing the chance of a negative earnings surprise. Bank management then has to balance between these variables.

Shareholder return as an incentive to internationalize does not necessarily imply that banks have to increase earnings (growth) by internationalizing; the lowering of variability might be enough to increase shareholder value. In this view, support investments might be defined as internationalization activities that lower earnings, but are beneficial to the market valuation of the bank because variability of earnings is lowered. Also, internationalization activities focusing on activities with similar earnings, variability and high correlation between home and host country do not a priori create additional shareholder value. Either economies of scale are expected (lowering the required rate of return) or non-financial motives such as asset seeking are sought after.

3.2.13.   Financial systems

Financial systems, financial development and internationalization are intertwined. In general three different financial systems can be identified: bank oriented, market oriented and government/institution directed financial systems. With market oriented financial systems (for example the United States or the United Kingdom), the allocation process is mainly determined by market prices, and a substantial part of the banks' main activities is performed by capital markets. With bank oriented financial systems (for example Germany or France), the price process still is important, but the bank itself also plays an important part in the allocation process. Finally, in government/institution directed systems (such as Japan), banks can be instrumental in achieving the government's objectives.

Hypothetically, differences between financial systems and changes within financial systems might also be an incentive for banks to internationalize. Table 3.3 presents incentives to internationalize from and to (countries with) different financial systems than domestically.

In market oriented financial systems, the price mechanism plays a central role, allowing banks to securitize their loans but also forcing them to compete strongly than in the other financial systems. For example, the environment for funding is more competitive, leading to financial innovations and new products. Banks operating in such a financial system can export this financial innovation to other countries (in bank oriented and government/institution led financial systems). For banks not located in a country with a market oriented financial system, the financial innovation might be an incentive to internationalize (cf. the transfer of resources as an incentive to internationalize (Canals, 1997)). The long term banking relationships in bank oriented and government/institution directed financial systems can form a barrier to entry for banks from a market oriented system, they are therefore likely to concentrate on specialized services based on the financial innovation achieved domestically.

Finally, internationalization of banks in a government/institution directed financial system might be promoted by government. Governmental goals such as power and prestige are visibly promoted, combined with escapist motives to evade strict government regulation at home. Crédit Lyonnais' management built their internationalization

Table 3.3 Financial systems and incentives to internationalize

Effect on international activities of banks	Bank oriented	Market oriented	Government/ institution directed
Incentives for foreign banks to internationalize to financial system	• Difficult to gain market share due to banking relationships • Foreign banks compete in specialized services	• High market share • Competition in all services • Acquire product innovation	• Low market share • Competition in specialized services
Incentives for domestic banks in financial system to internationalize	• Evade domestic regulation • Exploit advantage of long term banking relationship	• Exploit comparative advantage gained by price efficiency and product innovation	• Create national champion • Evade domestic regulation

Table 3.4 Change in financial systems as an incentive to internationalize

		Transition from		
		Market oriented	Bank oriented	Government/institution directed
Transition into	**Market oriented**		(+) Larger and more liquid securities market (–) Decrease of spread between home and host country (+) Price efficiency becomes more important than client relationship	(+) Larger and more liquid securities market/privatizations (–) Decrease of spread between home and host country (+) Price efficiency becomes more important than client relationship
	Bank oriented	(+) Increase in spread between home and host country (+) Client relationship becomes more important than price efficiency		(+) Similar institutional relationship between financial intermediary and bank (–) High entry barrier to be part of institutional arrangement
	Government/ institution directed	(+) Increase in spread between home and host country (–) Increase in entry barriers for foreign banks, part of institutional arrangement	(+) Similar institutional relationship between financial intermediary and bank (–) High entry barrier to be part of institutional arrangement	

Note: (+) Positive incentive to internationalize, (–) Negative incentive to internationalize

strategy in the 1980s and early 1990s on surpassing Deutsche Bank with the tacit support of the French government. This combination serving both goals implicitly inhabits a moral hazard for bank management.

Table 3.4 suggests some positive incentives to internationalize and incentives to abstain from internationalization when financial systems change. If a bank has operations in a country were the financial system changes, positive incentives then indicate motivation to further expand activities, whereas negative incentives indicate a motivation to decrease activities or even exit the host country.

The (perceived) change from a bank oriented or institution directed system to a market oriented system in a host country can be an important incentive to internationalize: a larger part of assets will be securitized, raising the volume and liquidity of the securities market.

The change to a market oriented system increases first of all the size of the market, and might also lower entry barriers because activities related to long term relationships and strategic stakeholders diminish in importance. By the end of the 1990s the expected imminent restructuring of corporate Germany heralding a more market oriented economy was viewed as a huge opportunity for investment banking activities. American investment banks Goldman Sachs and JPMorgan increased their activities in Frankfurt in the wake of these anticipated changes (that subsequently did not materialize).[3] The argument for the home country is more complex. If the financial system in the home country were to change from bank oriented to market oriented, the opportunities to raise funding for internationalization activities would increase. On the other hand, such a change would invoke an increase of the domestic securities market, in itself decreasing the need to internationalize.

3.3. Shaping international organizations

Banks have a wide range of organizational forms to choose from when establishing a presence in a foreign country, with different control aspects (Anderson & Gatignon, 1999): diffused interests (alliance, affiliates, representative office), balanced interests (consortium, syndicate, joint venture) and dominant equity interest (agency, subsidiary, branch). Pecchioli reviews the characteristics of these organizational modes (Pecchioli, 1983; see also Robinson, 1972). Banks cannot use all available organizational forms though; licensing or franchising as an organizational form to internationalize does not apply for banks. The lack of patent or copyright protection on most banking innovations means that banks are often constrained from exploiting them abroad through these forms (Ursacki & Vertinsky, 1992).

3.3.1. Choosing the organizational form

Research on the choice of organizational form suggests that bank size, regulation, the relationship with its clients, the extent of other foreign activities and relative costs are all issues raised above to explain (modulation between establishing) organizational forms.[4] The organizational form chosen by the bank in the foreign country might be a good indicator of the level of commitment in the host country, since it reflects the banks' willingness to make a costly and long term investment (Blandon, 1998; Ursacki & Vertinsky, 1992). The choice between the various organizational forms depends on a number of factors mentioned in earlier discussion: 1) regulatory and legal structure, 2) entry barriers, 3) strategy, and 4) relative costs.

- First, the *foreign regulatory and legal structure* influences the choice of organizational form to a large degree. From the viewpoint of the home country, restrictions on the type of organizational form usually stem from considerations relating to problems with supervision and monitoring banks' positions booked in a foreign center, and the implications for the extension of parental responsibility (Pecchioli, 1983). Specific requirements may determine the choice of organizational form (Curry, Fung & Harper, 2003). For example, minimum capital requirements have to be met, perhaps different from the host country banks' capital requirements. Foreign taxation may also be an important factor in the choice of organizational form: the tax treatment of directly controlled foreign branches can differ from the tax treatment of foreign bank subsidiaries. Finally, the (desired) legal liability structure in the host country also influences the choice of organizational form.
- Second, *entry barriers* in combination with the type of activity the bank wants to undertake are instrumental for the choice of organizational forms. Host countries may impose entry barriers with a view to retaining effective control over, and protecting the local banking system. Where limited entry restrictions apply, they are usually modulated to take account of the possible benefits to be derived from certain types of foreign banking presence. For example, the United Kingdom and Switzerland allow foreign banks only on condition of reciprocity, i.e. British or Swiss banks are guaranteed entry in the entrant's home market (Baldock, 1991 cited in Curry, Fung & Harper, 2003).
- Third, decisions about the structure and organization of a foreign network are primarily based on a bank's overall *strategy*, in particular with regard to its involvement in trade-related business, global funding policies, the servicing of multinational customers and the extent of involvement in local currency business. Given the choice of organizational form, the change of organizational form also has an important signaling effect to the customers in the home country. Signaling may be more important for relatively large banks. A priori it is to be expected that banks with more assets tend to establish relatively more subsidiaries and/or branches since they have the capital and therefore the opportunity to commit to such responsibilities.

Another signaling factor (as well as a cost factor) is the publication requirements for regulators attached to different organizational forms. Due to the size and organizational impact, foreign mergers and acquisitions are likely to have the largest impact on a bank's strategy. The European Central Bank (2000b) examined motivations for foreign mergers and acquisitions (Table 3.5).

Table 3.5   Rationalizations for international M&As

	International bank M&As: similar foreign financial activities as domestically	International conglomeration: different foreign financial activities from domestically
Main motive	• Size, i.e. the need to be big enough in the market	• Size • Economies of scope through cross selling
Other motives	• Matching the size of clients and following clients • Possible rationalization within administrative functions	• Risk and revenue diversification • The M&A offers few rationalizations because institutions are in different countries and subject to different regulations and practices

- The decision for a particular organizational form can also be influenced by *relative costs* on a firm level. Major costs are rents, salaries and communication costs. If the banking activity in the foreign country tends to require extensive face-to-face communication, communication costs tend to be disproportionally high if conducted from the head office for all but very large transactions (Ursacki & Vertinsky, 1992). Banks seeking to gain market share for smaller transactions may have little choice but to establish subsidiaries or branches instead of representative offices, unless they are very close to the host market. The relative costs of different organizational forms are difficult to estimate; relative costs can also be viewed on a more aggregated level: how large must the market in the host country be, or what potential exports from the home country can be accommodated to set up activities in the host country?

3.3.2.   Organization patterns

Banks which decided to enter new markets or to strengthen their market position have had a wide range of options available to them as to how they could proceed in implementing their foreign banking activities. Looking back at activities for the case studies, there has been a strong rise in the number of each of the approaches used. Three bank specific developments in organizational form stand out: branch network, alliances and joint ventures, and internet.

Branch network

In general, the objective to build a branch network has been to assist foreign clients, finance activities more cheaply or to evade home country regulation. Activities in financial centers were set up, usually starting with London, New York and Singapore or Hong Kong. This was then expanded to second tier financial centers and economic centers in Europe, the United States, Asia and Latin America.

Table 3.6   Development of branch networks

Period	1970s	1980s	1990s
Incentive	• Breakdown consortium	• Increase trade and exports	• Growth in Asian (capital) markets
	• Trade related, service existing clients	• Liberalization of capital markets • Opening up markets (Spain)	• Opening of Eastern European markets • Increase volume in securities markets
Example Banks	• Citicorp, BankAmerica, Lloyds, Barclays, ABN,	• AMRO, NMB, WestLB, Crédit Agricole	• Deutsche Bank, Dresdner Bank

Alliances and consortium banks

Consortium banks were mainly a feature of the late 1960s and 1970s. With these joint ventures, banks tried to create a platform to service foreign clients and undertake corporate finance activities, while sharing the costs of building such an activity independently. In the beginning of the 1980s banks like AMRO and Midland relied on the consortium banks to provide an alternative for a foreign branch network. Later in the 1980s a number of banks expanded their foreign networks by buying out the other shareholders in the consortium banks.

Banks also acquired detailed information of the partner banks during these alliances. This could be concluded from the observation that ING successfully acquired several InterAlpha partners from the mid-1990s for its expansion in Europe.

Table 3.7   Selected alliances

Alliance to acquire or share specific skills	Alliance to ensure (future) market position
• Royal Bank of Scotland – Santander (1990–2004) • BNP-Dresdner (1988–2000) • Société Générale – BSCH (2000)	• BBVA – UniCredito (2000) • AMRO – Generale (1988) • Commerzbank – Banco Hispano Americano (1973, 1990)

The nature of alliances changed from the 1990s. Alliances between banks either had to develop specific skills neither bank could achieve alone, or serve as a defensive move in the wake of expected restructuring in the European banking market. This usually was accompanied by relatively small equity share exchanges.

The reappearance of alliances and joint ventures in the 1990s was more specific than in the 1970s and was also accompanied by mutual equity stakes. Banks opted for mutual equity stakes to forge a stronger link with the other bank than an alliance; the mutual equity stake effectively represented an option to a first right to negotiate with the other bank when consolidation in the (European) banking market was considered.

Internet

From the late 1990s, the branchless Internet banks as an organizational form gained importance. Internet banking was initially viewed as a cost saving measure, providing the opportunity to close down branches while retaining the bank's customers. Other banks have developed internet banking into a low cost distribution form to expand in mature markets, such as ING Direct, Comdirect or DB24. Other activities were less successful though. Aiming to capture the high end of the consumer market, HSBC formed in 2000 a one billion US dollar joint venture with US securities firm Merrill Lynch to offer online brokerage services to wealthy clients. HSBC wanted to win new customers by outsourcing research and brokerage services to Merrill. However, the activity was quietly disbanded in 2003. Since then most banks have successfully developed internet retail banking activities. The furthest developed is ING Direct, active in nine countries with 145 billion euros or 40% of ING total entrusted funds. ING Direct has developed a successful business model and has developed into a successful internationalization model on its own, for example buying the French savings activities of internet bank Egg in 2004.[5]

4
The World's Largest Banks

4.1. Introduction

Internationalization is shaped and moved by the world's largest banks. Chances are, when walking in a main street in a city somewhere in the world, whether Europe, South America or Asia, that the branch or ATM in sight is probably owned by one of the world's 25 largest banks. The "six handshakes" idea finds its counterpart in banking: a customer somewhere in the world is probably always within six blocks of one of the world's largest bank branches. Who are the world's largest banks, what are their characteristics, and what are their (dis)similarities? This chapter presents an overview of the bank sample and discusses its key indicators.

The sheer size is impressive: outside their home countries the 25 largest banks in the world held over 10.2 trillion US dollars in assets, employed 916,000 staff and generated 36% of their total banking income in 2004. The banks combined take up a major share of the assets, capital and profits of the world's 100 and even 1,000 largest banks as reported yearly by The Banker.

The group is representative for the banking industry's internationalization because choosing the largest banks has several important advantages over a similarly, smaller sized sample (Healy, Palepu & Ruback, 1992). Although the group is a small fraction of the total number of banks in the world, the total dollar value of the selected changes in internationalization accounts for a significant portion of the dollar value of merger activity. Second, if there are economic gains from internationalization, they are most likely to be detected when the international banking activities are large. Finally, public concern about the internationalization of banks is typically triggered by the largest transactions, making them an interesting research subject in their own right.

4.2. Who form the world's largest banks

The banking group consists of the five largest banks measured by total assets in the Netherlands, Germany, France, United Kingdom, United States, Switzerland, Spain and Japan, as determined in the benchmark year 1995. These banks have been involved in internationalization activities between 1980 and 2004. In the case of both the Netherlands and Switzerland initially only three banks were included for the benchmark year 1995, due to the high concentration of banking activities in these countries.

One bank was added to the Dutch sample: Fortis, the Belgian/Dutch bank whose administrative headquarters are in Belgium but has extensive Dutch operations. For the United Kingdom, HSBC has been included as a UK bank in 1995. The bank relocated to the United Kingdom in 1992 after the acquisition of Midland bank. Therefore, HSBC has been included from 1992 onwards in the sample. This leads to an initial list of 37 banks for the benchmark year 1995, whose key characteristics are listed in Table 4.2. Including predecessors, the total sample for 1980–2004 consists of 44 banks.

The banks in the sample have several characteristics in common. First, most banks have not only been among the largest banks in their countries in 1995, but also between 1980 and 2004. All banks combined have taken up a major share of the assets, capital and profits of the world's 100 largest banks. Also, between 1980 and 2004 all banks have been engaged in international banking activities.

In this study, internationalization patterns are not differentiated by banking type because most banks in the sample are universal banks, providing a broad range of commercial banking services. European banks have historically provided the widest range of financial services, while US banks have historically offered a more limited range of financial services converging over time to universal banks as regulation changed.

A limited number of (mostly European) banks also have become part of, merged with, or came to own insurers. In the study, the bank activities of the bank-insurers are considered. Table 4.1 lists the most noteworthy combinations of banks and insurers.

Bank-insurers do not always form stable organizational relationships though. Credit Suisse prepared in 2004 the sale of Winterthur;

Table 4.1 Combinations of insurers and banks in sample between 1980 and 2000

Year	Country	Activity
1988	United Kingdom	Acquisition of insurer Abbey Life by Lloyds Bank
1989–90	Netherlands/ Belgium	Formation of Fortis through merger of Dutch bank VSB and insurer AMEV with Belgian insurer Groupe AG and bank ASLK
1990	Netherlands	Acquisition of insurer Interpolis by Rabobank
1991	Netherlands	Formation of ING Group through merger of NMB Postbank with insurer Nationale Nederlanden
1997	Switzerland	Acquisition of insurer Winterthur by Credit Suisse
1998	United States	Formation of Citigroup by merger of Citicorp and insurer Travelers group
2000	Germany	Acquisition of Dresdner Bank by insurer Allianz

Citigroup divested in 2005 nearly all its insurance activities and returned to banking. Even Rabobank effectuated a looser relationship with Interpolis in 2005, merging Interpolis with Dutch insurer Achmea in return for a 37% stake in the Eureko, Achmea's holding company.[1]

Asset growth and distribution on a country level are presented in Table 4.3. Total reported assets increased from 2,258 billion US dollars in 1980 to 24,645 billion US dollars in 2004. Total assets increased with an 11.5% annualized growth rate from 1980 to 1990 leveling off to 7.1% between 1990 and 2002. In 2003 and 2004 the growth rate strongly increased to 23%, generating an annual average asset growth of 10.2% over the total period. The difference in asset growths is caused by a combination of:

- *Change in currency*: Fluctuations in the currencies have increased or decreased relative positions in US dollar terms. The surge in the Japanese yen in the late 1980s substantially increased the size of Japanese banks in dollar terms, while the appreciation of the euro relative to the dollar in 2003–04 increased the relative size of European banks.
- *Saturation*: Due to their large size, it may have become more difficult to maintain high levels of asset growth.

Table 4.2   Key indicators banks in benchmark year 1995

Country	Bank	Total assets, min US$ dollar	Capital and reserves, % total assets	Profit before tax, % capital and reserves	Costs, % total income	Staff
France	Crédit Agricole	381,386	5.35	11.881	63.12	74,380
	BNP	320,954	5.94	3.27	74.96	53,600
	Crédit Lyonnais	334,911	2.27	5.51	83.36	59,018
	Paribas	268,618	4.63	–0.64	82.30	25,841
	Société Générale	322,194	3.42	10.27	74.10	45,374
Germany	Bayerische Hypobank	207,229	3.06	14.85	59.23	16,239
	Commerzbank	280,527	3.05	9.69	70.36	25,826
	Deutsche Bank	500,898	3,89	12.71	71.56	74,119
	Dresdner Bank	336,273	2.85	14.50	74.09	46,890
	Bayerisch Vereinsbank	247,472	2.89	12.97	64.31	22,188
	Westdeutsche Landesbank	294,826	2.98	8.73	74.91	9,670
Spain	Argentaria	106,641	5.05	12.89	52.78	16,715
	BBV	115,429	5.38	19.10	60.02	34,178
	BCH	91,597	4.48	5.10	71.18	29,369
	Santander	358,536	4.21	12.12	63.14	34,310
Switzerland	Credit Suisse	358,536	4.21	12.12	63.14	34,310
	SBC	250,569	4.89	9.68	73.55	27,236
	UBS	336,193	6.17	8.44	69.19	29,071
United Kingdom	Barclays	261,681	4.37	27.91	70.17	92,400
	HSBC	351,457	6.80	23.31	55.69	101,070
	Lloyds TSB	204,213	4.78	25.79	65.99	91,044
	National Westminster	287,541	6.74	7.75	69.07	72,500
	Standard Chartered	60,348	5.15	32.98	59.20	26,953
Netherlands	ABN AMRO	338,785	6.13	11.47	67.48	63,694
	Fortis	174,571	6.19	13.16	74.18	30,388
	ING Bank	153,217	6.49	10.93	70.87	28,015
	Rabobank	181,956	6.18	10.99	67.07	37,437
United States	Bank of America	232,446	8.70	22.58	61.51	79,900
	Chase Manhattan	121,063	7.37	20.70	67.47	33,618
	Chemical Banking	182,926	6.51	24.89	59.15	39,078
	Citicorp	269,000	7.28	28.52	59.44	85,300
	JPMorgan	184,879	5.65	18.24	67.72	15,613
Japan	Dai Ichi Kangyo	519,193	3.70	8.37	46.61	18,069
	IBJ	383,301	3.25	–8.02	45.01	5,362
	Mitsubishi Bank	514,187	4.53	3.76	60.03	14,977
	Sumitomo Bank	528,217	3.46	1.44	83.30	18,104
	Bank of Tokyo	250,102	5.23	5.28	47.38	17,538

Source: Annual reports, the Banker top 1000 1995, issue July 1996.

- *Change in monetary regime*: Total assets are positively correlated to the level of money supply, whose growth has been more restricted in the 1990s than the 1980s.
- *Change in management focus*: Many banks shifted their management goals from asset growth to profitability and a healthy capitalization. The early 1980s witnessed a high correlation between asset growth and profitability, this relationship completely breaks downs in the latter part of the decade.

Table 4.3   Distribution of assets in sample

	1980			1990			2000			2004		
	Assets	%	N	Assets	%	N	Assets	%	N	Assets	%	N
France	452	20.0	5	1,295	18.9	5	1,743	12.4	4	3,289	13.4	3
Germany	349	15.5	6	995	14.5	6	2,791	19.9	5	3,412	13.9	5
Spain	na	na	na	195	2.8	3	600	4.3	2	1,205	4.9	2
Switzerland	122	5.4	3	494	7.2	3	1,268	9.0	2	2,475	10.0	2
United Kingdom	362	16.0	6	907	13.2	6	2,252	16.0	6	4,077	16.5	5
Netherlands	163	7.2	4	482	7.0	4	1,559	11.1	4	3,134	12.7	4
United States	442	19.6	6	653	9.5	6	1,909	13.6	3	3,752	15.2	3
Japan	368	16.3	5	1,844	26.9	5	1,925	13.7	4	3,301	13.4	3
Total	2,258		35	6,865		38	14,047		30	24,645		27

Note: Total assets in billion US dollars. N is the number of banks in the group for the country. Spanish banks in 1980: missing data.

- *Change in regulation*: Change in regulation and change in management focus are intertwined. The implementation of the capital adequacy rules from 1988 onwards provided a regulatory framework for new management drivers. For example, when banks evaluated granting new loans, it also became important to consider the effect on capital reserves, effectively lowering asset growth.

If the distribution of assets in the sample per country for 2004 is compared to 1980, then the asset share of French banks has decreased, as have American banks. German banks have shown the largest increase, followed by Swiss and Dutch banks. Japanese and English banks maintained roughly the same asset share in 1980 and 2000, but Japanese banks dominated the sample in 1990 with 26.9%.

The number of banks is relatively small but represents a large portion of the world's banking assets, profits and capital if compared to the top 100 banks and top 1,000 banks as compiled by The Banker. The sample dominates the 100 largest banks in terms of total assets, capital and profits before tax, averaging between 48% and 54% for the reported periods, compared to the top 100 banks.

4.3.   Key financial developments

The group shows strong underlying dynamics. Banks have increased considerably in size in Switzerland and the Netherlands if compared to GDP, while their share has remained stable in countries like Japan or the United States. Gross income showed on average the same growth rates as assets; employee growth was for the whole period lower than asset or income growth, moderately picking up in the 1990s. This suggests an increase in scale and productivity for the whole period, and for the 1990s a shift to relatively more labor intensive activities in the sample such as retail banking.

Average gross income as a percentage of assets has been relatively stable during the whole period, with structural differences in levels between countries. The composition of income has changed considerably for most banks, shifting from interest income to non-interest income. Costs showed no change on average between 1980 and 2000. On a country basis, significant trends can be observed: American and English banks have reduced their costs considerably, especially since the 1990s, while Dutch, Japanese and Swiss banks have increased their costs considerably since the 1990s.

Also, provisions have had a major impact on profitability. From 1982 onwards general provisioning levels were raised peaking in 1987 and 1989 as the LDC debt crisis was resolved. In the 1990s Japanese banks stand out with high provisioning levels. The 1998 Russia LTCM crisis raised provisioning levels once again, but also shows some learning effects: due to less concentrated exposures compared to the 1980s, no individual bank stands out.

Finally profitability, i.e. profit before tax as a percentage of capital and reserves, on average moved between 15% and 20% between 1980 and 2000 with strong swings in 1987–89 due to high levels of provisioning not only affecting profits but also capital strength. The average bank increased its capital strength between 1984 and 1994. The key financial indicators are now considered in further detail.

4.3.1. Key figures, asset growth and asset size

The banks in the sample reported total assets of 2,258 billion US dollars in 1980; the asset size of the sample increased assets fivefold to 14,049 billion US dollars in 2000. The average bank in the sample showed a compounded annual growth rate of 10.4% during that period; average gross income showed similar growth rates of 11%. Growth in the number of employees on the other hand was lower between 1980 and 2000. The average number of bank employees increased by 1.6% per year between 1980 and 1990. Between 1990 and 2000 this rate of increase picked up to 6.0% on a yearly basis.

The growth rates of both average gross income and total assets have been particularly strong between 1984 and 1987. This has partly been the result of exchange rate movements of the US dollar, illustrated in

Table 4.4   Basic statistics

Year	Assets, mln US dollar	Capital, mln US dollar	Income, mln US dollar	Staff, number	No. of banks
			Group		
1980	2,258,400	81,967	49,926	1,053,812	35
1985	3,084,101	107,807	93,652	1,343,561	36
1990	6,865,307	282,540	187,496	1,458,559	38
1995	10,087,788	476,007	296,041	1,519,569	37
2000	14,049,324	695,218	452,683	2,144,080	30
2004	24,645,078	1,183,613	704,627	2,314,853	27
			Average per bank		
1980	64,525	2,341	1,783	33,993	35
1985	85,669	2,994	2,675	37,321	36
1990	180,665	7,435	5,357	41,673	38
1995	272,642	12,865	8,001	42,210	37
2000	468,310	23,173	15,089	71,469	30
2004	912,780	45,523	26,097	85,735	27

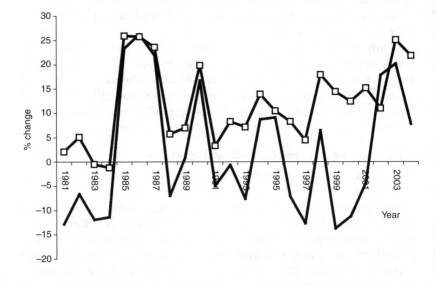

━☐━ % change average asset growth, US dollar   ━━ % change US dollar/deutschemark

Figure 4.1   Total average assets and yearly growth rate
Note: A positive (negative) percentage change of US dollar/deutschmark indicates a depreciation (appreciation) of the US dollar against the deutschmark.
Source: OECD. Exchange rates at end-of-year value

Figure 4.1 where the yearly average asset growth is compared with the yearly change of the US dollar/deutschmark exchange rate, assuming the German currency to represent continental Europe.

Average asset growth has been consistently higher than changes in the exchange rate movement. For the 1980s the parallel movement of asset growth and exchange rate indicate that translating total assets reported in local currencies to US dollars produced a major currency translation effect, boosting year on year growth rates in US dollars. In the 1990s asset growth and exchange rate movements diverged, indicating a shifting focus to other regions as well as an increased use of hedging policies.

The banks have been selected in the sample based on their size. To assess the magnitude of large banks, total assets can be compared to GDP. This ratio serves as a proxy for the relative importance of banking intermediation to the economy,[2] and suggests that disintermediation is not visible in our sample, perhaps the opposite (Figure 4.2). From 1980 to 2004 banking assets in the sample as a ratio to GDP have been stable in Japan and the United States. An increase is visible in the other countries, implying that asset growth was larger than GDP growth.

For most countries, the ratio of bank assets to GDP suggests that banks in the sample have accumulated assets at a rapid pace. The ratio of bank assets to GDP is the highest for banks in the sample located in countries with smaller economies, Switzerland and the Netherlands, supporting the small home market as an incentive to internationalize.

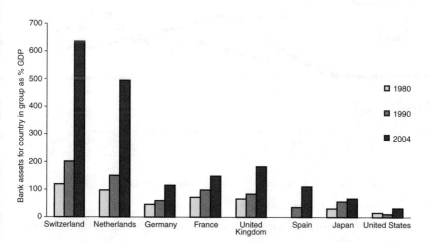

Figure 4.2   Bank assets in sample as a ratio of GDP
Source: GDP figures, *OECD Economic Outlook*. Figures for Spain in 1980 not available

4.3.2.   Change in income structure

The largest banks managed to increase their gross income slightly over the two decades. The composition of gross income changed between 1980 and 2000: net interest margin (loans) declined for banks, especially in the 1990s, while non-interest income (fees and commissions) steadily increased between 1980 and 2000. Banks now generate the majority of their income from fees and commissions. The shift from interest income to non-interest income on average has not led to a structurally higher gross income over the whole period. Between 1980 and 1983, gross income increased from 2.8% to 3.2% mainly due to an increase in non-interest income. After 1987 a volatile period set in with gross income showing results between 2.8% and 3.3%, moving towards to 3.3% once more in the latter half of the 1990s.

Table 4.5 presents the sources of income for banks per country, and per five-year period. Banks in the United States have enjoyed the highest net interest income as a percentage of average assets.[3] Net

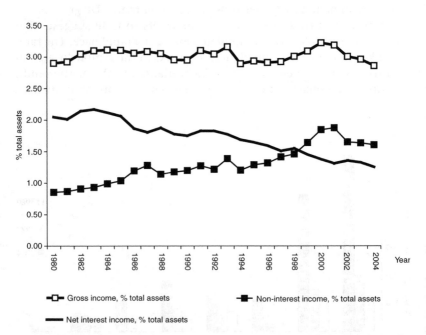

Figure 4.3   Net interest income, non-interest income and gross income for banks in sample
Note: Gross income, non-interest income, net interest income weighted by total assets in US dollars.

interest income of American banks steadily increased from the early 1980s for almost a decade. Starting out as one of the most attractive earning possibilities in 1980, net interest margin earned by British banks constantly decreased in the next decades. The trend for German and Dutch banks has developed similarly over the period, showing a real but modest decline since 1995. Japan on the other hand has shown the lowest income potential throughout the period. For all banks, the net interest margin in 1996–2000 was lower than in 1981–85. The table also shows that the relative decrease in net interest margin varied among countries. The table allows us to identify some simple consequences. If banks had wanted to exploit differences in net interest margin to internationalize, then Japanese banks should have felt the greatest urge to develop activities outside Japan, which was the case until 1992. The choice of host country might be of lesser importance since benefits could be gained in each country. German and Dutch banks would have an incentive to set up activities in the United Kingdom and the United States. Banks

Table 4.5 Key indicators income structure of banks in sample per country

		France	Germany	Spain	Switzer-land	United Kingdom	Nether-lands	United States	Japan
Gross income,	1980–84	3.13	2.28	na	2.33	4.54	2.85	3.48	1.66
% total assets	1985–89	3.23	2.47	na	2.59	4.95	2.84	5.10	1.55
	1990–94	2.96	2.41	4.16	3.21	4.64	3.25	5.76	1.46
	1995–99	2.60	1.99	3.85	2.89	4.12	3.11	5.21	1.84
	2000–04	2.41	2.00	4.05	2.92	3.51	2.69	5.13	2.04
Net interest	1980–84	2.36	1.52	4.39	0.85	3.12	2.15	2.47	1.26
income, %	1985–89	2.04	1.60	4.10	0.95	3.13	2.04	3.00	0.91
total assets	1990–94	1.82	1.46	2.79	1.16	2.61	2.13	3.09	0.99
	1995–99	1.39	1.02	2.32	0.75	2.26	1.86	2.62	1.06
	2000–04	0.81	0.78	2.25	0.79	1.93	1.48	1.95	0.97
Non-interest	1980–84	0.76	0.76	0.87	1.49	1.42	0.69	1.01	0.38
income, %	1985–89	1.13	0.87	1.19	1.65	1.82	0.80	2.09	0.64
total assets	1990–94	1.14	0.95	1.38	2.05	2.03	1.11	2.67	0.47
	1995–99	1.21	0.97	1.53	2.14	1.86	1.25	2.59	0.79
	2000–04	1.60	1.22	1.80	2.14	1.58	1.21	3.18	1.07
Non-interest	1980–84	24.26	32.64	16.58	63.74	31.24	24.77	29.07	22.78
income, %	1985–89	34.88	33.77	22.31	63.61	36.67	28.78	41.12	41.66
gross income	1990–94	39.76	41.19	32.97	63.21	43.77	33.23	46.86	31.55
	1995–99	47.77	47.32	38.72	73.48	45.28	40.02	52.07	40.38
	2000–04	67.24	55.85	44.59	72.35	45.33	43.62	61.65	50.20

Note: Averages weighted by total assets in US dollar, except non-interest income as % gross income, weighted by gross income in US dollar. na: not available.

setting up activities in Japan cannot have been motivated by interest income differentials; and banks in the United Kingdom stood only to gain from activities in the United States, after 1990. Finally, if banks in the United States had set up foreign activities, they must have been motivated by other incentives than the exploitation of net interest margin.

The shift from interest income to non-interest income is in general viewed as the banks' response to disintermediation (Figure 4.4), where the line represents the percentage of non-interest income to gross income. For the largest banks the shift from interest income to non-interest income has gradually moved from 30% on average in 1980 to almost 56% in 2004. This structural change of business model eased somewhat in 1990–94, and 2002–04. During 1990 and 1994 non-interest income decreased slightly; economic recessions in 1991 in the United States and 1994 in Germany slowed down growth of capital market activities while net interest margins were upheld. This temporarily increased the relative importance of interest income. After 1994 the trend towards an income structure with relatively more fee income was reinstated. For the 2002–04 period a similar reasoning applies.

A large number of banks changed the ratio of interest income to non-interest income. To illustrate this, the ratio of non-interest income

Figure 4.4   Non-interest income, percentage of gross income
Note: Non-interest income as percentage of gross income weighted by gross income in US dollar.

as a percentage of gross income is displayed in Figure 4.5 for 1990 (horizontal axis) and compared to 2004 (vertical axis). Markers on the diagonal line would indicate banks whose ratios have not changed between 1990 and 2000. Three banks (Credit Suisse, Commerzbank and Fortis) are below the diagonal line, indicating a relative decrease of non-interest income. In the case of Fortis, the acquisition of Belgian Generale Bank in 1998 increased its dependency on interest margin considerably. An opposite change of profile is shown by BNP, whose acquisition of Paribas in 1998 raised its dependency on non-interest income considerably. Similar explanations can be given for Deutsche Bank (acquisition of investment bank Morgan Grenfell in the United Kingdom and investment bank Bankers Trust in the United States) and Dresdner (acquisition of British investment bank Kleinwort Benson).

The number of banks which have increased their non-interest income to gross income ratio and also raised gross income equals the number of banks which increased their non-interest income to gross income ratio but did not increase gross income. There is no visible relationship between change in gross income and change in the share of non-interest income.

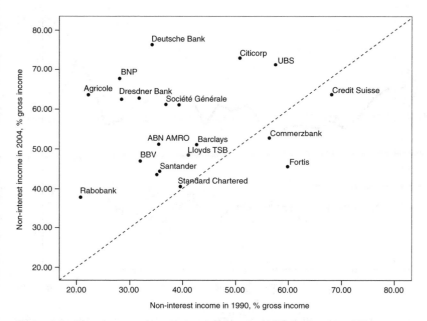

Figure 4.5   Non-interest income as percentage gross income in 2004 versus 1990

4.3.3.   Economies

Profitability is influenced by the operational costs banks incur, the provisions they have to make on their loans and the development of the bank's capital. Internationalization is linked to more asset growth. Theoretically, more assets should enable more economies of scale advantages such as lowering costs. The operating expenses of a bank are usually summarized in a cost to income (CI) ratio.[4] American and British banks lowered their operating expenses (and decreased their internationalization activities) while German and Dutch banks saw their operating expenses increase (as well as their internationalization activities).

The swings in CI ratio are not uniformly distributed among banks: on a yearly basis there is no relationship between the change in CI ratio and the dispersion of CI ratio among banks, measured by the yearly standard deviation of CI ratios of the banks in the sample. The combination of a changing CI ratio and decreasing standard deviation suggests that the CI change is influenced by general market events and

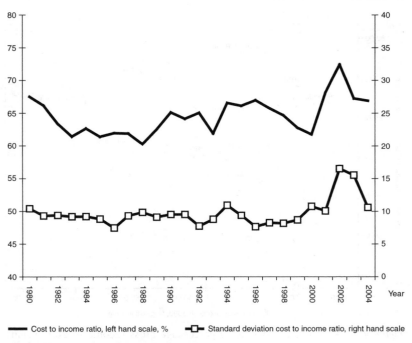

Figure 4.6   Cost to income (CI) ratio

applies to a large group of banks in the same way. Between 1990 and 1992, and 1994 and 1996 such periods were observable. In both periods, the CI ratio decreased. Generally, a lowering of the CI ratio tends to be accompanied with an increase in the standard deviation, suggesting that a minority of the banks cause the major changes in CI ratio shifts. From 2000 the CI ratio and its standard deviation increased, suggesting that the economic slowdown and stock market decrease has had a wide range of different consequences for the banks. From a country perspective, the CI ratio has varied between countries as well as between periods (Figure 4.7).

British and American banks showed a strong decrease in CI ratio between 1990 and 2004, German, Dutch and Japanese banks on the other hand showed the strongest increase. Based on this sample, banks from the same country tend to show similar CI ratios, probably due to different institutional settings.[5] Significant differences in CI ratios between the United Kingdom, United States, Japan and the other European countries are found, whereas no significant differences between the United States and the United Kingdom are observed.

The existence of economies of scale suggests that aggregate costs are lowered when the right amount of asset size is chosen (Van Dijcke, 2001). Internationalization activities to increase scale advantages has not led to a lower CI ratio. This relationship is not traceable per bank

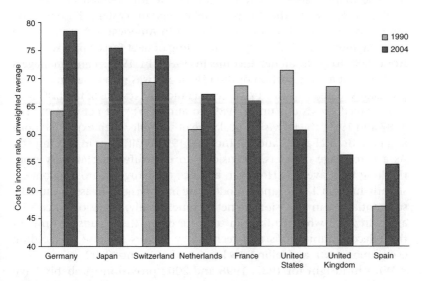

Figure 4.7   Average cost to income ratios, per country

or per period between 1990 and 2004. The composition of the sample might result in a non-relationship between the CI ratio and asset size: if efficiencies occur through scale enlargement it probably takes place with smaller banks, which are not part of the sample. Also, the relative weakness of UBS in 1997 and Bankers Trust in 1998 preceded the emergence of the two largest banks at the time (Danthine, 2000). The creation of Japanese Mizuho in 2000 is another example of banks with weak financial positions merging into larger banks. The findings for the world's largest banks agree with the research about the relationship between bank size and efficiency, and the limited evidence to support it.[6] Similarly, no relationships have been found in this sample when the level of CI is related to the level of gross income to assets and/or the composition of income.

4.3.4. Provisions

The banks experienced pronounced swings in provisions over time, drawing extensive (negative) publicity at times. The years 1981, 1987, 1989 and 1997 stand out as milestones that are closely linked to banks' internationalization activities.

Figure 4.8 represents total provisions as a percentage of net income, and as a percentage of total assets. Provisions rose in 1981 from 31% to 38% of net income because of the debt crisis in Eastern Europe. The increase in provisioning is especially visible for German and French banks, which were the main stakeholders in Eastern Europe. The announcement by Mexican and other Latin American governments to defer payments and following rescheduling of debt forced provisions up from 38% to 47% of net income in 1982. In 1987, bank managers realized that a large portion of the LDC loans was not to be repaid, and provisions soared to over 71% of net income. The resolve of the LDC debt crisis forced provisions up in 1989, to almost 61% of net income. For 1987 and 1989, the provision peaks are observable when expressed both as a ratio of total assets and net income. 1998 is different in this respect. As a percentage of assets, provisions do not differ substantially from the long term average. However, absence of change in gross income, a slightly higher CI ratio, and a modest rise in provisions to assets caused a substantial rise in provisions to net income. Finally, provisions increased again in 2002 when banks had to write down their loans to firms in the telecommunications and technology sectors because of receding economic growth and falling stock market levels since 2000.

With hindsight for 1987, 1998 and 2002 provisions probably have been overdone. In these years the provision levels the year after were

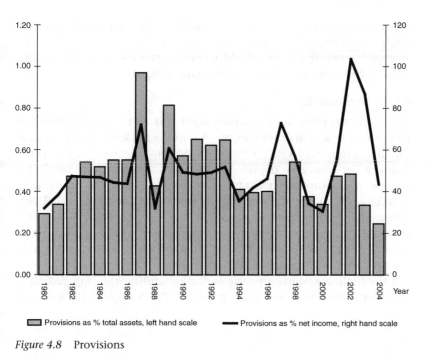

Figure 4.8 Provisions

Table 4.6 Top five highest provisioning in 1987, 1989 and 1998

Rank	1987		1989		1998	
1	Manufacturers Hanover	3.04	Lloyds	4.08	Dai Ichi Kangyo	1.81
2	Lloyds	2.83	J.P. Morgan	2.29	IBJ	1.32
3	Midland	2.57	Manufacturers Hanover	2.20	Tokyo Mitsubishi	1.23
4	Chase Manhattan	2.41	Midland	2.05	Sumitomo Bank	1.19
5	Standard Chartered	2.19	Chase Manhattan	1.61	Standard Chartered	0.91
Average sample		1.17		0.86		0.49

Source: Annual reports.

extremely low, suggesting a "big dip" strategy: bank management real-ized that extra provisions were unavoidable, and probably included other possible negative events for the near future in the provision amount.[7] On a bank level, provisions have not been uniformly as high for all banks. On a yearly basis the standard deviation is the highest for the three top provision years (1987, 1989, 1998), indicating that while these crises have raised provisions for all banks, they have increased provisions dramatically for some banks. This is demonstrated in Table 4.6. The highest provision rates for 1998 do not reflect the average increase due to the LTCM/Russia crises but are country specific, reflecting the domestic banking problems in Japan.

4.3.5.   Profitability

Profitability is calculated as profits before tax as a ratio of capital and reserves, or as a ratio of total assets. A number of elements are familiar: the low extremes of 1987, 1989 and 1998 can be traced back to provisioning. Differences in the two profitability indicators point to relative changes in the capital/assets ratio, displayed in Figure 4.9. For the total sample, profitability has been high between 1981 and 1986 (17–18%), followed by a transitional period in 1987–89. From 1990 onwards profitability has been relatively stable, averaging 11–13%, followed by a decline to under 10% in 1998 and an uplifting in 1999–2000, with a similar pattern emerging for 2001–04.

If the highest and lowest periods of profitability are compared, then the French and Japanese banks stand out. The French banks achieved

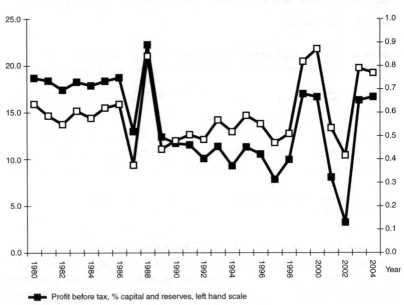

 Profit before tax, % capital and reserves, left hand scale
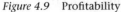 Profit before tax, % total assets, right hand scale

Figure 4.9   Profitability
Note: Profit before taxes are weighted by total assets, capital and reserves in US dollar.

the highest profitability in 1981–85, and the lowest in 1991–95. Even more pronounced are the Japanese banks, reporting the highest profitability between 1986 and 1995, followed by a period of negative profitability. For both groups of banks, periods of relatively high profitability were followed by relatively low profitability.

4.3.6. Capitalization

The difference in profitability for the period up to 1986 and from 1989 onwards can also be related to a change in capitalization: when capital increases at a different pace than profits, then this affects the profitability ratio. Capitalization of the banks was under pressure in the early 1980s, to rise over 5% in 1995. Deterioration in 1996 and 1997 is probably due to a combination of temporary higher asset growth and more sophisticated capital management. Temporary asset growth can be the result of acquiring assets at a higher market value than the one the bank is valued at, on average decreasing capital.

A changing approach to bank capital management resulted from the growing focus on bank solvency at the end of the 1980s, leading to the Basle Accord where standards were introduced how to measure capital and to calculate risk based capital. Also, a distinction was introduced between core capital (tier one, the basis provided by shareholders and retained profits) and secondary capital (reserves, preferential securities). Figure 4.10, representing tier one capital, shows that the adoption of new capital adequacy rules was a gradual process. In the latter half of

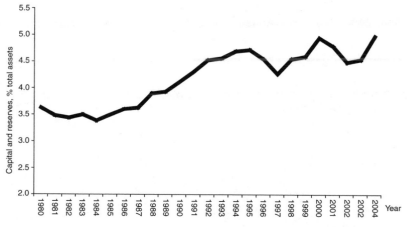

Figure 4.10 Capitalization
Note: Capital and reserves as percentage of total assets, weighted by total assets in US dollar.

the 1990s new financial instruments were introduced, designed to serve as tier two capital, shifting (rather expensive) capital away from tier one to tier two. In June 2004 the Basle II framework was finalized, designed to improve risk management by using models based on past performance to help set the level of capital banks are required to hold by regulators. This approach could advance the efficiency of financial systems by improving the allocation of capital; the framework should be implemented by the beginning of 2008.[8]

5
Internationalization Patterns

5.1. Introduction

In 1980 Bank of America reported record earnings and became a year later the largest bank in the world, measured by assets. The bank positioned itself as a prominent international bank, active in most major and economic centers where the "World Banking" division generated 52% of the bank's profitability and held 43% of the assets outside the United States. The strategy backfired in the early 1980s: management had difficulties coping with the organization, and the foreign expansion turned out to be overambitious, having lent considerably to South American countries.

Rumors about its capital adequacy forced the share price down, even prompting a takeover bid from a smaller bank in 1985. Seven years later, the bank was not among the largest 25 banks in the world, a position it achieved again in 1998. Coming close to bankruptcy, the bank transformed itself over the next decade, divesting foreign activities and expanding domestically whenever deregulation permitted this. After a string of domestic takeovers, where only the name survived, the highly profitable Bank of America bought FleetBoston in 2004, and its foreign assets dropped under 8%.

Continental European banks generally pursued an opposite internationalization trend. Founded as a bank primarily for financing German foreign trade in 1870, Deutsche Bank held 14% foreign assets in 1980, mainly in financial centers for investment banking and Luxemburg for tax purposes. The bank embarked the next two decades on an ambitious internationalization strategy. In 2004, more than 70% of its assets were outside Germany, positioning itself as a European retail bank and international wholesale bank. The growth in the capital markets was primarily accomplished in two large steps: the acquisition of Morgan Grenfell in 1989, and the acquisition of Bankers Trust in 1998. By 2004, Deutsche Bank strongly remained committed to its internationalization strategy, despite lagging profitability, its inability to expand its domestic market share, and its struggle to absorb the large foreign acquisitions.

What underlying trends and strategies can be distilled from this? This chapter moves away from an anecdotal approach. For each bank in the sample the degree of internationalization (DOI) is calculated. The DOI is calculated as an unweighted average of foreign assets to total assets ratio, foreign gross income to total gross income ratio and foreign employment to total employment ratio. Trends are analyzed and the internationalization of banks is examined from different angles: changes in internationalization as well as differences in internationalization between countries.

For the sample as a whole, the average DOI in the 1980s remained between 28% and 30%. There were distinctive underlying dynamics during this period; Japanese and European banks increased their DOI while American and British banks decreased theirs. From 1990, the overall DOI of the largest banks increased to almost 40% in 2000, mainly the result of accelerated internationalization activities of European banks. The individual indicators of DOI (foreign assets ratio, foreign income ratio, foreign staff ratio) suggest that internationalization up to the early 1980s was income driven, while the internationalization activities in the 1990s were both asset driven and employee driven. In other words, setting up and acquiring investment banking and corporate finance activities took place in the 1980s, while the major component of the internationalization activities of banks in the 1990s consisted of acquiring retail banks.

5.2.   How to measure internationalization

When is a bank truly internationalized, or a "global player"? Estimating the DOI of a firm or bank is to some extent arbitrary. There are different approaches to measure a bank's DOI; an initial approach could be to construct a single item indicator. Sullivan (1994) reviewed 17 studies which all applied a single item indicator to measure the DOI, i.e. foreign sales to total sales. However the use of a single item indicator increases the potential error of measurement, because it is more sensitive to external shocks. An alternate approach is to combine several indicators into one index. Depending on the choice of indicators, this might provide a better approximation of the DOI, but the choice of indicators may be restricted on data availability rather than theoretical induction (Sullivan, 1994).

This study applies three single item indicators that are combined in a composite index to analyze the DOI of a bank. The DOI is one of the most cited indicators for internationalization (cf. United Nations Conference on Trade and Development, 1998; Van Tulder, Van den Berghe & Muller, 2001). The index is expressed as a percentage and calculated as an unweighted average of 1) foreign assets to total assets ratio, 2) foreign gross income to total gross income ratio and 3) foreign employment to total employment ratio.[1]

The general appeal of the DOI is that the DOI is presented in one scale, which by definition moves between 0 and 100. Also an internationalization index that incorporates income, staff and assets captures a richer picture of the bank's foreign activities than that which would be captured by income, staff and assets separately (cf. Sullivan, 1994). Another attractive characteristic is that the DOI dampens the effect of finance companies or offshore funding constructions if a ratio were only based on foreign assets relative to total assets. A substantial amount of assets can a priori be expected to be located in tax havens or countries with lenient fiscal regimes. Such reported assets would be accompanied by low number of employees. Combining both employees and assets in the DOI would then create a more balanced view. The same argument also applies to investment banking activities that are concentrated in financial centers outside the home country; these activities tend to generate a relatively high degree of income with fewer employees. When interpreting the DOI, several disadvantages have to be taken into account: technological change, geographical boundaries, and data availability.

- *Technological change.* The construction of a DOI index cannot take account of the effects of technological change. Changes in technology can for example raise productivity and increase the assets or income per employee; if these changes are distributed evenly over the total bank organization then its effect on the DOI is probably limited. If the ratio of foreign assets per foreign employee increases in the same amount as the ratio of domestic assets per domestic employee, then technological change has no effect on the DOI. From the mid-1990s however technological advances have had other geographic distribution effects. For example, the development of "internet" banks like ING Direct implies that the share of foreign assets and foreign income increases while staff and operations working for the internet bank basically remain at home. This might potentially depress the true extent of internationalization measured by the DOI.

- *Geographical boundaries.* For Fortis, Belgian/Dutch corporate structure creates a problem to determine what region is home or foreign. This is solved in the database by denoting Benelux as home. Similarly, HSBC is the only bank not disclosing information for the home country, instead reporting Europe as "home region".
- *Data availability.* Not all banks have consistently reported detailed information on foreign assets, staff, income or profitability. Banks like SBC, UBS or Deutsche Bank did not always report this information although they progressed significantly with their internationalization activities. A general remark is usually found in the financial report stating something like "due to the integrated nature of our activities worldwide a geographical breakdown does not provide additional information"; the information provided by British and American banks in the 1980s proves otherwise. Data collection from other sources provided valuable additional information, like the foreign banks in the United States that have to report their balance sheets to the Federal Reserve.

5.3.   Internationalization since the 1980s

Table 5.1 presents the key internationalization indicators for selected years between 1980 and 2003. The average bank in the sample has operated roughly one-third of its banking activities outside the home country between 1980 and 2000. The average DOI was almost 29% in 1980, remaining stable throughout the 1980s and early 1990s, and increased from 1995 onwards, rising to 41% in 2004. These percentages are consistent with figures reported in the annual "Global Top" listings of the Banker. Other comparisons however are not available; the DOI for non-financial firms has been better documented. For the top 100 transnational (non-financial) corporations, as compiled for the UNCTAD World Investment Report, the average DOI moved between the 50–55% range between 1995 and 1998. Another measure of internationalization is the one compiled by the SCOPE project, where the DOI is determined for the 200 largest (non-financial) firms worldwide. For the year 1995 an average DOI is reported of 29.7% agreeing with the banks' DOI to some extent; this however might simply be a coincidence.

Table 5.1 Key statistics of internationalization indicators of total sample, selected years

Statistic	Year	Foreign/total assets	Foreign/total gross income	Foreign/total employees	DOI
		%	%	%	%
Average	1980	34.8	47.6	20.9	28.9
	1985	35.1	40.2	20.4	28.6
	1990	32.5	32.2	23.1	28.3
	1995	36.1	33.4	26.7	31.9
	2000	39.5	40.1	40.9	39.0
	2004	41.3	37.9	44.8	40.7
Weighted	1980	34.9	48.8	21.3	35.0
Average	1985	35.0	41.1	24.2	33.4
	1990	34.2	33.1	25.0	30.7
	1995	36.9	34.5	29.7	33.7
	2000	41.1	40.6	43.2	41.6
	2004	41.7	36.2	49.0	42.3
Median	1980	35.6	53.4	13.8	28.9
	1985	34.2	40.5	13.8	30.4
	1990	31.1	36.0	20.2	29.3
	1995	31.7	31.9	26.7	30.1
	2000	33.4	35.6	37.4	34.2
	2004	38.6	37.9	47.3	44.2

Note: The average indicators and DOI are calculated as arithmetic average; the sum divided by the number of cases. For the weighted average indicators, foreign/total assets for one bank is for example weighted by the share of total assets of a bank in total assets of the sample, and then aggregated for all banks. For the DOI, the unweighted average of the weighted averages of indicators 1, 2, 3 is then calculated.

The decrease in average DOI in the 1980s is mainly due to the decrease of foreign gross income. This decrease can largely be ascribed to English and American banks, on the one hand reducing their activities in LDC loans and selling off related activities outside the home country, while on the other hand increasing the share of domestic activities. Figure 5.1 shows the trend in more detail, displaying average and median values for DOI.

Initially in 1983–84 DOI was at its highest, declining until 1991. From that period, DOI increased again, reaching higher levels (both for median and average DOI) than in 1980. Between 1980 and 1993, median DOI was higher than average DOI, indicating that there were relatively many banks with a low DOI. On the other hand, between

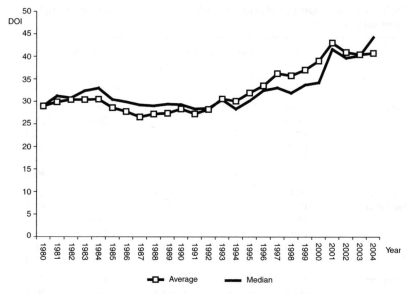

Figure 5.1   Average DOI development between 1980 and 2004 in %

1994 and 2000 average DOI was higher than median DOI, suggesting a concentration of banks with relatively high DOIs.

The country averages for DOI can also provide useful information; if banks in a country are considered as separate groups, then the development of internationalization activities of banks has differed between countries. There is a certain country of origin effect observable in international banking.[2] At the beginning of the 1980s, American and British banks showed the highest DOI. In the 1980s, the DOI decreased systematically for American banks, while this applied to British banks from the mid-1980s.

The ascent of Japanese banks in the late 1980s in the international banking arena also filled a relative void created by American and British banks in the 1980s. The internationalization activities of Japanese banks increased until the early 1990s, their descent followed from the mid-1990s.

Continental European banks showed the strongest increase in DOI between 1980 and 2000; the largest banks from the Netherlands, Germany, Spain, France and Switzerland steadily increased internationalization in the 1980s, which accelerated in the mid-1990s. From 1994 onwards, the DOI increased steadily, mainly propelled by German,

Table 5.2   Average DOI values per country

	1980 Average	N	1985 Average	N	1990 Average	N	1995 Average	N	2000 Average	N	2004 Average	N
France	19.7	5	24.9	5	26.7	5	30.5	5	31.3	4	37.5	3
Germany	8.4	6	8.9	6	12.1	6	23.2	6	39.0	5	42.7	5
Spain	a	a	a	a	20.3	2	21.3	4	57.7	2	56.1	2
Switzerland	31.9	3	31.6	3	41.3	3	42.7	3	67.3	2	68.8	2
United Kingdom	44.2	5	46.0	5	37.9	6	44.3	5	36.5	6	40.3	5
Netherlands	18.3	3	21.6	4	23.2	4	29.7	4	47.6	4	48.1	4
USA	49.0	6	39.7	6	31.7	6	32.8	5	27.2	3	24.7	3
Japan	28.0	5	28.1	5	33.1	5	34.2	5	27.2	4	18.3	3
Average/Total	28.9	33	28.6	35	28.3	37	31.9	37	39.0	30	40.7	27

Note: a: No data for Spanish banks prior to 1990; N: number of banks.

Dutch, French and Swiss banks. On average the DOI for British banks has increased in the 1990s; however the increase is caused by the addition of HSBC in the sample in 1992. The bank had a higher DOI than Lloyds, National Westminster and Barclays, but also increased its DOI throughout the 1990s while the other British banks did not.

In the 1980s American banks reduced their DOI by divesting foreign activities, while domestic acquisitions in the 1990s reduced the average DOI of American banks. American banks tended to show decreasing DOI at the end of the 1990s when domestic mergers in the United States raised the relative weight of domestic activities between 1990 and 2000.

The individual components of DOI provide additional information (Figure 5.2). Foreign income was relatively high in the early 1980s, decreasing between 1983 and 1989, steadily increasing again since 1991. Foreign assets showed a similar pattern, but with less volatile changes than foreign income, especially in the 1980s. On the other hand, the ratio of foreign employees was relatively stable in the 1980s, but steadily increased in the 1990s. The three indicators suggest that internationalization up to the early 1980s was income driven, setting up and acquiring investment banking and corporate finance activities, while the internationalization activities in the 1990s were both asset driven and employee driven, acquiring retail banks.

From 1980 to 1990, a number of banks set up foreign activities in financial centers concentrating activities there such as brokerage or corporate finance. Large loans (to foreign countries or foreign firms) were concentrated in those centers, leading to high assets to employee

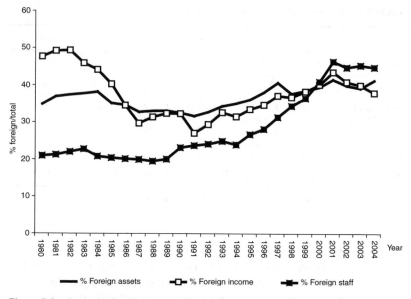

Figure 5.2   Average development of key internationalization indicators
Note: Variables are calculated as arithmetic average.

ratios. Besides that, assets were also located in centers outside the home country for fiscal reasons, needing few employees administering large assets. This has been especially the case for German banks, leading to a relatively high ratio of assets to employees. In the 1990s new activities were also developed; acquisitions in retail banking took place at a more rapid pace than in the earlier decade, creating more labor intensive activities for the banking organizations abroad which lowered the average foreign to total assets ratio. Overall, the developments of the three indicators to construct the DOI suggest that the composition of internationalization activities at the end of the 1990s has become more stable (in terms of relationship between foreign assets, income and staff) than in the early 1980s.

The DOI varies significantly between banks. If the DOI of banks in 2000 is compared to 1990 a large number of banks have increased their internationalization activities (Table 5.3). The bank with the largest DOI in 2000 as well as 1990 is the English Standard Chartered Bank; Bank of America has the lowest DOI in 2000. Banks in Continental Europe such as Deutsche Bank, ABN AMRO, UBS and Credit Suisse have increased their foreign activities the most during this period. One Continental European bank, Crédit Lyonnais, reduced its foreign activities as part of

Table 5.3 DOI for banks in selected years

Bank	DOI						No. of DOI observations
	1980	1985	1990	1995	2000	2004	
France							
Crédit Agricole	2.3	4.1	3.9	5.4	17.8	18.3	25
BNP	27.6	34.5	30.5	31.3	47.6	49.4	25
Crédit Lyonnais	11.3	25.4	32.5	41.4	25.1	–	23
Paribas	28.1	30.4	39.4	41.0	–	–	19
Société Générale	29.2	30.0	27.4	33.3	34.8	44.6	25
Germany							
Bayerin Hypobank	4.7	4.5	4.4	8.5	–	–	18
Commerzbank	14.8	15.6	17.7	17.4	26.4	13.7	25
Deutsche Bank	9.3	11.1	23.5	41.8	59.0	69.6	25
Dresdner Bank	8.3	8.5	8.4	25.2	32.4	30.8	25
Hypovereinsbank	–	–	–	–	36.1	51.5	7
Vereinsbank	4.9	5.3	6.4	11.5	–	–	18
Westdeutsche Landesbank	8.5	8.6	12.3	34.5	41.1	47.8	25
Spain							
Argentaria	na	na	–	8.7	–	–	8
BBV	na	na	11.4	28.9	55.9	44.2	18
BCH	na	na	–	18.9	–	–	7
Santander	na	31.9	29.3	28.7	59.4	68.1	20
Switzerland							
Credit Suisse	26.7	28.7	47.5	46.4	69.2	66.3	25
SBC	41.2	36.1	38.5	42.6	–	–	18
UBS	27.8	30.1	37.8	39.2	65.5	71.3	25
United Kingdom							
Barclays	51.5	36.3	44.2	32.7	28.5	22.2	25
HSBC	–	–	44.3	60.5	56.3	63.3	15
Lloyds TSB	40.8	34.4	18.8	14.5	15.0	4.5	25
Midland	21.3	46.6	14.1	–	–	–	12
National Westminster	34.6	37.2	29.2	32.7	24.1	–	21
Royal Bank of Scotland	–	–	–	–	15.3	26.8	9
Standard Chartered	72.6	75.6	76.9	80.9	79.7	84.8	25
Netherlands							
ABN	30.5	33.0	–	–	–	–	10
ABN AMRO	–	–	32.7	47.3	74.9	67.8	15
AMRO	13.5	20.9	–	–	–	–	10
Fortis	–	–	28.8	25.3	33.6	48.9	15
ING (bank)	–	–	–	30.1	61.6	54.5	13
NMB Bank	11.0	20.9	16.8	–	–	–	12
Rabobank	–	11.4	14.5	16.1	20.2	21.2	24
United States							
Bank of America	48.3	36.0	21.8	14.5	7.5	5.6	25
Chase Manhattan	51.7	44.8	31.8	30.1	27.9	26.6	25
Chemical Banking	38.4	32.9	15.3	18.8	–	–	16
Citicorp	53.6	45.5	41.2	55.5	46.1	41.9	25
JPMorgan	47.7	44.1	41.7	45.3	–	–	20
Manufacturers Hanover	54.5	35.1	38.6	–	–	–	11
Japan							
Dai Ichi Kangyo	28.9	29.6	39.6	29.1	19.1	–	21
IBJ	12.0	27.7	26.2	27.6	28.6	–	21
Mitsubishi Bank	31.4	34.3	33.5	27.8	–	–	16
Mizuho Group	–	–	–	–	–	16.8	4
Sumitomo Bank	36.3	31.1	35.0	32.5	20.5	9.5	25
Tokyo Mitsubishi	–	–	–	–	40.5	28.8	9
Tokyo	31.3	17.7	31.3	53.8	–	–	16

na: not available; – : bank was not in the sample in the year(s) presented in the table, due to mergers and acquisitions a restructuring strategy. Apart from Europe, Japanese banks have also reduced their foreign activities as a share of total activities.

The development in DOI can be analyzed by calculating the DOI changes for five-year periods, and clustering them (Table 5.4). For the five-year periods displayed, over two-thirds of the observations show changes in DOI ranging between −10% and +10%. The period 1990 versus 1985 stands out, where 17 out of 33 banks reported a negative change in DOI. For the comparison of 1995 to 1990, all negative changes in DOI have led to overall levels of DOI in 1995 lower than 40%. Whether this 40% signifies something relevant remains to be examined.[3] When the DOI change was positive, the dispersion in resulting DOI levels also became greater. German Dresdner Bank set up most of its internationalization activities in that period, while internationally active banks like ABN AMRO and HSBC increased their international activities by more than 10%. An outlier here is once again English bank Standard Chartered, showing the highest DOI without expanding its foreign activities. As one of the last remaining British overseas banks, it historically has enjoyed such high levels of DOI.

From 1995 to 2000 there are far more positive changes in DOI than from 1990 to 1995. Two Swiss banks show the largest change in internationalization, UBS and Credit Suisse. Major growth acquirers in the previous period like ABN AMRO repeated the high levels of increase for 1995 to 2000. A few American banks (Citicorp, Bank of America) showed negative changes, albeit for different reasons. Citicorp remained highly engaged in international activities, broadly balancing foreign and domestic growth of activities, while the foreign activities of Bank of America decreased in importance through the domestic merger with Nationsbank and active divestitures in 1998.

Table 5.4   Change in DOI

Period	< −25%	−25% to −10%	−10% to 0%	0% to 10%	10% to 25%	> 25%	Total
'80–'84	0	4	8	18	2	1	33
'85–'89	1	4	12	13	3	0	33
'90–'94	0	2	9	15	8	0	34
'95–'99	0	3	7	8	4	5	27
'00–'04	0	4	8	8	4	0	24
Total	1	17	44	62	21	6	151

Note: The number of observations varies due to mergers and acquisitions. For example, Paribas existed in 1995 but merged with BNP in 1999, dropping out of the dataset when 2000 is compared to 1995.

Table 5.5   Major changes in DOI between 1980 and 2004

Bank	Year	DOI change	DOI EOY	Event
Large increases				
Santander	1997	19.54	53.13	South American acquisitions
ABN AMRO	1997	18.60	69.85	Acquisition Brazilian Banco Real
Hypovereinsbank	2000	17.34	36.11	Acquisition Austrian Bankverein
HSBC	1992	16.87	58.40	Acquisition Midland Bank
ING (bank)	1998	15.75	56.24	Acquisition German BHF Bank
Westdeutsche Landesbank	1995	14.63	34.54	Acquisition English Cook Travel
Credit Suisse	1990	14.29	47.53	Acquisition Swiss Bank Leu
Tokyo	1990	13.72	31.31	Loan expansions
Midland	1981	12.38	33.74	Acquisition American Crocker Bank
Large decreases				
Dai Ichi Kangyo	1999	−10.93	15.02	Foreign divestitures
Lloyds TSB	1995	−12.44	14.50	Acquisition TSB
Crédit Agricole	2004	−12.45	18.39	Acquisition Crédit Lyonnais
Crédit Lyonnais	1999	−12.72	27.79	Sell off foreign activities
Sumitomo Bank	1985	−13.17	31.13	Acquisitions in Europe and the United States
Barclays	1991	−16.78	27.48	Divestiture American retail banking
Barclays	1985	−17.39	36.38	Merger Barclays and Barclays DCO
Santander	1994	−19.55	26.32	Acquisition Banesto
Midland	1990	−20.05	14.19	Sell off/swap foreign activities

More than in previous periods there seems to be a positive relationship between change in DOI and resulting level of DOI: banks with already higher levels of DOI tend to expand their foreign activities most between 1995 and 2000. For 1995 to 2000 this seems to be a tendency for the whole sample, for 1990 to 1995 this is only valid for DOI levels above 40%. An explanation for this might be that some kind of experience curve exists: organizations with DOIs above a certain level are better equipped to absorb more foreign activities.

5.4.   Home bias

Internationalization in its truest form should alleviate any differences between foreign and domestic markets. Driven over time by technological progress, deregulation and worldwide standardization of financial services practices, a home bias effect should decrease in importance. It is probably more realistic to expect a persistent home bias. There are potential advantages to be gained with decreasing the home bias (Buch, Driscoll & Østergaard, 2004). Buch et al. apply the mean-variance approach to determine geographical optimal bank portfolios and compare these optimal portfolios to the actual cross border assets of banks from 1995–99. They find that banks overinvest domestically to a considerable extent and that cross border diversification entails considerable gain.

A home bias also exists when domestic activities are more stable than foreign activities: ratios such as assets per employee should show lower variability for domestic activities than for foreign activities. Practically, a home bias might be expected for political reasons: a bank has more stakeholders in the home country than outside the home country. Changes in activities are therefore more easily executed outside the home country, leading to a higher variability. Also, if banks have concentrated corporate banking or investment banking activities outside the home country, then these activities might have a higher correlation with economic cycles than for example domestic retail activities.

Domestic and foreign indicators differ, supporting the existence of a home bias. If assets per employee are calculated for foreign, domestic and total activities (Figure 5.3), average total assets per employee increased from about two million US dollars in 1994 to six million in 1995. Domestic assets per employee were on average one million

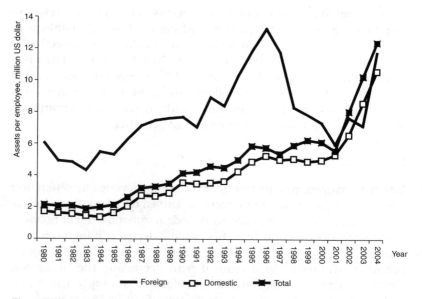

Figure 5.3   Foreign assets per employee
Note: Variables are calculated as arithmetic average.

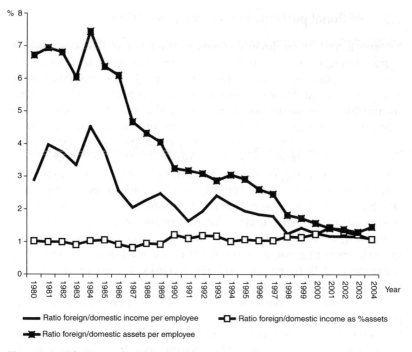

Figure 5.4 Foreign to domestic ratios

lower. Throughout the period, foreign assets per employee were higher than domestic assets, with a deviation between 1993 and 1996 where a strong increase and decrease took place. The growth in 1993–96 for foreign assets is not easily explained; the decrease after 1996 might be explained by an increase in foreign retail banking acquisitions, lowering the assets per employee ratio. Similar results are found when income per employee ratios are calculated.

Assets per employee have been steadily converging; this may be due to a number of reasons. Fiscal deregulation has effectively reduced the number of offshore havens and finance companies of banks outside the home country, activities with a high asset per employee ratio. Also, banks might have recentralized activities from the 1980s, bringing back corporate banking or investment banking activities to the head office. Finally, the acquisitions of foreign retail banks have increased in the 1990s, lowering the ratio. Income per employee is volatile, but foreign income is structurally higher than domestic. On the other hand, income as percentage of assets is similar for foreign and domestic activities.

5.5.   Regional patterns in internationalization

Internationalization developments in the last two decades could be better described by *regionalization* rather than *globalization* within the three main economic regions of Europe, Japan and Asia-Pacific, and the United States (Ruigrok & van Tulder, 1995). Internationalization of banks between 1995 and 2000 has shown uneven patterns across regions (De Nicoló, Bartholomew, Zaman & Zephirin, 2004); the share of foreign controlled assets increased significantly in the United States, several countries in Western Europe and non-Asian emerging countries. In other continents the increase of internationalization was limited, or even decreased as in Africa (De Nicoló, Bartholomew, Zaman & Zephirin, 2004). Are internationalization activities mainly focused in the region where the bank is located, or is it more broadly based? What have been the geographic areas of growth, and have they differed between American, Japanese and European banks? Have banks shifted their activities from one region to another?

On an individual bank level, there are too many gaps to form a general understanding of the trends. We can however construct continuous series by representing regional asset growth in the sample as an index where regional asset information per bank is grouped for American, European and Japanese banks. In this study, regional breakdown by assets reported by banks has been supplemented with additional sources, such as the publication of foreign owned assets in the Federal Reserve Structure data, or annual reports from separately reporting subsidiaries.[4] To construct such an index, the asset weighted growth rate for the banks per region in the sample is calculated as follows:

- Year-on-year percentage change for assets in each reported region, if available, is calculated. For comparison, all data is converted into US dollar.
- To prevent distortions in the data, large changes due to a change in data availability have been filtered out. For example, from 0 in t to 100 in t+1 or vice versa results in interpretable figures unless there is an indication that these assets have been completely divested (which would be included), or that the bank has reclassified the geographical information.
- For each region, an asset weighted average of these percentage changes are calculated and then indexed.

Figure 5.5 shows the regional indices for European banks as a group. Between 1980 and 1995, growth rates in all regions except the Middle East/Africa have been similar, circa 10% per year. Asset growth in America stayed stable during the 1980s, increasing faster than the other regions from 1989 to 1995 onwards. From 1995, growth rates diverged; the pace further increased for European banks acquiring Asian and American assets, while for domestic and European assets similar – pre-1995 – growth rates were upheld. Activities in the Middle East and Africa were reduced, especially between 1980 and 1985. The international boycott of the South African government by the United Nations between 1984 and 1986 forced many banks to sever their links with their South African subsidiaries. Also, reduction of project finance after the 1979 oil crisis and the reducing economic importance of the African region contributed to the permanent reduction.

The growth of European assets shows a consistent and subdued rise from 1985 until 2000; only from 2001 onwards growth increased strongly. In the light of European integration, European asset growth has not been a distinguishing feature for European banks. If Europe

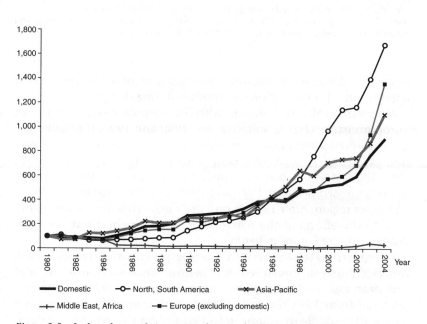

Figure 5.5   Indexed growth in regional assets for European banks
Note: Growth rates indexed at 1980 = 100. Growth rates calculated in US dollar, and weighted by domestic, foreign assets in US dollar. N varies per region.

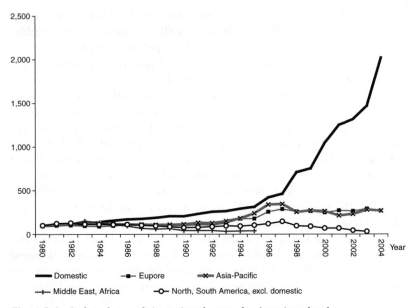

Figure 5.6 Indexed growth in regional assets for American banks
Note: Growth rates indexed at 1980 = 100. Growth rates calculated in US dollar, and weighted by domestic, foreign assets in US dollar. N varies per region.

was a crucial element in the internationalization of banks then growth opportunities for this region were limited during that period.

American banks have shown different regional growth rates from European banks (Figure 5.6). Between 1980 and 1990, the banks as a group showed slight negative growth for most regions, with the exception of assets in the Middle East/Africa that steadily declined until 1995 the last year when such information was available.[5] Regional assets increased between 1991 and 1997, especially for the European and Asian region. After 1997 growth declined. While this can be attributed to the effects of the Asian crises, such an effect has not been visible with the European banks.

The growth rate of American assets, especially Central and South American assets, remained far behind that of European and American assets. While a slight growth set in from 1991, growth also declined from 1998 onwards. The declining growth rate has been partly attributable to American banks, and on the other hand devaluation of the American currency reducing the value of asset holdings in US dollar.

For Japanese banks, regional indices could not be constructed. Japanese banks have reported limited geographical information, especially if compared to European and American banks. European banks formed a larger group, while American banks had to comply regulatorily to provide such information. Japanese banks on the other hand did not have to report geographical information and formed a much smaller sample; the available data suggests that Japanese banks' assets in the United States declined between 1980 and 1984 but showed high growth rates between 1985 and 1998, leveling off the period after. Foreign asset growth rates were higher than American growth rates suggesting that European assets must have enjoyed high growth rates also.

Over time European, American and Japanese banks shifted their regional dependence, but did not substitute one regional growth strategy for another. European banks have been most active in their own geographic region, while this has been the case to a far lesser degree for Japanese and American banks. While American banks expanded their activities in Europe and vice versa, both banking groups have also expanded activities in the Asian region, while Japanese banks may have done this reciprocally in the 1980s but reduced the foreign activities over time. In other words, internationalization in the geographic home regions is specific for European banks.

To illustrate this, the banks have again been treated as three groups (American, Japanese and European), and the available regional distribution of assets has been calculated, weighted by total assets for five-year periods (Table 5.6).

European banks have decreased the relative weight of their domestic assets, especially in 1995–2004. Benefactors were European activities, increasing to 14.1% between 2000 and 2004. The expansion was also relatively focused on American assets, gaining an average 9.3% in asset weights if 2000–04 is compared to 1985–89 (cf. De Nicoló, Bartholomew, Zaman & Zephirin, 2004). On a bank level, exceptions can be found to this general trend. For example, Crédit Agricole consistently expanded both European and American activities. Lloyds on the other hand did the opposite between 1981 and 1988, decreasing its European and American activities. Midland Bank's activities showed a consistent increase in European activities, while its American activities with the exception of 1982–85 remained below 10% of total assets. The main growth in the foreign banking activities of Credit Suisse took place in Europe, where the bank systematically expanded its activities from 20% to 40% of total assets while keeping its share of American assets relatively stable.

American banks took another approach, decreasing their assets in all regions. Although American banking activities were acquired by American banks in the 1990s, the regional importance of these banking activities actually decreased to an average 4.6% between 1995–99, more than half the percentage of 1980–84. Based on Table 5.6, Japanese banks in the sample did not expand to a great degree in the Asian region. Most activities were concentrated in the American region, while Europe steadily gained influence. However, this observation might be influenced by the currency movements.

Table 5.6   Average regional bank assets for different time periods and bank groups

Home region	Region	1980–84	1985–89	1990–94	1995–99	2000–04
Europe	Home	65.2	66.8	66.4	59.6	54.5
	Europe*	4.9	5.4	10.0	11.6	14.1
	North, South America	5.1	3.5	5.5	8.6	12.8
	Asia, Pacific	6.5	9.8	7.0	8.2	7.4
	Middle East, Africa	6.6	1.8	1.3	0.8	2.0
	Rest of World	11.7	12.7	9.8	11.2	9.2
		100.0	100.0	100.0	100.0	100.0
United States	Home	49.9	63.8	67.5	62.6	74.5
	Europe	17.9	13.0	14.7	16.7	2.0
	North, South America*	10.8	7.2	6.1	4.6	0.6
	Asia, Pacific	8.7	6.0	6.9	8.7	1.8
	Middle East, Africa	2.3	1.3	0.6	0.4	0.3
	Rest of World	10.4	8.7	4.2	7.0	20.8
		100.0	100.0	100.0	100.0	100.0
Japan	Home	66.6	66.7	67.3	74.6	82.3
	Europe	1.5	7.4	6.4	4.3	4.2
	North, South America	21.3	6.1	5.4	6.1	8.0
	Asia, Pacific*	na	5.9	4.7	3.7	3.2
	Middle East, Africa	na	na	na	na	na
	Rest of World	10.6	13.9	16.2	11.3	2.3
		100.0	100.0	100.0	100.0	100.0

*Excluding domestic assets
Note: Average of asset weightings for bank sample, five-year average, weighted by total assets in US dollar.
na: not available.

6
Internationalization Strategies

This chapter identifies internationalization patterns of banks: what did they have in common, and how did they differ? Commonalities and differences for clients and products are first reviewed, after which organizational form and phases in internationalization are discussed. Integration is pursued by applying the previous findings to five stylized types of realized internationalization strategies.

6.1. Identifying internationalization strategies

In total 44 case studies were analyzed, spanning 25 years. For each bank the internationalization activities were also tabulated, identifying phases in activities, the geographical area or region of activity, and additional information about the clients, products and organizational form used. The results are presented in a framework, combining bank strategy phases. Within this framework, four major phases for internationalization activities are identified. Each realized internationalization strategy will be discussed in more detail including a schematic representation of the phases involved in such a strategy with two case studies to illustrate the arguments.

A bank's strategy is determined by a large number of variables which cannot be easily molded into a framework (Canals, 1997). Walter (1988), Smith and Walter (1997) and Canals (1997) have developed strategic frameworks for banks. Smith and Walter (1997) developed a three dimensional matrix, which can be drawn up for each banking organization: a client-arena-product (C-A-P) matrix. The C-A-P classification is useful to analyze the activities of a bank or any firm in general. Smith and Walter do not derive general strategic typologies from their framework, although it builds on the strategy research of

Porter (1985). Banking "is a complex web of markets, services and institutions that is not easily subjected to systematic analysis" (Canals, 1997). Instead, they state essential attributes to exploit opportunities within the C-A-P framework. These include the adequacy of the institution's capital base, the institutional risk base, quality of human resources, its access to information and markets, its technology base and managerial culture, and the entrepreneurial quality of its people.

Canals (1997) investigated internationalization strategies of banks and presented an internationalization model which is based on three main incentives, the combination of which he hypothesizes to be instrumental for the internationalization of banks. In his view, scale, customer service and resource transfer are the main incentives for international activity. Canals (1997) further linked motives to organizational form of internationalization activity. Alliances are the best way to transfer resources or skills, and acquisitions are a modus operandi for increasing scale. If on the other hand customer service is an important objective, then the development of branches are quite likely. Canals stressed that "the strategic options banks have open to them vary depending on their resources and their home country [...]. The reason for this variety of strategic options is related not only to each bank's starting position, resources, skills, and weaknesses, but also to the financial model in which it operates." (Canals, 1997).

The risk of simplifying strategic nuances may weigh up to the analytical advantages of creating a comparative framework to develop general observations. Although each framework has its merits, there is no general framework which can be straightforwardly applied to internationalization strategies for banks. Therefore, the strategic framework for internationalization strategies in this study builds on the determination of strategy phases developed by Fujita and Ishigaki (1986), and De Carmoy (1990), combining banking strategies with strategic conduct into phases. Additionally, we limit ourselves to the identification of realized strategic activities compared to intended strategies (Mintzberg, Quinn & Ghoshal, 1995): information on realized strategies is publicly available and the measurement of realized strategies allows more comparisons between banks.

Within this framework four major strategies for internationalization activities are identified: entry, expansion, consolidation and restructuring. For each bank, a chronology of domestic and foreign banking events (mergers, acquisitions, divestitures and so on) was also set up, and its effect on the change in DOI registered. This information was then used to identify "phases" in the different strategies. Table 6.1

Table 6.1 Phases of international organizational activity

Strategy phase		Description	Effect on bank organization	Effect on bank's DOI	
				DOI level	DOI change
1 Entry		A new activity in a new market, a new activity in an existing market or an existing activity in a new market.	Change/expansion of organizational structure, new strategic goals.	0–20%	0–10%
2 Expansion	Broad	Above average growth of capital commitment to activities.	Targeting of several markets, combined with several acquisitions.	20–60%	0–20%
	Focused	Above average growth of capital commitment to activities, combined with selective disinvestments in activities and/or markets.	Specific targeting of one or few markets, perhaps combined with one large acquisitions.	20–80%	0–20%
3 Consolidation	Balanced growth	Average growth of capital commitment to activities, aiming to maintain current marketposition and/or financial targets.	Change in internationalization dependent on difference between home and foreign growth rates.	All levels	–5–+5%
4 Restructuring	Refocus	Period of reformulating strategy or restructuring the organization as a result of a crisis of some sort. Restructuring of activities does not lead to disinvestments and serves to increase profitability and/or lower the cost base.	Staff cuts, change of organizational structure and refocusing of strategic goals.	20–80%	–5–+5%
	Refocus & exit	Period of reformulating strategy or restructuring the organization as a result of a crisis of some sort. Average growth of capital commitment to activities,combined with selective disinvestments in activities and/or foreign markets toincrease profitability or lower the cost base.	Staff cuts, change of organizational structureand refocusing of strategic goals. Disinvestments in the markets which are no longer targeted. Freed capital is used to invest in remaining activities or to generally shore up solvency.	All levels	–10–0%
	Exit	Period of reformulating strategy or restructuring the organization as a result of a crisis of some sort.Sale or shut down of activities and markets to raise capital and/or reinvest in other existing activities.	Staff cuts, change of organizational structure and refocusing of strategic goals. Disinvestments in the markets which are no longer targeted. Freed capital is used to increase solvency.	40–80%	–20–0%

shows the phases; based on the case studies additional information has been added in the right columns: the range of DOI during a phase and the change in DOI during the phase.

Grouping banks on the basis of these phases and the resulting DOI development led to five distinct types of realized internationalization strategies, and are discussed in the next paragraph. In general, a stylized strategy is bound to ignore specific choices that banks have made, but on the other hand offers the advantage of defining commonalities in internationalization activities more clearly.

6.2.   Internationalization strategies

Before discussing the five internationalization strategies, the case studies also suggest the following stylized internationalization cycle: starting in the 1970s, bank internationalization originally consisted of setting up banking activities in financial centers and economic centers. Part of this was related to incentives such as "follow-the-client" or aimed at increasing overall profitability. Additionally, restructuring and expansion in the domestic markets might have been cumbersome for some and impossible for others, further stimulating internationalization. Regulatory idiosyncrasies in the home market might be one explanation for this, but also the existence of a home bias "inertia": restructuring the domestic retail networks in the early 1980s might have been more difficult with vested interests in the home country such as labor unions. In particular, banks in smaller countries had to expand abroad for fear of anti-trust regulation at home.

For most banks during the 1980s, international expansion supported their domestic strategies and was relatively small compared to the home country. So banks did not have to attract additional capital. When banks initiated larger acquisitions in the late 1980s and 1990s, external capital became more important as a source of financing. Domestic and foreign shareholders not only provided additional capital to expand, they also followed management more closely, and pressed for changes when expected results were not delivered. An increasing shareholder role and foreign profitability that was below expectations, led bank managers to change objectives in the mid-1990s: profitability should be internally generated, the domestic base strengthened and foreign activities divested if they did not contribute satisfactorily to total profitability.

Grouping banks on the basis of these phases and the resulting DOI development led to five distinct types of realized internationalization

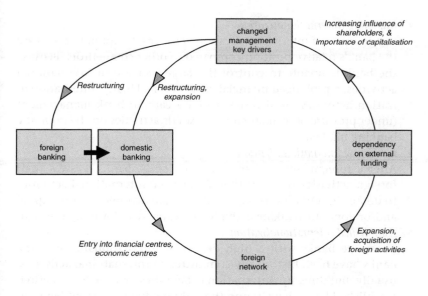

Figure 6.1   Stylized internationalization patterns of banks

strategies. In general, a stylization strategy is bound to ignore specific choices that banks have made, but on the other hand offers the advantage of defining commonalities in internationalization activities more clearly. The five archetypes selected are:

- *Accelerating internationalization*
  Banks initially develop internationalization activities by setting up branches in major economic and financial centers. As a next step international activities are expanded by increasingly large foreign bank acquisitions. Finally, the bank has to restructure to consolidate the large foreign acquisitions and to regain or increase its profitability.
- *Moderate internationalization*
  Banks with *Moderate* internationalization strategies consider internationalization as a support activity of the total bank organization. They develop a foreign branch network and bank activities in major foreign economic and financial centers; acquisitions and establishment of other international bank activities are a reaction to the internationalization activities of other banks, especially banks with *Accelerating* strategies. Ultimately, restructuring also sets in to consolidate activities and (re)gain profitability.

- *Imploding internationalization*
  Fast increase of internationalization activities, to uphold or increase the bank's relative position compared to other competitors. Because the bank is unable to control the large increase in international activities, a prolonged financial crisis occurs. Finally, internationalization activities are divested to raise capital; bank management (under pressure of regulators) refocuses its activities on the domestic banking market.
- *Retreating internationalization*
  After a foreign financial or economic crisis, banks reassess their foreign activities and shift their focus from international activities to domestic activities. Foreign activities are divested to raise capital and/or domestic banking activities are expanded, lowering the DOI.
- *Established internationalization*
  These are banks with a high degree of internationalization; the banks have been historically committed to international activities, usually building up international activities over a long period. Established banks have found the right configurational fit between foreign and domestic activities.

The five types represent the internationalization of all banks in the sample, and is classified in Table 6.2. Besides the two banks representing *Imploding* internationalization, the number of banks' models of internationalization is evenly spread between the other four types. Next, the stylized types of realized internationalization strategies are discussed.

The strategy types have a long time period in common spanning 20 years, which might be considered a long time for a strategy. Such a long time period is not uncommon,[1] but has some implications: the bank is in the analyses treated as an organization with a sense of historical memory; changes or events in the past bear their mark on strategic thinking today.

If unweighted DOI averages are compared per strategic type, then *Established* banks show the highest DOI throughout the period only to be surpassed by *Accelerating* banks in 2000. On the lower end are the *Moderate* banks, showing the lowest average DOI throughout the period to be surpassed by the *Retreating* banks in 1998. *Accelerating* and *Retreating* banks are negatively related: for the *Accelerating* banks DOI increased, especially after 1989. *Retreating* banks show steadily declining levels of DOI, from 1983 onwards. The five internationalization strategies are now considered, each illustrated with two case studies.

Table 6.2 Banks and their model of internationalization

Accelerating	Moderate	Imploding	Retreating	Established
• Hypovereinsbank	• Argentaria	• Midland	• Manufacturers	• Tokyo
	• AMRO	• Crédit	Hanover	Mitsubishi
• BCH	• Fortis	Lyonnais	• Chemical	• ABN
• ING Bank	• Bayerische		Banking	• HSBC
• ABN AMRO	Hypobank		• Mitsubishi	• Tokyo
• NMB Bank	• Vereinsbank		Bank	• SBC
• BBV	• Agricole		• Bank of	• JPMorgan
• Paribas	• Commerzbank		America	• BNP
• Credit Suisse			• Barclays	• Citicorp
• Deutsche Bank	• IBJ		• Chase	• Société
	• Rabobank		Manhattan	Générale
• Dresdner Bank	• Royal Bank		• Dai Ichi	• Standard
	of Scotland		Kangyo	Chartered
• Santander	• Mizuho		• Lloyds TSB	
• UBS			• National	
• WestLB			Westminster	
			• Sumitomo	
			Bank	

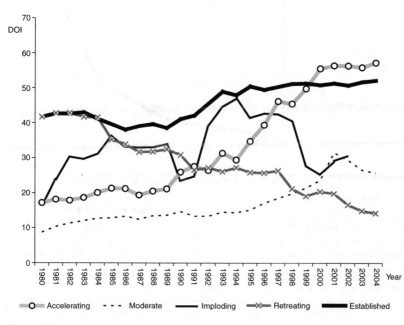

Figure 6.2 DOI per strategy type, unweighted average

6.3. Accelerating strategy

The first model fits banks that started internationalization at a moderate pace, increasing the degree of internationalization in one or more subsequent steps, after which a period of consolidation set in (Figure 6.3).

In the first period (stage A in Figure 6.3), the DOI generally moved between 10% and 20%. Foreign activities comprised a branch network in main financial centers and economic centers. For European banks, activities were set up in centers such as Luxembourg, Switzerland, Paris and London to gain access to the Euromarkets and more advantageous sources of finance than in the domestic market. The bank's objective has been to seek resources, acquire skills and funding. Also, market seeking was an important objective, expanding the existing services to be offered to domestic related clients in foreign countries. This stage also includes banks who have actively participated in consortium banks, building their branch networks in the late 1970s partly on the basis of restructured or dissolved consortium bank networks.

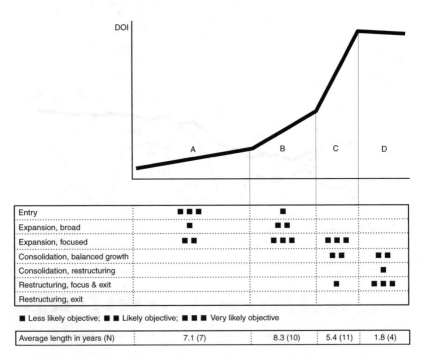

Figure 6.3 Stylized model of accelerating internationalization

In the second stage (B), internationalization quickly gathered pace and DOI reached levels of 20% and 40%. Weighing up between domestic and international investments, banks increasingly chose international expansion. Drivers for this change in Europe were the perceived convergence of financial markets, forcing banks to acquire foreign activities to have a European foothold (just in case) and also to reestablish relative domestic positions. The change from stage A to stage B is consistent with "obtaining a foothold strategy". Information about the foreign market is obtained by making small investments, precursor of larger investments in the following years (Molyneux, 2003).

A number of banks have a third stage (C), accelerating the already strong growth of internationalization activities. Here, the acquisitions get larger in size, pushing DOI levels to 60% and 80%. The acquisitions in the second stage probably have been integrated relatively smoothly. The increase took place for a number of banks between 1995 and 2000 (ABN AMRO, UBS, Credit Suisse); the funding opportunities in the stock market might have helped as well.

The strong organizational changes in stages B and C have to be absorbed at some point, signaling a consolidation or restructuring period (D). A trigger for this could be threefold. First a financial crisis could force bank management to reconsider its geographic-product portfolio. For example, the Asian crises of 1998 made Barclays and ING (further) downscale their investment banking activities, leaving shareholders with the impression the (geo-graphic) span of risk control was not an optimal one. Second, funding opportunities for further expansion might be limited because the stock market is no longer a viable option, forcing the bank to concentrate more on organic growth opportunities than growth by acquisitions. Third, banks might have hit an internation-alization ceiling: raising internationalization above a certain level raises questions like representativeness of the management board, and the validity of the location of the headquarters. In other words, raising the DOI above a certain level might in some respects be a threat to sitting management.

Bank management at this stage is general refocused: it redefined the C-A-P areas it would like to excel, finding that it acquired a number of activities in the previous years that would not fit anymore in the bank organization. Key ratios as solvency, stability of earnings, profitability and loan provisions become more important management drivers, forcing divestments in some activities.

6.3.1.   Accelerating strategy: Deutsche Bank

Deutsche Bank "fits the stereotype of the European bank in search of a truly global strategy" (Canals, 1993). Founded as a bank primarily for financing German foreign trade in 1870, it had established offices in Shanghai, Yokohama and London by 1873. The bank had been internationally active from its beginning, also being confronted with two seizures of activities during the First and the Second World Wars. Postwar internationalization was resumed in 1957, after Deutsche Bank had been realgamated (Gall et al., 1995). In the 1960s there was a growing interest in international alliances with a view to promoting foreign business. In 1963, Deutsche Bank was the first German bank to enter a loose cooperation (EAC) that evolved into EBIC. Deutsche Bank integrated its Asian activities into a joint venture of the EBIC group in 1972, until 1978 when the 14 branches were renamed Deutsche Bank (Asia). In 1970, a subsidiary was established in Luxembourg. The expansion and restructuring of the foreign branch network continued in the 1970s and 1980s (Gall et al., 1995).

Throughout the 1970s, Deutsche Bank systematically set up its branch network worldwide. Although it seemed that this development was largely over in the early 1980s, Deutsche Bank continued to open branches, or convert representative offices to branches. While this might represent an assets seeking strategy, it did not have the intensity of the "flag-planting competition" of British banks. The bank's lack of representation in the Scandinavian countries may be explained that business there can be easily conducted from Germany and London, even abstaining from purchasing possibilities during the Swedish banking crisis in 1992 (Gall et al., 1995). In 1986, Deutsche Bank started a reorganization to increase efficiency, formulating the following corporate objectives (Canals, 1993):

- Increase market position in securities trading, expanding the services offered.
- Continue development of commercial bank activities, increasing the bank's presence in other high growth international markets.
- Strengthen the bank's position in retail banking, developing new distribution channels and services.

The strengthening of retail banking took place in the same years, when the 100 Italian branches of Bank of America were acquired. The Italian subsidiary would further expand in 1993 with a majority stake in Banca Popolare di Lecco, a profitable northern regional bank also with 100 branches.[2] In 1988 the partner in Dutch bank Albert de Bary was bought out, and the bank began building up its branch networks in Argentina and Brazil. It also acquired a further 100 branches in Spain (Gall et al., 1995). In 1993 it acquired Banco de Madrid from Banesto, adding another 300 branches in Madrid and Central Spain while overtaking Crédit Lyonnais as the largest foreign retail bank in Spain, and challenging the growth strategy of National Westminster and Barclays in the country.[3]

In 1998, Deutsche Bank paid 1 billion deutschmark for Crédit Lyonnais Belgium. While Crédit Lyonnais achieved more than half the asset sale amount imposed by the European Commission in exchange for state aid,[4] Deutsche bank established its third substantial retail branch network outside Germany, besides Spain and Italy. It was unsuccessful in acquiring a retail network in France, and decided in 1999 to set up 15 branches for wealthy customers.[5]

The growth in the capital markets was primarily accomplished in two large steps: the acquisition of Morgan Grenfell in 1989, and the acquisition of Bankers Trust in 1998. In the 1970s and 1980s, Deutsche Bank established subsidiaries in the major financial centers for capital market activities.[6] The major shift to investment banking started in the

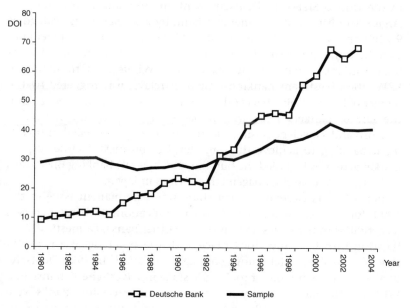

Figure 6.4   DOI of Deutsche Bank

1980s, when it acquired a 4.99% stake[7] in British investment bank Morgan Grenfell, aiming to gain access to London investment banking know-how (Gall et al., 1995). In 1989 the situation changed when French financial group Indosuez bought a 14.9% stake from a British insurer, with an option to buy another 10%. Deutsche Bank seized the opportunity, to present itself as white knight, and by the end of 1989 Deutsche Bank had acquired a controlling share of the bank. The full acquisition amounted to 2.7 billion deutschmark, the bank's biggest post-war investment (Gall et al., 1995). The bank integrated existing capital market activities in Morgan Grenfell, a process that took several years to complete.[8] Subsequently, the bank's headquarters for its investment banking activities were transferred to London, "emphasizing London's pre-eminence over Frankfurt as an international financial center".[9]

In 1992, Deutsche Bank announced the restructuring of its capital market and private banking operations, creating a holding company to bring together its North American activities. Employing 1,200 people in that region, Deutsche Bank's aim was to become a sizeable participant in the wholesale banking activities, focusing on corporate finance, securities and derivatives trading, foreign exchange and asset management.[10] This was achieved with the sale of Bankers Trust, the eighth largest bank in the United States, to Deutsche Bank in 1998 and at the time the largest acquisition of an American bank by a foreign bank, valued at 9.7 billion US dollars. Bankers Trust had been trying to build a medium-sized investment banking business in the United States, having shed its retail banking activities some years earlier. Where the termination of BZW, the investment banking unit of Barclays, was triggered by the merger of Salomon Brothers and Smith Barney (part of Travelers group), the sale of Bankers Trust was probably triggered by the merger of Citicorp and Travelers, raising the amount of capital needed in investment banking to achieve the same kind of business.[11] Other capital market activities included the building of wholesale banking operations in Australia, and asset management activities in Japan.

Increasing its German market share was a permanent issue in the 1990s for Deutsche Bank. With German unification, the bank increased its activities in the new states, as did the other banks. Domestic diversification into insurance took place with the purchase of a majority stake in Herold Versicherungs company in 1992.[12] In 1996 Deutsche Bank created a stir when it took a 5% stake in Bayerische Vereinsbank. With the German economy recovering from a recession, banks were concentrating on low-risk, and thus low profit, loans, striving to cut costs and gain business from wealthy customers. The prospect of an acquisition launched speculation about a restructuring of the German banking scene, and the stake might have signaled that Deutsche Bank intended to be a major participant in that process.[13] In the end however, Bayerische Vereinsbank ended up merging with Bayerische Hypobank the next year.[14]

Playing down prospects for a merger of its retail banking operations with Dresdner Bank at the launch of its retail operation Deutsche Bank 24 in late 1999,[15] a few months later the bank announced that a merger of its domestic retail activities with Dresdner was discussed. Although the banks agreed on the domestic approach of the merger, talks eventually failed because Deutsche Bank's plan intended to fold Dresdner Kleinwort Benson (the investment banking unit of Dresdner) into its own investment banking operation. Combined with the proposed restructuring to save costs, it would have effectively closed down Dresdner Kleinwort Benson, a consequence which met considerable resistance at Dresdner's board.

Table 6.3 Activities of Deutsche Bank

Period	Phase	Objective	Arena
'80–'85	Entry	• Build worldwide network to service client	Major financial and economic centers
		• Maintain commercial bank network	Domestic
		• Expand capital market activities	United Kingdom, United States
'86–'98	Broad expansion	• Increase domestic market position	Domestic
		• Expand wordwide network to service large corporations	Major financial and economic centers
		• Growth in retail banking	Spain, Italy, Belgium, France
		• Increase capital market activities	United Kingdom, United States
'99–'04	Restructure, refocus	• Increase domestic market position and profitability	Domestic
		• Restructure foreign activities	Whole organization
		• Divest strategic industrial shareholdings	Domestic

The restructuring of domestic operations had to be done alone, and Deutsche Bank created "Deutsche Bank 24", its retail banking unit, by combining retail and direct bank activities (clicks and bricks) in 1999. The direct banking activities had already been set up in 1995, reacting to the start of the direct bank of Commerzbank (Comdirect).[16] After restructuring, profitability increased in 2000, and the bank slowly moved away from the concept that retail banking was a costly but necessary burden for the bank. With its domestic presence established, Deutsche Bank planned to venture into online brokerage in seven European countries.[17]

By 2004 Deutsche Bank had essentially become a global operating investment bank with a relatively small retail banking network, its business model resembling Goldman Sachs rather than Citigroup. Earning most of its profits with investment banking, *The Economist* aptly summarized Deutsche Bank's current state as "while trying to broaden its horizons, it has shrunk them; by going global, it has ceased to be local".[18]

6.3.2.   Accelerating strategy: Santander

In the early 1980s Banco de Santander had branches in six countries and representative offices in another eight. Expansion in South America started as early as 1983, when the former colonies of Spain and Portugal began to privatize and open their banking system to foreigners. The expansion in South America was lasting but in Asia the bank moved too fast. In the 1980s the bank opened offices in East Asia, these were closed soon afterwards for lack of business.[19] Until 1987, its international growth was modest, spurred by internal loan growth. The pace changed in the late 1980s when Santander prepared to compete in deregulated Spain and the single European market; the bank purchased two German organizations in 1987: CC-bank, a consumer finance bank, and Visa Card Services. In 1988, the bank established an alliance with Royal Bank of Scotland, encompassing the joint development of products and also a share swap between the banks giving Santander a 9.88% stake in Royal Bank of Scotland at the end of 1994.[20] Also, in the late 1980s alliances were formed with Kemper and Metropolitan Life Insurance.[21] Santander focused on the home market in the 1990s. In 1994, Santander acquired a 60% stake in financially distressed Banco Español de Crédito (Banesto), taking full control in 1998. Santander swiftly began to reduce Banesto's international exposure in Argentina, Chile and Mexico, as well as its real estate holdings. Industrial holdings were reduced to a minimum level, as a necessity for maintaining client relationships (McDonald & Keasey, 2002).[22]

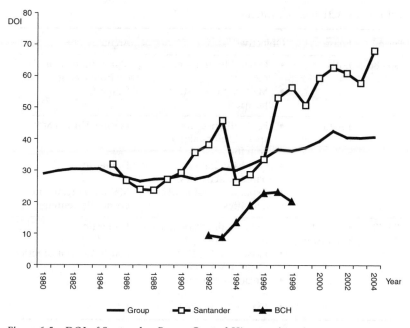

Figure 6.5 DOI of Santander, Banco Central Hispano Americano

Regional expansion took place in 1990, when Portuguese Banco de Comercio e Industria was acquired, "the Portuguese market [...] already being considered a natural extension of the Spanish market" (Canals, 1997). In 1991 the bank ventured into the United States with a 10% equity participation in First Fidelity, a large commercial bank in the north east of the United States.[23] The American continent became the center focus of international expansion. In 1994, Santander was licensed as a broker on the US stock market, and it expanded its presence in Puerto Rico, owning the second largest bank at the end of 1994.[24] In the same year, several branches were opened in Mexico. Santander first opened representative offices in 1955 in Mexico, gradually increasing its presence in that region with offices in Argentina, Brazil, Chile and Venezuela. In 1978 the first subsidiary of Santander was set up in Chile. From there on, Santander would mostly expand by making acquisitions in the region. In the early 1990s, South America was selectively targeted with the Chilean acquisitions of Fincard (1993) and Financiera FUSA (1995), merging them with Banco Osborne (1996). Santander was actively engaged in investment fund

Table 6.4   Activities of Santander

Period	Phase	Objective	Arena
'80–'86	Entry	• Expand foreign branch network	Major financial and economic centers
		• Maintain domestic position	Domestic
'87–'93	Broad expansion	• Form alliances for specialized banking activities	Europe, United States
		• Diversify domestic banking activities	Domestic
		• Expand capital market activities	Major financial and economic centers
'94–'04	Focused expansion	• Increase domestic market position (1994, 1999)	Domestic
		• Expand in South and Central America	South, Central America
		• Create European alliances (2000 onwards)	Europe
		• Expand in home region	Portugal

and pension fund business, in countries such as Chile and Argentina, establishing leading market positions in those countries (Canals, 1997). Following the acquisition of Banco Totta and Acores in 1999, BSCH obtained a 12% share of the Portuguese banking market (McDonald & Keasey, 2002).

The year 1998 proved to be difficult for Santander which had built up extensive holdings in South America; 51% of the bank's income in 1998 originated in that region. In that year, most South and Central American economies slipped into economic recession and Santander saw its profitability slip. Expecting its future to be further threatened by the coming transition to the Euro, Santander approached its smaller domestic rival, Banco Central Hispanoamericano, for a merger. Santander merged in 1999 with Banco Central Hispanoamericano to form BSCH.

In 2000 BSCH focused on expanding in Europe and Latin America. In Europe it formed an alliance with Société Générale to buy investment fund management firms, targeting the United States.[25] In the same year Santander purchased a controlling share in Banespa, the largest of Brazil's privatized banks, for 3.7 billion US dollars, almost four times the minimum asking price. Until this purchase, Spanish banks had been less aggressive in entering the Brazilian market than they had been elsewhere in Latin America (McQuerry, 2001). BSCH also bought Banco Meridional, the leading bank in the state of Rio Grande du Sol, as part of its strategy to concentrate on the seven richest states in the south east of Brazil. BSCH aimed to achieve a 10% market share there, and was halfway with the acquisition of Banco Meridional. BSCH also purchased banks in Peru and Columbia for the same reason (McDonald & Keasey, 2002). Also in 2000, BSCH bought Gruppo Financiero Serfin, Mexico's third largest bank, controlling 30% of the Mexican banking market.

In 2004 Santander completed the largest cross border bank merger in Europe to date, acquiring UK Abbey for 15.5 billion US dollars, with 741 branches and 18 million customers. With Abbey Santander bought a retail bank with a high cost base, 62% compared to 47% for Santander. This offered ample opportunities for Santander in combination with the Spanish bank's successful technology platform Parthenon to improve performance.[26] The Abbey deal completed two decades of transformation where Santander is now regarded as one of the best retail banking groups in the world, growing from the world's 152nd bank in market capitalization to the 13th largest, and seventh in assets.[27]

6.4. Moderate strategy

Banks with a stable growth of internationalization activities tend to consistently increase their DOI over time. Here too, the first stage is the build up of a branch network, with levels of DOI remaining between 10% and 20%. Where other banks accelerate their growth, mostly by acquisitions, these banks prefer to continue a strategy combining greenfields and/or small acquisitions. In some cases they are simply restricted by earlier actions (Commerzbank's internationalization activities lagged behind its domestic competitors because it had accumulated less reserves in the 1980s) or focus: Argentaria was created as a domestic oriented bank, and Rabobank had a strong domestic base. At some point, usually when the acceleration in internationalization activities took place for the *Accelerating* banks, these banks also attempted to catch up with their competitors and strongly increase their foreign activities. Rabobank set up an investment banking unit in London in 1995, and Commerzbank, previously focused on Europe, set out to buy a Taiwanese bank. At this stage, DOI generally moved between 20% and 40%.

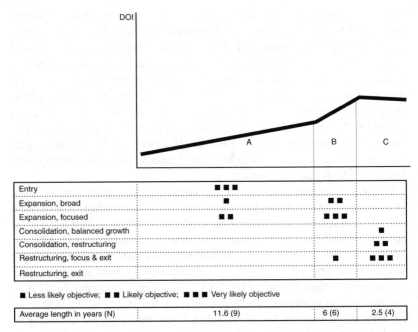

Figure 6.6   Stylized model of moderate internationalization

Reorientation with these banks generally took place ahead of restructuring with *Accelerating* banks: the low degree of internationalization is probably caused by a more risk averse approach to foreign activities, allowing little room to absorb more volatile results. Also, a relatively late acceleration of internationalization activities might have soon created the awareness that size or infrastructure to effectively compete in markets with other banks could not be achieved without considerable amount of investments. A reorientation takes place (C), focusing on its core activities. Rabobank downscaled its investment banking activities and focused on agricultural finance as an international niche strategy, aligning its international activities with its domestic strengths. Commerzbank set out to keep a confined geographic scope, maintaining a European branch network to support its German clients.

6.4.1.   Moderate strategy: Rabobank

On the subject of internationalization, the newly formed cooperative Rabobank in 1972 trod far more carefully than AMRO bank or ABN bank. Foreign activities to serve its domestic clients formed the core of its internationalization strategy in the 1970s and 1980s (De Boer & Graafsma, 2002). To join the international capital market operations, Rabobank set up activities in London and New York. Rabobank took a stake in the London and Continental Bank, a consortium bank located in London in 1972. The other major financial center, New York, was covered through a short-lived joint venture with Bank of America in New York by establishing Rabomerica International in 1974. Rabobank bought out its partner in the joint venture two years later, optimistically stating that its goals were easily achieved (Sluyterman, Dankers, van der Linden & van Zanden, 1998). In the following years, Rabobank actively participated in consortium banks and alliances, with UNICO as a linking pin within this strategy.[28]

In 1980 Rabobank became a partner in London based BEG Bank, also a consortium bank. Here it was confronted with the same problems AMRO Bank faced with consortium banking a few years earlier, and in 1980 the strategy broadened: foreign expansion through greenfields and acquisitions became additional means of international expansion, though the concept of alliances was not abandoned.

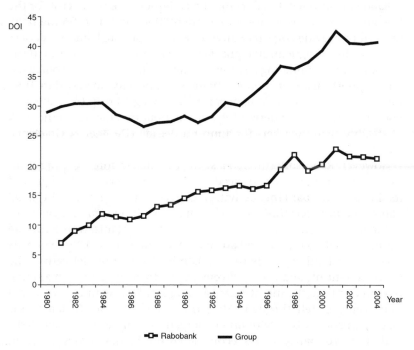

Figure 6.7 DOI of Rabobank

An important change in internationalization was the approval of the cross guarantee system in 1980, making all banks and other legal entities within the Rabobank organization mutually liable for each other's liabilities. This strengthened Rabobank's solvency considerably, making it possible to achieve the highest international credit rating ("Triple A"). From 1980 onwards, capital and reserves grew at a faster pace than total assets, providing scope for Rabobank to expand activities abroad (Pohl & Freitag, 1994).

Over the next ten years Rabobank opened a string of offices in the major OECD countries. 1990–95 was a period of redefinition: it participated fully in the bankassurance wave by acquiring Dutch insurer Interpolis, creating the third all-finance provider in the Netherlands. It was the starting point for a three pillar strategy: in the home market, Rabobank built its organization into a broad financial service provider, strengthening the retail, corporate finance and asset management side. Second, it remained loyal to the legacy of earlier decades. Rabobank strengthened ties with existing UNICO partners, especially German DG Bank and Spanish bank Banco Popular.

Rabobank also redefined its foreign activities. The rising costs of the foreign branch network forced a reorientation, and in 1996 the bank decided to provide corporate, investment and private banking services to clients in the agricultural, pharmaceutical and food industries in the major regions,[29] initiating a string of acquisitions worldwide. Somewhat more opportunistic, its London branch was heavily upgraded in 1997 into an investment banking department, trying to reap the fruits of a booming securities underwriting and distribution climate on the back of steadily rising markets for almost a decade (De Boer & Graafsma, 2002).

However, Rabobank suffered a string of setbacks forcing it to reconsider its strategy: two announced large scale mergers fell through and its investment banking activities delivered poor results. In 1998 Rabobank unsuccessfully contemplated a full-fledged merger with Achmea, a Dutch insurer with a cooperative organization structure similar to Rabobank. More bad news accumulated in 1999 when its investment banking activities in London were not delivering the expected returns, and no improvement was to be expected. An alternative, to combine the investment banking activities with DG Bank in a joint venture, fell through. Also, the domestic cost efficiency was lagging in comparison with other competitors. These events signaled a period where management reconsidered the bank's strategy, and in anticipation of a new direction, investment banking activities were

Table 6.5 Activities of Rabobank

Period	Phase	Objective	Arena
'73–'80	Entry	• Domestic growth strategy	Domestic
		• International expansion to service existing clients	United States, United Kingdom, Germany
'80–'94	Broad expansion	• Development branch network	Western, Eastern Europe
		• Domestic diversification (insurance)	Domestic
'95–'98	Focused expansion	• Foreign expansion, agriculture corporate finance	United States, Australia
		• Diversification into asset management	Domestic
'99–'02	Restructuring, refocus and exit	• Rationalization of domestic growth strategy, focus on cost control	Domestic
		• Scale down investment banking to corporate finance for existing clients	Domestic, United Kingdom
'02–	Focused expansion	• Foreign expansion, agriculture corporate finance	United States, Australia
		• Maintain domestic market position	Domestic
		• Expand asset management activities	Europe, Asia, United States

scaled down significantly and costs cutting measures announced. The restructuring was beneficial to the solvency of the bank: while the DOI decreased from 1999, capital growth increased.

Asset management heralded the continued commitment to international operations when Rabobank bought two American asset managers and a hedge fund boutique in 2001 and 2002, as well as a small Swiss private bank. In 2004 Rabobank agreed to cooperate with pan-European insurer Eureko, in a deal initially restricted to health insurance. In Poland a large financial participation in the leading agricultural bank BGZ was acquired, while in India the bank took an equity stake in an Indian retail bank. The bank faced resistance however when it announced its intention to acquire US based Farm Credit Services. Rabobank's commitment to further international growth remains unwavered however; its chairman predicted in early 2005 that in ten years the bank's international side will be bigger than the Dutch side, building on Rabobank's two-tier strategy: strengthening its domestic All-Finanz activities, with the ambition to become the largest "Food and Agri" bank.[30]

6.4.2. Moderate internationalization: Dai Ichi Kangyo and Mizuho

Dai Ichi Kangyo Bank (DKB) became for a while the world's largest bank in terms of assets in the mid-1980s. The bank was the result of a government sponsored merger in 1971, combining Dai Ichi and Nippon Kangyo Bank. This created the country's largest bank, partly as a reaction to American banks that in the 1960s moved into Japan and gradually gained market share in the Japanese lending market.[31] The merger created a strict balance of power between the former bank executives, slowing growth of the bank, especially outside Japan.[32] In the 1960s DKB further developed banking activities in Taiwan.[33] DKB's competitors avoided setting up activities in Taiwan, in an effort to win favor with the mainland Chinese. DKB on the other hand set up activities in Taiwan, assuming that dual contacts would be an asset with the

Table 6.6   Activities of Dai Ichi Kangyo Bank

Period	Phase	Objective	Arena
'80–'92	Broad expansion	• Build worldwide network for capital market activities and to service client • Maintain commercial bank network • Acquire commmercial bank and finance activities in the United States	Domestic United States, United Kingdom, Germany
'93–'96	Consolidation	• Restructure organization to regain profitability • Set up commercial banking activities in South East Asia	Western, Eastern Europe Domestic
'97–'00	Restructuring, refocus & exit	• Diversification of banking activities • Merger with IBJ and Fuji into Mizuho to restructure bad loans • Divest banking/finance activities in the United States to raise capital	Domestic Domestic, United Kingdom

possible reunification between Taiwan and China. Also controversially, the bank assisted foreign firms entering the Japanese markets.[34]

In general, the foreign expansion of DKB was export led, setting up branches. The bank did not favor acquiring foreign banks, "believing that existing operations often came with unwanted obligations".[35] A major exception took place in 1980, when DKB purchased the Japan-California Bank. The bank entered capital markets in the United States relatively late, when it started its own company in 1986 (the Dai Ichi Kangyo Trust Company) by purchasing 125 million US dollars in corporate loans from a New York based bank.[36] By 1986, the bank had surpassed Citicorp as the largest bank in assets, owing much to the appreciation of the yen relative to the US dollar. Its international operations also expanded; the bank opened a representative office in India[37] and by 1987 the bank had established a New York securities subsidiary, an investment consultancy in London and a subsidiary in Hong Kong.

Compared to IBJ or Sumitomo, DKB was relatively well represented in the Japanese retail banking market, where it had 363 branches in all 47 of Japan's prefectures, the biggest network of any Japanese commercial bank and one of the highest concentrations in the heavily populated Tokyo area.[38] DKB participated in the property and lending boom of the 1980s, leaving the bank in the early 1990s with bad loans and devalued assets. DKB tried to offset reduced lending to business by targeting consumer business, but then Japanese families suffered a crisis of confidence.[39]

In response to the difficult domestic situation, DKB restructured its foreign banking activities in 1993, shutting down its Indian operations. DKB further targeted new foreign markets, established offices in Indonesia and China, and strengthened its foreign activities to attract new local business rather than foreign business of Japanese clients. In anticipation of the Japanese program of financial reform, DKB divested a part of its non-performing loans and posted its first-ever loss in 1997. In that year, the bank suffered additional problems when top executives resigned in the light of a payoff scandal linking DKB to racketeers.[40]

In 1989, the bank had paid 1.28 billion US dollars to acquire control of CIT, a US based commercial financing subsidiary, from Manufacturers Hanover who needed to raise capital. Similar to Manufacturers at the time, DKB raised capital in 1997 when it publicly offered 22% of CIT Group. In 1998, it sold another 30%,[41] and in 2001 Tyco International eventually took control of CIT.

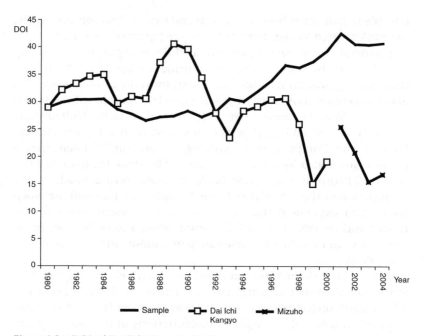

Figure 6.8   DOI of Dai Ichi Kangyo Bank

Foreign activities were further restructured in 1998, closing down the Milan and Madrid offices and reviewing its Paris office.[42] In the same year DKB bought Kankaku Securities to offer investment services to retail customers, and formed joint ventures with JPMorgan to offer mutual funds through DKB's domestic branches. In 1998, Fuji Bank and DKB agreed to form an asset management alliance and jointly buy the pensions and custody business of Yasuda Trust, a bank affiliated with Fuji Bank. A full merger between the banks was not ruled out at the time;[43] as losses continued for both banks DKB agreed to merge with Industrial Bank of Japan and Fuji Bank to form the world's largest bank under the Mizuho name in 2000. In the light of this merger, JPMorgan and DKB ended their joint venture.

The turnaround for Mizuho took place from 2003 onwards, after the bank reported the largest net loss in the country's history, totaling 21.6 billion US dollars. Despite remaining structural problems, 2004 signaled an improvement in Mizuho's financial health, when the bank announced it was to start repaying 20% of the borrowed government funds to shore up its capital in the late 1990s.[44]

6.5. Established strategy

What *Accelerating, Moderate* and *Imploding* internationalization have in common is that initially the level of DOI was low: the bank had to acquire a market position in international banking, and had three routes to choose from. For *Retreating* and *Established* internationalization, the bank's initial position was different. The level of DOI was high, and while *Retreating* banks chose to focus on domestic activities, *Established* banks continued their commitment to international activities, maintaining a DOI level between 30% and 50%. This was the case for JPMorgan, Citicorp and HSBC in the 1980s and 1990s, or ABN in the 1980s.

Established banks were not immune to change: economic and financial crises, and shifting focus on international banking activities led at times to restructuring activities. However, the banks typically did not decrease their DOI by more than 10%, illustrating their commitment to foreign banking activities. This also indicates that the banks have in general balanced international and domestic growth of banking activities.

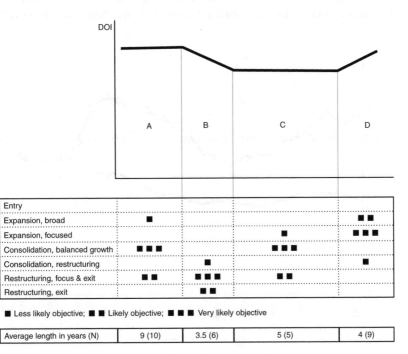

Figure 6.9 Stylized model of established internationalization

6.5.1.   Established internationalization: Citigroup

If financial experts were to name one "global universal bank par excellence", it would likely be Citicorp (Canals, 1997). In the 1960s, the expansion of international banking business followed American clients expanding in Europe. Also, the bank aimed to offer a full range of financial services, a strategy which was not common among banks during that period (Canals, 1997). During the 1970s, the bank grew in complexity, expanding the bank's business along the formulated I's: institutional banking, individual banking, investment banking and information technology.

The 1980s were a difficult period for Citicorp, coping with an economic recession in 1981–82 and 1989–90. In the early 1980s, volatile interest rates for funding, and interest rate ceilings hurt the profitability of consumer banking activities such as credit cards and mortgages.[45] From 1982 loans extended to emerging markets, and transformed into the LDC crisis, began to affect the financial performance of Citicorp. In 1987 John Reed, chairman of Citicorp, announced that his bank was establishing a 3 billion US dollar reserve against LDC loans, creating the largest quarter loss in banking history.[46] In the same year, the stock

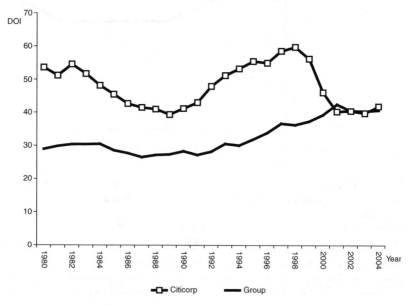

Figure 6.10   DOI of Citicorp

market crash in October meant heavy losses for the bank. Another strategic choice was the purchase of Quotron, an electronic data vendor of stock market information. Quotron clients were also competitors of Citicorp, and the company lost 40% of its clients inducing a net loss of 1 billion US dollars for the bank (Barnet & Cavanagh, 1994).

Citicorp refocused, aiming to stay dominant in its chosen main businesses: consumer banking worldwide, international banking, and securities and transactional banking such as foreign exchange.[47] The scope of activities in the investment banking division was cut back. On the other hand, the retail banking unit was to be expanded, which was profitable and less risky, growth was also to be achieved abroad. In the early 1990s, Citicorp was the US bank offering the most financial services; the retail unit was particularly strong in mortgages and credit card services. In those years, an aggressive program of cost cutting, and divestiture of non-strategic activities was pursued.[48] To emphasize Citicorp's role in foreign operations, Onno Ruding, a former Dutch finance minister and executive at ABN AMRO, was brought in as vice

Table 6.7 Activities of Citicorp

Period	Phase	Objective	Arena
'80–'91	Restructuring, refocus & exit	• Restructure foreign activities	Europe, Asia, South America
		• Internal restructuring, cost cutting measures	Domestic
		• Focus on consumer banking, reduce investment banking	Domestic
'92–'97	Expansion, broad	• Expand foreign activities	Europe, Asia
		• Focus on domestic retail and corporate clients	Domestic
		• Diversification in financial services	Domestic
'98–'04	Expansion, focused	• Expand in consumer finance	Domestic
		• Expand in investment banking	United Kingdom
		• Expand in foreign consumer and corporate finance services	Mexico, Japan

chairman to attract more foreign capital and promote its role in financial transactions in Europe (Rogers, 1993). By the end of 1992, the bank operated in 92 countries and had about 88,000 employees (Canals, 1997).

Fragmentation of the banking market (creating opportunities to create more efficiency by cutting costs), rising share prices (increasing merger and acquisition opportunities) spurred a consolidation wave in the US banking market from the early 1990s onwards. Its zenith was reached when in April 1998 Citicorp agreed to be acquired by Travelers for 82.5 billion US dollars, the largest acquisition in the banking history of the United States.[49] A driver for the merger was the cross selling of retail financial services.[50] Travelers Group evolved in the 1980s and 1990s as a financial services firm, diversifying in areas as life insurance, mutual funds, (secured and unsecured) consumer loans and credit cards. In 1997 Travelers bought Salomon and formed investment bank Salomon Smith Barney. The newly formed company was acclaimed to be the world's largest financial services firm, being a full service bank for customers in 100 countries. Citicorp and Travelers received regulatory approval for the merger, provided that the US Congress drop its restrictions against banking and insurance combinations. This was achieved in the Gramm-Leach-Bliley Act in 1999.

The merged company was renamed Citigroup and set out to balance retail activities on the one side and wholesale and investment banking on the other side. Retail activities were strengthened with consumer finance acquisitions in the area of sub prime lending, an old focus of Travelers: in 1999 Commercial Credit Company was acquired and also 100 branches of Associates First Capital Corporation. Continuing this development, Citigroup bought the largest listed US finance company, Associated First Capital, for over 31 billion US dollars. Associated First Capital specialized in making loans to consumers who have difficulty obtaining bank credit. With the acquisition, Citigroup also attained a stronger foothold in Japanese consumer finance.[51] This prompted the *Financial Times* to remark that "Citigroup now more looks like a finance company than a bank when it comes to consumer financial services, particularly in the United States" (Silverman, 2000).

Outside the United States, the bank stepped up its acquisition pace in Japan and Europe. In Japan it raised its stake in Japan's third largest broker, Nikko Securities, to almost 21% considering cooperation in a broad range of financial services. The two organizations already had an investment banking joint venture operating in Japan.[52] Citicorp had long been active in Japan, forming for example in 1986 an alliance

with Dai Ichi Kangyo to share each other's ATMs, act as financial intermediary, and distribute Citicorp's Mastercard in Japan (Smith &
Walter, 1997).

Citicorp also had a long history in the United Kingdom, entering the
market in the 1970s, when Citibank acquired 49% of Grindlays as part
of a rescue operation in 1974 (most of Grindlays' operations were outside the United Kingdom). Citibank was actively developing the Eurocurrency markets, and ventured into the corporate domestic market.
The UK market had some attractive traits, such as the structurally high
interest rates, the low degree of financial products compared to the
United States and the ongoing deregulation (Hindle, 1980).[53] Citibank
announced in 1980 that it would revamp all its 40 UK offices providing
a "comprehensive range of savings and loans products under one roof"
and introducing new products.[54]

The importance of the United Kingdom was reinforced in 2000,
when European investment banking was expanded with the 2.2 billion
US dollar acquisition of the investment banking unit of Schröder in the
United Kingdom. Citigroup intended to make its investment banking
unit, Salomon Smith Barney, into a serious player in Europe's M&A
market,[55] effectively doubling Salomon's equity and investment
banking activities in Europe. It also bought Polish bank Handlowy, one
of Central Europe's largest corporate banks.[56]

Within the home region, Citigroup purchased Mexican Grupo
Financiero Banamex in 2000. The company was the country's largest
financial services group, also having a Californian subsidiary. The purchase served as a "reverse internationalization": Citigroup intended to
use the bank to reach the growing market of Mexicans and Hispanics
living in the United States (McQuerry, 2001).

From 2001 Citigroup's ambitious growth plans became more
subdued. Several financial scandals hit the bank, most notably Enron,
disrupting the European bond market and having to close down its
private banking operations in Japan due to a series of serious
breaches.[57] The subsequent reorientation led to dissolving the bank-
insurance merger from 1998 by selling Travelers Life and Annuities,
and essentially all of its international insurance business. Citigroup
motivated the move by pointing to the unattractive growth prospects
of the insurance market and the low return on capital compared to its
other businesses.[58] However, compared to other insurers the results
were acceptable; *The Economist* suggested that the sale might also be a
consequence of the financial scandals, trying to steer clear of potential
future conflicts of interest.[59]

6.5.2. Established internationalization: HSBC

Hongkong and Shanghai Bank was originally founded and headquartered in Hong Kong, exemplified by the 9% stake holding of the Hong Kong Monetary Authority.[60] Being set up in 1865, the bank initially financed and promoted British imperial trade. Hongkong and Shanghai Bank began expanding its activities in the late 1950s by acquiring the British Bank of the Middle East and Indian Mercantile Bank. In 1965 it bought 62% of Hang Seng, Hong Kong's second largest bank. In the late 1970s and into the 1980s, China began to open up for foreign business. The bank bought operations in North America to capitalize on business between China and the United States and Canada, much of which was transacted through Hong Kong since China lacked financial infrastructure until the 1980s.

HSBC, having first opened an US agency in 1875, acquired 49% of Marine Midland of New York, a bank in need of capital. In 1985, HSBC bought the branches and assets of the failed New York Golden Pacific Bank, taking a stake in 1986 in Westchester Federal Savings Bank, and acquiring in 1987 the remaining 51%. Acquisition intensified again in the mid-1990s, buying four banks between 1995 and 1999 (Tschoegl, 2000). In 2000, it engineered a major acquisition, the Republic National Bank of New York. In Canada, the bank purchased Hongkong Bank of Canada in 1981, most of the assets and liabilities of the Bank of British Columbia in 1986, and Lloyds Bank of Canada in 1990. The Hongkong Bank of Canada was the largest foreign Canadian bank by the end of 1990 (Jones, 1993).

During the 1980s, HSBC also had to face the problem of its home base. In 1984 the British government negotiated an agreement under which the entire Hong Kong colony would be returned to China in 1997, but with a guarantee of economic continuity for 50 more years. The agreement did not boost confidence in the viability of a Hong Kong under Chinese rule, and by the time of the Tiananmen Square massacre in Beijing in 1989, businesses and people were emigrating. HSBC already had a modest presence in the United Kingdom and joined other commercial banks to acquire brokers, buying a 29.9% stake in London securities firm James Capel & Co. in 1984, taking full control in 1986 (Jones, 1993). Three years earlier, HSBC had also tried to gain a foothold in the United Kingdom by making a failed takeover bid for Royal Bank of Scotland. In 1987, pressed to reduce its dependence on Hong Kong, it took an equity stake in Midland, then UK's third largest bank entering a cooperation agreement with the possibility of a full merger in 1990. Midland Bank was purchased in 1992 and

– as part of the agreement to buy Midland – in 1993 HSBC formed HSBC Holdings, transferring its headquarters from Hong Kong to London.

The strategy of HSBC in the mid-1990s has been to build the world's biggest financial services group, presenting itself as a contender of Citigroup.[61] HSBC took a different approach to investment banking than competitors like JPMorgan and Deutsche Bank, building a far more modest investment banking unit, emulating Barclays Capital Market's activities. HSBC began to expand further in Asia, where it established the first Malaysian foreign owned subsidiary with 36 branches. HSBC moved back to China, where it had withdrawn after the Communist regime took control in 1949, opening branches in Beijing and Guangzhou.

In 1997 it expanded to South America, buying banks in Argentina, Brazil, Mexico and Peru. The motivation of HSBC's expansion to South America seemed to be related to the strategy of risk diversification through geographical diversification, further decreasing its dependency on Asian activities (De Paula, 2002). In Brazil it bought Bamerindus in 1997, the fifth largest bank in Brazil with the country's second largest branch network,[62] planning to challenge local banks but eventually toned down and sought to increase its customer base to include more high income customers (De Paula, 2002).[63] Negative financial effects of the Asian crises in 1998 were cushioned by HSBC's non-Asian operations, but

Table 6.8   Activities of HSBC

Period	Phase	Objective	Arena
'81–'92	Broad expansion (1)	• Build presence in North America	United States, Canada
		• Gain market share/shift homebase to Britain	United Kingdom
		• Maintain market share in Hong Kong	Domestic
'93–'04	Broad expansion (2)	• Restructure domestic activities	Domestic
		• Expand in South East Asia	China, Malaysia, South Korea
		• Expand in Europe in commercial banking (CCF)	France
		• Expand in the United States by acquisitions	United States

the share price suffered from investor nervousness. The Hong Kong Monetary Authority even bought 9% of the bank to halt the fall of the stock exchange.

International expansion continued when the bank announced in 1999 that it would buy a controlling stake in South Korea's government-owned Seoulbank. It also bought Republic New York and Safra Republic Holdings, doubling HSBC's private banking business and adding 426 branches in New York State. In 2000, HSBC bought Credit Commercial de France for 11 billion euros, adding 1 million French customers and completing Europe's largest ever cross border banking acquisition.[64] Also in 2000, HSBC formed a 1 billion US dollar joint venture with US securities firm Merrill Lynch to offer online brokerage services to wealthy clients. HSBC wanted to win new customers by outsourcing research and brokerage services to Merrill, attempting to achieve through a partnership what Citigroup had tried to do with acquisitions.

HSBC's American expansion continued with the 15 billion US dollar acquisition of consumer finance group Household in 2002. By 2004 HSBC had managed to acquire more than 50 businesses over a period of 12 years at a total value of 50 billion US dollars, aiming for future growth in Asia and North America, two regions where HSBC's chairman argued that the growth will be concentrated in the coming decades.[65]

6.6.   Retreating strategy

Retreating banks have already acquired high levels of internationalization in an earlier period. They have built a branch network supporting their domestic clients, but also other activities like commercial bank networks. The decline of internationalization is triggered by a crisis; for American and British banks in the early 1980s this was the LDC crises.

Banks then began a period of reorientation: their main concern was to stop the loss making activities, depressing their profitability, solvency as well as their market value. American banks reduced their LDC exposure throughout the 1980s, while playing an active role in the loan restructuring committees until 1985 to salvage some of the loans. Regulatory authorities tended to play an active role, stimulating the decrease in foreign activities by allowing more domestic mergers and acquisitions to achieve scale and more cost-cutting opportunities. This hastened the decline in DOI in stage B (see Figure 6.11). This also suggests that internationalization was not the preferred growth strategy

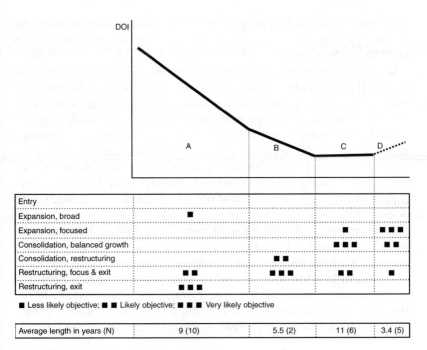

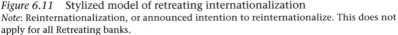

Figure 6.11 Stylized model of retreating internationalization
Note: Reinternationalization, or announced intention to reinternationalize. This does not apply for all Retreating banks.

for these banks in the first place. This is especially the case for American banks, when the regulation on interstate banking was lifted, allowing domestic mergers.

After a period of consolidation, working through the domestic merger, bank management became interested again in internationalization. Chase Manhattan bought JPMorgan in 2000 to this end, Bank of America set up investment banking activities in London from 1999 onwards, and domestic oriented banks like Lloyds announced that it might once again reconsider international activities in 2000.

6.6.1. Retreating internationalization: Bank of America

In 1980 Bank of America reported record earnings and became the largest bank measured by assets a year later. More than 45% of its assets were located outside the United States, indicating an active internationalization strategy. Seven years later, the bank was not among the largest 25 banks in the world, a position it achieved again in 1998. By

1998, foreign assets had dropped to 11%, a steady decline since the 1980s caused by an active combination of increased domestic mergers and foreign divestitures.

Bank of America built a strong position in California, having been restricted in branching out to other states. In the 1970s, the bank had established a presence in all major financial centers, with commercial branch networks in Europe and Latin America. The bank acquired Seafirst, a Washington based bank in 1983, and diversified into securities buying Charles Schwab. The 1980s demonstrated that the asset seeking strategy of the 1970s and early 1980s had major flaws: operating expenses were hard to control,[66] management had difficulties coping with the organization, and the foreign expansion turned out to be over ambitious,[67] having lent considerably to LDCs.

Between 1985 and 1987 the bank had to reveal losses. Rumors about its capital adequacy forced the share price down, even prompting a takeover bid from smaller bank First Interstate in 1985. This event did not succeed but forced a change in management.[68] Subsequently a restructuring program was announced with three goals (Canals, 1997). First, the retail and commercial banking unit was strengthened, since Bank of America had an extensive distribution network. Second, poorly

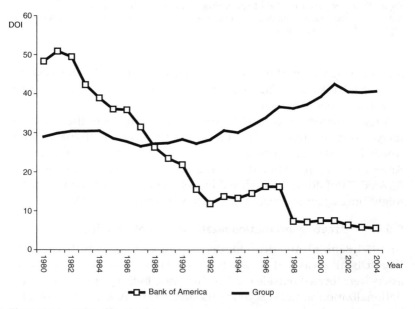

Figure 6.12   DOI of Bank of America

performing lending activities were divested or cut back. Third, international activities also cut back. Divesting foreign activities raised capital – the retail branches of Bank America d'Italia were sold to Deutsche Bank,[69] as was German Bankhaus Centrale Credit. At home FinanceAmerica, the bank's consumer finance arm was sold to Chrysler and the trust business went to Wells Fargo.[70] In 1987 Charles Schwab was sold back to the founder, and new capital was issued, mainly invested in by Japanese institutions.

After cutting costs and restructuring bad loans, the bank returned to profit in 1988 and steadily increased its financial performance. In 1990 the operations of Bank of America were expanded into seven other states by acquiring thrifts.[71] In 1992 Bank of America acquired Security Pacific, the largest US banking merger at that time. Loan losses, unsuccessful diversification in investment banking and overexpansion in Australia had hurt the bank badly. Internationally, Bank of America had retreated since the mid-1980s. The number of European staff decreased from 7,500 to 1,700 in 1994, the number of Latin American countries it was active in decreased from 20 to 6.

In acquiring Californian bank Security Pacific it gained an Asian network of 22 branches. The branches were kept, aiming at a niche strategy serving large customers from the United States. Other foreign activities were rationalized, selling the British securities firm of Security Pacific[72] in 1992 to ABN AMRO. As a result of the merger, Bank of America increased its position in California, increasing total assets by 56%. The bank acquired additional banks and mortgage businesses, and in 1994 Continental Bank was bought, expanding Bank of America with a large corporate banking franchise.[73] In 1996 the bank restructured: 120 branches in California were to be closed, reducing staff by 3,700. To raise capital, Bank of America spun off its credit card operations in a 1996 IPO; it also sold its institutional trust and securities services and a consumer finance unit. It acquired investment banking group Robertson Stephens in 1997, which was soon afterwards sold to BankBoston.

Bank of America and Nationsbank announced their merger in 1998. Nationsbank emerged as a regional bank from North Carolina, expanding by acquiring assets, branches and (defunct) banks from the savings and loans crises of late 1980s and early 1990s, nearly doubling its assets when the FDIC chose the bank to acquire Texas' largest (defunct) bank. From 1993, it diversified into securities trading (1993) and investment banking (1997), further expanding its network by acquiring more regional banks.[74] The merger was domestically driven and came in a

Table 6.9   Activities of Bank of America

Period	Phase	Objective	Arena
'80–'84	Growth strategy, internationally diversified	• Diversify in financial services (securities)	Domestic
		• Maintain a global network	Europe, Asia, South America
		• Expand domestic branch network	Domestic
'85–'98	Restructuring, domestic focus	• Reduce foreign activities	Europe, Asia, South America
		• Focus on domestic retail and corporate clients	Domestic
		• Mergers with regional banks (1992, 1994, 1998)	Domestic
'99–'02	Renewed focused international expansion	• Divest foreign consumer and private banking	Europe, Asia
		• Expand investment banking unit	Domestic, United Kingdom
		• Diversify in financial services (securities)	Domestic
'03–	Domestic expansion	• Expand domestic market share, acquire FleetBoston	Domestic

period when consolidation in the US banking market was considered to be increasing. Combining Bank of America, the fifth largest bank in the US with a strong West Coast presence, and Nationsbank, the third largest bank with a strong presence in the south eastern part of the United States, created the largest and most broadly based bank in the United States at the time, controlling 8.1% of consumer deposits, double its nearest competitor.[75]

Just after completing the merger, the bank had to write down a 1.4 billion US dollar bad loan to investment firm D.E. Shaw, being financially hit similar to LTCM by the Russian crisis. The Russian crisis, and the merger activities between Nationsbank and Bank of America led the bank in early 1999 to restructure its foreign activities, selling its private banking operations in Europe and Asia to UBS,[76] and its consumer banking business in Asia to ABN AMRO.[77] Simultaneously, it announced that it planned to expand its securities activities at home as well as in the United Kingdom, attempting to build it up internally.[78]

Its international activities were modest and dwarfed by the subsequent acquisition of FleetBoston. Bank of America paid 47 billion US dollars for this bank, a large domestic retail bank. The combination had a 10% market share of domestic deposits. With FleetBoston, Bank of America completed a transformation spanning two decades from one of the largest global banks to one of the largest domestic banks in the world.

6.6.2.   Retreating internationalization: Lloyds TSB

As with Barclays, Lloyds' interest in international activities dates from the 1910s. After failing to pursue a domestic merger with Martins in 1968,[79] Lloyds Bank was in need of a new strategy. Lloyds subsequently planned a "progressive 'group' concept – a bank with a strong domestic base, fit to withstand growing pressure from foreign, particularly American, banks, and able to counter-attack abroad by having its own branches" (Pohl & Freitag, 1994). Internationalization took off after Lloyds acquired a controlling stake in BOLSA, active in South America, and merged it with Lloyds Bank Europe into Lloyds Bank International in 1974. Its American presence started in California, buying First Western Bank and Trust, and First State Bank in 1974.[80] Having acquired the New Zealand Bank in 1966, the group concept showed a presence in 50 countries in the 1970s. In 1978, Lloyds entered investment banking through the formation of Lloyds Merchant Bank (Rogers, 1999). German private bank Schröder, Munchmeyer, Hengst & Co was purchased a few years later.

In the early eighties the strategy needed revision. Besides accumulating problem loans through BOLSA, the bank had also accumulated a large portfolio of non-performing commercial real-estate loans during the years. As the smallest of the four largest British banks, its portfolio of non-performing loans to South American countries was one of the biggest and it had less capital as a buffer to write down the loans than any other domestic competitor (Rogers, 1999). Although its problems were not that different from the other British banks, its cushions were smaller and change of management in 1983 prompted a reorientation. Shareholder value would be leading, concentrating on activities that earned a high return on capital by growing business that were performing well and divesting or closing down businesses that were not performing (Pohl & Freitag, 1994).

This meant a retreat from international and wholesale activities, as well as an increased focus on the retail client. Lloyds closed down its investment bank, Lloyds Merchant Bank, in 1987 and also closed many branches in the United States, Europe and South East Asia. In 1986, Lloyds Bank sold Lloyds Bank California to Sanwa Bank (Tschoegl, 2000). Late 1987, Lloyds withdrew from market making in British government bonds and Eurobonds, withdrawing its application for a licence to trade securities in Tokyo (Rogers, 1999).

Retail financial services were expanded through a series of acquisitions. In 1988, it expanded its insurance activities with the purchase of Abbey Life Insurance, designed to build a larger customer base and increase the product range (and profitability) for retail clients (Pohl & Freitag, 1994). Lloyds failed to take over Midland in 1992, which would have considerably expanded its domestic network, but the bank was outbidded by HSBC and unprepared for the hostility of Midland managers in the wake of cost cutting measures.[81] The purchase of Cheltenham and Gloucester in 1995 added to its home mortgage business, and the acquisition of Trustee Savings Bank (TSB) in 1996 expanded its customer base and provided selling opportunities for its savings and insurance products (Rogers, 1999).

Lloyds stepped up the pace in 2000 to increase its market size, as well as its range of financial products. Although the bank kept the option of

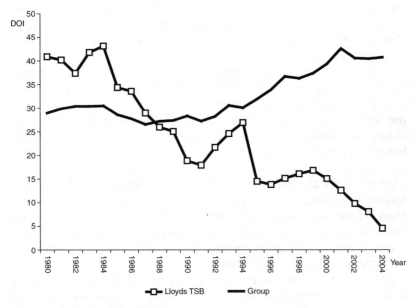

Figure 6.13   DOI of Lloyds TSB

a European merger or acquisition open,[82] the major activities were domestic. Scottish Widows, the country's sixth largest insurer, was acquired in 1999, buying one of the strongest brands in the life insurance and pensions industry. Lloyds also gained access to a network of independent financial advisors that have recommended Scottish Widows products, and the ability of distributing their products through the 2,500 bank branches.[83,84] Scope for further domestic growth became limited however. At the end of 2000, Lloyds unsuccessfully attempted to acquire Abbey National, a former building society that had been trying to merge with Bank of Scotland to challenge the largest UK banks.[85] International activities were subsequently further divested. In 2003 Lloyds TSB sold The National Bank of New Zealand, and its Brazilian and French activities.[86]

Lloyds has been particularly successful in pursuing a domestic focus strategy during most of the 1980s and 1990s. Roger attributes this to an early recognition compared to its competitors that international asset growth and global investment banking did not equate profitability

Table 6.10   Activities of Lloyds TSB

Period	Phase	Objective	Arena
'80–'84	Consolidation, balanced growth	• Maintain strong domestic position	Domestic
		• Build international branch network	Main financial centers
		• Expand in commercial banking in selected countries	United States, Germany
'85–'99	Restructuring, refocus & exit	• Retreat from international activities	Europe, United States
		• Scale down capital market activities	Domestic
		• Gain market share, by diversification in financial services and acquisitions	Domestic
'00–'04	Restructuring, refocus	• Gain domestic market share (failed)	Domestic
		• Retreat from international activities	New Zealand, Brazil, France
		• Consider foreign mergers	Europe

growth (Rogers, 1999), and a first mover advantage by (re)embracing the domestic consumer, committing itself to retail banking when Barclays and National Westminster would address this issue almost a decade later (Rogers, 1999).

The retreat from international activities has not always been consistent: in 1986 it made a bid to acquire Standard Chartered, which would have diverted Lloyds considerably from its domestic retail strategy. The blocked attempt to acquire Abbey National indicated domestic growth opportunities could become less in the near future, prompting remarks from management that activities outside the home market might be contemplated again.[87] Yet by 2004, reinternationalization had not materialized in contrast to its domestic competitors HSBC, Barclays and Royal Bank of Scotland.

6.7.   Imploding strategy

Jean Deflassieux, senior international officer at Crédit Lyonnais in 1980, said that banking internationalization is "a bit like bicycling: if you stop going you fall off".[88] A strong rise and decline of internationalization between 1980 and 2000 applies to two banks: Crédit Lyonnais and Midland Bank. Within a short period, foreign activities were acquired to achieve status (stage A): Crédit Lyonnais aimed to achieve a similar market position as Deutsche Bank in the European banking market, while Midland felt it lagged in internationalization activities after years of consortium banking and alliances, and wanted a major foreign acquisition to be at par with the other British banks.

The rise in internationalization and change in market position came in both cases at a cost: the bank organization became uncontrollable, its problems surfacing in stage B. For example, the management of US Crocker Bank did not give its owner, Midland, full insight in its financial statements (Rogers, 1999). Midland was not able, and perhaps did not press hard, to gain disclosure about how its capital injection was spent. The influx of capital in Crocker created unbalanced loan growth, and poor disclosure meant that similar risks for Crocker and Midland were not controlled for the total organization. Crédit Lyonnais had similar problems: it did not have an administrative organization in place to manage the operational risks that increased with each additional foreign acquisition.

The decline of internationalization for both banks was a forced exit, as sudden as its entry. Midland had to take large provisions for the losses at Crocker, damaging Midland's solvency which was only

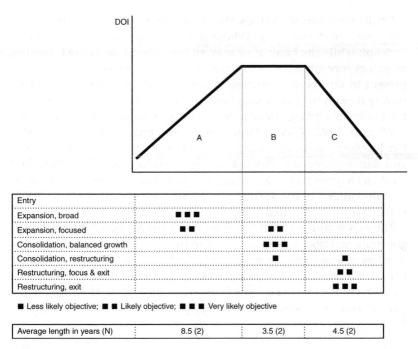

	A	B	C
Entry			
Expansion, broad	■ ■ ■		
Expansion, focused	■ ■		■ ■
Consolidation, balanced growth		■ ■ ■	
Consolidation, restructuring		■	■
Restructuring, focus & exit			■ ■
Restructuring, exit			■ ■ ■

■ Less likely objective; ■ ■ Likely objective; ■ ■ ■ Very likely objective

Average length in years (N)	8.5 (2)	3.5 (2)	4.5 (2)

Figure 6.14   Stylized model of imploding internationalization

stopped when Crocker was sold at a large loss. Crédit Lyonnais had to sell its European subsidiaries in return for state aid. After this forced exits, both bank's independence ended soon afterwards. The restructuring of Midland was undertaken by HSBC from 1992; the French government restructured Crédit Lyonnais from 1998, and redistributed its shares in a public offering in 2000 making it clear it would not object to a (domestic) takeover.

6.7.1.   Imploding internationalization: Crédit Lyonnais

The internationalization of Crédit Lyonnais was well underway in the 1970s, already having established a network in Latin America, Africa and for a short while the Middle East. In 1970 UBAF (Union des Banques Arabes et Francaises) was created and the Europartners alliance was formed between 1970 and 1973. With Europartner members, joint ventures were set up, such as the Credit-Commerz Bank in Saarbrücken in 1973 with Commerzbank. Branches in the major financial centers were created during the next years.

Crédit Lyonnais undertook the most ambitious growth strategy in the 1980s and the early 1990s. It embraced a universal banking concept: while the bank must play an important role in the financing as well as control of industrial companies, it believed in the need to be present in European countries, either through internal growth or by buying foreign banks (Canals, 1997). Between 1986 and 1993 this presence was developed, mainly by acquiring a score of banks between 1989 and 1992: Chase Banque de Commerce in Belgium (1989), Credito Bergamasco and Banco San Marco in Italy, Banca Jover (1991) and Banco Comercial Espanol (1990) in Spain, and particularly BfG Bank in Germany. During the same period, major stakes were acquired in companies via the Clinvest and Clindus subsidiaries.[89] In 1991, Crédit Lyonnais acquired Irish Woodchester (Marois, 1997).

The expansion of Crédit Lyonnais was actively steered by the French government. Haberer, bank president in the late 1980s, declared in parliamentary hearing that the government had asked him to expand Crédit Lyonnais' investment abroad and to assist state-owned industrial firms as they sought to compete outside France (Coleman, 2001, p. 337). Also, by pursuing an aggressive growth strategy prudent banking was not always

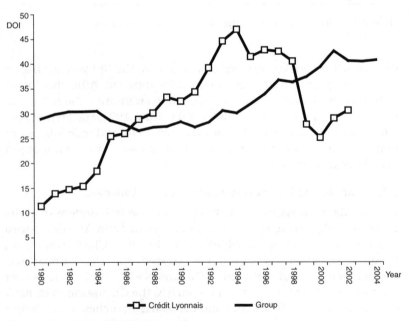

Figure 6.15   DOI of Crédit Lyonnais

followed, and bank management was actively involved in fraudulent activities (when finalizing the purchase of MGM by Paretti in 1990).

By 1993, Crédit Lyonnais owned 850 offices and branches in Europe outside France (Marois, 1997). This aggressive strategy proved to be a risky one after the economic slowdown in 1992. Industrial holding weighed down the bank's working capital while property loans generated heavy losses. Finally, insufficiently controlled subsidiaries caused serious setbacks both in France (SASEA) and abroad (MGM). After a change of management, staff was cut, operations streamlined and assets sold, including 48% in insurer Union des Assurances Fédérales. This was to little avail, and the heavy losses forced the French government to rescue the bank, first in early 1994 and then in April 1995. Low quality of bank management, an inadequate investment and loan monitoring process, and the bank's slowness to pull out of the investments in time when a company reached a point of no return all attributed to the bank's troubles (Canals, 1997).

Between 1993 and 1995, the government provided financial assistance which probably worsened the situation (Coleman, 2001). A "bad" bank (Consortium de Realisation, CDR) was created in 1995 to hold the worst assets of Crédit Lyonnais, but Crédit Lyonnais itself also had to make a substantial loan below market rates to CDR and provide CDR with good assets to ensure that CDR would be viable to carry out the required sell-offs. These decisions tied Crédit Lyonnais' hands, and the bank ran into further trouble in 1996. By 1998, total losses had reached 31.8 billion US dollars, the single largest commercial bank failure in the post-war period in the OECD and costing the taxpayer at least 20 billion US dollars (Coleman, 2001).

The French government now also had to negotiate with the European Commission, realizing that substantial financial assistance would be needed to salvage the bank. A financial restructuring plan was finally agreed on with the French government and approved by the European Commission in 1998, scheduling major sales of foreign assets (reducing its international network by 30% and halving its European assets) as well as the privatization of the bank by October 1999. The sale of German subsidiary BfG in 1999 completed the divestment of the foreign banking division. The bank refocused on three areas: retail banking in France, investment and corporate banking, and asset management and private banking. The public offering of shares took place in 1999, reducing the state's stake to 10% and creating a core shareholder group holding 33% with Crédit Agricole controlling a 10% stake.[90]

Table 6.11   Activities of Crédit Lyonnais

Period	Phase	Objective	Arena
'80–'84	Broad expansion	• Maintain domestic position • Build international network • Set up joint ventures with Europartners	Domestic Major financial and economic centers Europe
'85–'93	Focused expansion	• Build European branch network • Diversify in other financial services • Build up industrial shareholdings • Expand in investment banking	Continental Europe Domestic, Europe Domestic Major financial centers
'94–'03	Restructuring, refocus and exit	• Sale of European branch network • Refocus on retail banking, investment and corporate banking, asset management • Develop activities with core shareholders (from 1999)	Spain, Belgium, Netherlands, Germany Domestic Domestic

Crédit Lyonnais stated that it would pursue a strategy based on a number of partnerships with domestic and foreign financial institutions, mainly the members of its core shareholder group. The bank set up a series of joint ventures: two with Crédit Agricole in consumer lending and leasing, one with BBVA in cross border mergers and acquisitions, another with CDC in global custody, and one with Allianz-AGF for non-life insurance products.[91]

6.7.2.   Imploding internationalization: Midland Bank

Compared to the other large British banks, Midland's internationalization activities were modest until the 1960s when it aimed to cooperate more with European banks, and develop business within the British Commonwealth. The first led to the formation of EBIC, and subsidiaries formed with EBIC partners. The second pillar led to the formation of Midland and International Banks (MAIBL), together with the Commercial Bank of Australia, the Standard Bank, and the Toronto-Dominion Bank. This is claimed to be the first consortium bank (Pohl & Freitag, 1994), followed by the creation of a further 34 consortium banks by 1976, mostly based in London.

From the mid-1970s the emphasis of Midland changed to direct representation in the main foreign markets. It restructured its international activities by forming the Midland Bank International, and setting up representative offices. It founded Midland Bank SA in France in 1978, and bought from a controlling interest in German private bank Trinkaus and Burkhardt Citicorp in 1980 (Pohl & Freitag, 1994), which held branches in major cities in Germany and subsidiaries in Switzerland and Luxembourg. Also, Midland owned the travel company Thomas Cook. In 1982, Midland bought a majority stake in Handelsfinanz Bank in Switzerland. It also divested during that year, selling its shareholding in MAIBL to Standard Chartered, who became sole owner, and 40% of Samuel Montagu to American Aetna Life & Casualty Company, the largest US insurance company.

The sale of MAIBL was prompted by a change in its international strategy, seeking direct presence in the major financial centers to "diversify our interests and to better serve the needs of our rapidly growing clientele".[92] The United States and Europe were identified as areas of continued expansion and in 1981 Midland bought a majority stake in Crocker National Corporation of California, a large Californian bank with total assets of 80 billion US dollars. Midland bought the bank in an attempt to catch up in market position internationally after a slow start in the 1970s.[93] The acquisition took place "without taking into account Crocker's weaknesses and without developing controls over its operations. [...] Widely known as one of the low-performing banks in the US, with an abundance of poorly performing loans, [Crocker] proceeded to squander Midland's capital in more bad loans." (Rogers, 1999). Midland stated at the time of the acquisition that "our alliance with Crocker will preserve their operational autonomy and the infusion of capital will ensure that they are in a strong position to take advantage of any changes in the structure of banking in the United States" (Annual report 1980, p. 7). From 1982, Crocker reported large losses, adding to the LDC problems Midland had by also having extended loans to the problem countries, and creating a large portfolio of problem loans in the United States.

In 1984 Midland identified its strategy as 1) rehabilitating Crocker to financial health as soon as possible, 2) continue to have a strong position on the domestic market, 3) continue developing an international network to serve a wide range of customers, and 4) enter the new (capital) markets created as the UK financial markets were to be deregulated.[94] Restoring Crocker's profitability was left to another bank; in 1986 the bank was sold at a total loss of one billion US dollars[95] to

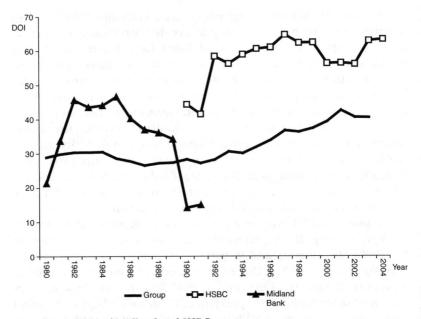

Figure 6.16   DOI of Midland and HSBC

American bank Wells Fargo. Midland never recovered financially, which contributed to its decline and subsequent acquisition by Hongkong and Shanghai Banking Corporation (HSBC).

From 1987 the bank made a series of reciprocal transfers of overseas business with HSBC, which acquired a 14.9% stake in Midland in that year. Under the agreement, HSBC had to maintain its investment for at least three years. Also, HSBC and Midland agreed to cooperate and transfer certain overseas assets and operations between the two banks.[96] During 1988, almost all of HSBC's commercial banking operations in Continental Europe were transferred to Midland, while a reciprocal activity took place in Asia. In return, Midland sold its Canadian activities to HSBC.

Midland experienced close to 12 years of losses, starting in 1980, before it was acquired by HSBC. Besides the acquisition of Crocker, other adverse developments contributed to its financial problems: the accumulation of LDC loans, a mismatch in treasury activities resulting in a large loss in 1990, high costs in domestic retail banking and HSBC's decision not to buy it in 1990, after much of Midland's planning had been based on the merger (Rogers, 1999).

Table 6.12 Activities of Midland Bank

Period	Phase	Objective	Arena
'80–'85	Focused expansion	• Gain sizeable presence in the United States	United States
		• Build network for corporate clients	Continental Europe, main financial centers
		• Maintain domestic position	Domestic
		• Build capital market activities with domestic deregulation	Domestic
'86–'92	Restructuring, exit	• Retreat from United States	Canada, Europe, South East Asia
		• Restructure foreign branch through alliance network with HSBC	Domestic
		• Increase domestic market position	Domestic

The two banks had moved towards greater integration since 1987. They were also complementary: Midland's strength was in the United Kingdom and Europe, while HSBC's was in South East Asia and in North America. Midland had a strong retail franchise, while HSBC was large in wholesale banking. Also important, HSBC was well capitalized, and Midland was not. A potential obstacle was that HSBC would have to move its headquarters to the United Kingdom in the event of a merger, but this seemed a realistic option in the wake of the return of Hong Kong to China. In 1990, economic conditions were worsening deterring HSBC from a merger, although it wanted to continue the existing relationship. In 1992, HSBC renewed its interest in Midland, shortly after Lloyds made a bid for Midland. Midland had rejected the bid, partly because Lloyds had rigorous cost saving measures in mind. In June 1992, HSBC acquired Midland at a cost of 3.9 billion pounds.

6.8. Internationalization strategies: financial indicators

Do the financial key ratios differ for the five strategies? Table 6.13 presents a number of key figures per strategy and per five-year period. Although *Accelerating* and *Retreated* banks are different strategies, they seem to have had similar growth targets: the average asset size in 1995–2000 is similar for *Accelerating*, *Retreating* and *Established* banks.

Table 6.13 Descriptives of realized internationalization strategy types

	1980–84 Mean	1980–84 Standard deviation	1985–89 Mean	1985–89 Standard deviation	1990–94 Mean	1990–94 Standard deviation	1995–99 Mean	1995–99 Standard deviation	2000–04 Mean	2000–04 Standard deviation
DOI										
Accelerating	18.35	8.78	20.70	9.93	28.19	12.60	43.07	13.93	56.30	12.37
Moderate	11.10	7.26	13.11	9.29	14.01	8.96	18.19	6.85	27.27	10.74
Imploding	26.22	13.99	33.78	6.59	32.41	13.19	39.02	6.34	28.27	2.83
Retreating	42.12	7.62	32.98	5.54	27.64	7.35	23.80	8.07	17.31	8.32
Established	42.25	16.09	38.98	15.87	45.24	16.10	50.54	16.51	51.40	16.63
Total assets, mln US$										
Accelerating	48,698	19,911	86,400	43,126	175,661	80,295	342,125	171,083	603,481	268,549
Moderate	54,474	22,346	113,388	67,895	181,809	104,272	265,179	124,895	577,637	236,427
Imploding	82,992	12,168	123,525	44,652	261,317	103,785	262,932	62,844	204,038	45,933
Retreating	83,617	24,959	166,497	114,173	267,227	168,380	364,928	126,057	743,098	297,638
Established	73,010	31,134	123,096	60,734	193,846	82,635	348,156	173,437	729,606	377,397
Asset growth, %, US$										
Accelerating	-1.00	8.23	23.44	17.70	16.20	20.61	14.14	17.89	12.19	16.57
Moderate	-2.73	6.43	22.29	15.85	16.17	23.23	10.61	24.56	24.81	46.48
Imploding	1.71	11.84	11.86	10.98	10.65	17.50	-10.90	12.98	15.44	23.57
Retreating	5.29	10.46	14.30	18.20	9.43	16.72	13.37	38.38	15.19	20.37
Established	2.58	7.10	13.65	13.64	9.05	15.96	12.39	16.78	16.19	18.62
Profitability, % capital										
Accelerating	12.14	7.00	16.68	8.41	13.60	7.51	12.52	6.72	9.90	12.68
Moderate	14.69	5.65	15.57	4.36	12.89	3.66	13.26	9.48	11.36	8.53
Imploding	16.63	7.10	9.77	13.19	-0.56	13.21	6.98	1.91	11.99	2.23
Retreating	18.88	4.91	13.93	19.80	12.96	10.37	14.87	19.78	13.84	24.55
Established	20.12	6.72	14.37	12.34	14.56	7.87	14.09	15.49	18.07	8.43
Capital ratio										
Accelerating	4.21	1.34	4.60	1.27	5.05	1.20	4.47	1.48	4.39	1.63
Moderate	3.23	1.20	3.64	1.32	4.63	2.52	4.20	1.08	5.12	1.49
Imploding	2.86	1.71	3.65	1.37	3.26	0.74	3.16	0.87	4.43	0.29
Retreating	3.90	1.22	4.13	1.30	4.90	1.48	5.45	1.86	4.78	2.05
Established	3.41	1.62	4.17	1.62	5.00	1.50	5.17	1.39	5.38	1.95
Total provisions, % capital										
Accelerating	12.17	7.98	14.20	6.72	11.65	6.16	8.85	6.94	8.75	6.93
Moderate	20.35	16.34	12.12	9.49	11.42	6.77	10.25	11.29	4.98	4.66
Imploding	33.08	23.32	25.76	12.95	25.41	8.87	16.46	3.93	8.94	3.58
Retreating	7.69	4.58	19.35	21.19	14.12	10.02	12.51	14.73	14.40	16.27
Established	18.26	17.58	17.32	16.55	11.78	8.89	10.12	10.51	6.78	6.38

Table 6.14 Realized internationalization strategies, per country

	United States	United Kingdom	Japan	France	Germany	Netherlands	Spain	Switzerland
Accelerating				Paribas	Deutsche Bank Dresdner Bank Hypovereinsbank Westdeutsche Landesbank	ING Bank ABN AMRO NMB Bank	BCH BBV Santander	Credit Suisse UBS
Moderate			IBJ	Agricole	Vereinsbank Commerzbank Bayerische Hypobank	Rabobank Fortis AMRO	Argentaria	
Imploding		Midland		Crédit Lyonnais				
Retreating	Chemical Banking Manufacturers Hanover Bank of America Chase Manhattan	Barclays Lloyds TSB National Westminster	Mitsubishi Bank Dai Ichi Kangyo Sumitomo Bank					
Established	JPMorgan Citicorp	Standard Chartered HSBC	Tokyo Mitsubishi Tokyo	BNP Société Générale		ABN		SBC

Table 6.15 Changes in internationalization strategy per strategy type, 1980–2004

Type	Successive internationalization phase	Entry	Entry, broad expansion	Broad	Focused	Focused & broad	Balanced growth	Restructuring	Exit & focused expansion	Exit	Total
		Entry		Expansion			Consolidation		Restructuring		
Accelerating	Expansion, broad	5									5
	Expansion, focused	2		8							10
	Consolidation, restructuring			1	4						5
Moderate	Expansion, focused		6								6
	Consolidation, restructuring		2		2						4
Imploding	Consolidation, restructuring					2					2
	Restructuring, exit							2			2
Retreating	Consolidation, balanced growth						1				1
	Consolidation, refocus						1			4	5
	Restructuring, exit & focused expansion								1	1	2
	Restructuring, exit						9			1	10
Established	Expansion, broad									1	1
	Expansion, focused			2						1	3
	Expansion, (re)focused			1	1						2
	Consolidation, balanced growth			1							1
	Restructuring, exit				2						2
Total		7	8	13	9	2	11	2	1	8	61

For the 1990s, *Retreating* and *Established* banks have been better capitalized, but also had higher loan provisions than *Accelerating* banks. *Moderate* banks have had a relatively high degree of provisions in 1981–85, probably leading to the relatively low capitalization of the banks during that period. This may be partly responsible for the low degree of internationalization: these banks did not have the financial cushions (anymore) in the early 1980s to engage in international activities. If herding has taken place in the 1990s, then it surely was a risk-controlled one: exits were more swiftly decided on than with other bank types.

Also, does herding apply to the five different realized internationalization strategy types? An incentive identified in Chapter 3 to internationalize was herding. Herding takes place when a bank imitates the actions of other banks; an incentive to herd might exist if other banks may know something about the return of foreign bank activities that the bank does not know; the bank may also have an intrinsic preference for conformity and follow (domestic) competitors.

Herding on a country level might exist. Table 6.14 shows banks in the sample, grouped per country and per realized internationalization strategy. *Established* and *Retreating* internationalization strategies tend to be concentrated with American, British and Japanese banks, while *Moderate* and *Accelerating* realized internationalization strategies tend to be clustered around German, Dutch, Spanish and Swiss banks.

Have changes in internationalization activity been concentrated in time for the banks? For 44 banks, 61 large strategic changes have been identified between 1980 and 2004; the yearly occurrence is shown in Figure 6.17.

The number of strategic changes has structurally increased in the 1990s. The five years with most changes are 1983, 1991, 1994, 1998 and 2003. Some of these years are readily interpretable: in 1983, banks changed their internationalization strategy as a result of the LDC crisis; in 1991 renewed strategies were set out after domestic consolidation (Netherlands, United States); in 1998 banks reassessed their investment banking activities and their commitment to domestic banking after the Asian crisis.

The numbers of strategic changes in internationalization activities for these five years add up to 29, almost half of the 61 strategic changes in total. This supports the herding hypothesis. Most of the strategic changes were initiated by accelerating and retreating banks, each accounts for approximately one-third of all changes in strategy. To give an idea of the underlying numbers for Figure 6.17, Table 6.15 presents

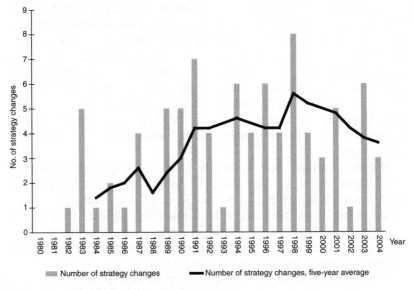

Figure 6.17   Number of strategic changes

the number of strategic changes for the five strategy types between 1980 and 2004.

The columns in Table 6.15 show the different internationalization phases previous to the strategic changes, while the rows show the internationalization phases following the strategic change. Most of the strategic changes were initiated by accelerating and retreating banks, where the banks changed their focus on expansion. As might be expected, an important aspect for retreating banks has been the shift from balanced growth to restructuring, exiting foreign banking activities: each accounts for approximately one-third of all changes in strategy.

7

Performance and Shareholder Wealth

7.1. Introduction

This chapter investigates the relationship between shareholder return as a performance measure of banks and the DOI. Through internationalization, a bank might aim to improve its profitability, or realize more stable profitability through geographical diversification. The goal of this chapter is to determine if international activities have delivered a better performance than home country activities, and what relationships exist between performance measures of banks and DOI. Also, internationalization strategies should improve shareholder return as a performance measure. We establish a theoretical link between internationalization and shareholder return. Discussing these models in more detail, we find that either profitability growth or the reduction of the risk premium through geographical diversification should improve shareholder return. We evaluate the following performance measures:

- foreign versus domestic profitability;
- the relationship between internationalization and total profitability;
- geographical diversification advantages;
- internationalization and shareholder performance.

Five types of realized internationalization strategies were identified based on the case study analyzed. Is a difference in realized shareholder return detectable?

7.2. Why internationalization should increase profitability

The relationship between internationalization and performance has been extensively investigated, focusing on two research questions. Is there a relationship, and if so, what is the shape of that relationship? Organizations might show learning effects when their commitment and involvement in foreign activities increase, resulting in different benefit-cost trade-offs for the organization.[1] In the last decade, researchers have developed different scenarios for explanation, hypothezing about two primary non-linear relationships: quadratic (J, U, inverted J, inverted U) and cubic curves.

The J curve assumes that over time banks can learn to minimize the additional costs associated with foreign expansion (Ruigrok & Wagner, 2003). This means that internationalization costs outweigh benefits until banks gain experience and learn to deal with them. Consequently, banks will reach an inflection point along the expansion path where incremental benefits start to outweigh incremental costs. This is visualized as a J- or U-curve. This scenario implies that banks undergo a period of performance deterioration before experiental knowledge can lead to higher performance levels.

On the other hand, an opposite J- or U-curve can be hypothesized, contending that banks do not need to explicitly address initial internationalization costs through organizational learning, but deploy their home based skills and resources to achieve economies of scale and/or scope, without large cost increases. Thus, at the start of internationalization, the incremental benefits of internationalization should outweigh the incremental costs. However, as banks intensify their foreign expansion, not only do coordination and monitoring costs increase exponentially and become difficult to address through organizational learning, but learning costs may outweigh value generated. In other words, an internationalization threshold is identified at the point where incremental costs of internationalization start to outweigh incremental benefits, implying that banks should not overstep this (degree of) foreign expansion.

Besides a J- or U- curve, a horizontal S shape has also been proposed to explain the link between performance and internationalization, aiming to reconcile the conflicting quadratic curve types. Here, two types of costs associated with internationalization are identified. Type 1 costs are fixed and modest costs at low DOI, stemming from the liabilities of foreignness and newness: unfamiliarity with trade laws, consumer ethnocentricity, new consumer tastes and cross cultural communication costs. Type 2 costs, visible at high DOI stem from the significant coordination and monitoring demands caused by intense market complexity, dynamism and uncertainty. The horizontal S logic argues that learning to address the Type I costs is necessary and cost effective, but learning to successfully manage extreme levels of internationalization (Type 2 costs) is not. Banks should aim at learning to deal with initial costs of foreign expansion but avoid extreme levels of foreign market dependence. Ruigrok and Wagner (2003) conducted a meta analysis of the relationship between performance and internationalization. Using data from 62 studies, covering 174 samples, they found empirical support for a non-zero, positive impact at the aggregate level. As to the form of that relationship, no clear conclusions could be drawn.

We can define the relationship between internationalization and performance as

$$p_T = f(w, p_F, p_H) \tag{1}$$

Where p is profit before tax as a percentage of total assets, the subscripts denote (T)otal, (F)oreign, and (H)ome. w is defined as foreign assets as a percentage of total assets. Whether w, p_F, p_H are related or not, the accounting definition holds by definition, stating that total profits before tax is an asset weighted average of foreign and domestic profits before tax:

$$p_T = w.p_F + (1 - w).p_H \tag{2}$$

Equation (2) is a simple test for the linear relationship between profitability and internationalization. If $p_F > p_H$ we should observe a linear, upward sloping relationship between total profitability (p_T) and the DOI (w). The opposite holds for $p_F < p_H$. In other words, not assuming any learning effects or economies of scale exploitation leads to a hypothesized linear relationship between internationalization and performance. Table 7.1 shows the four possible combinations of relationships.

While internationalization might not improve overall profitability, another argument is that internationalization leads to more *stable* profitability through geographical diversification. Rugman (1976) found that a higher ratio of foreign to total operations is positively related to a lower variability of earnings to book value, concluding that internationalization is risk reducing. Literature on commercial banks in the United States generally finds that larger, more geographically diversified institutions tend to have better risk-return trade off (Berger, DeYoung, Genay & Udell, 2000; Goldberg, 2001). Buch et al. (2004) calculated efficient country-allocation portfolios, and compared these with the actual allocations reported by banks. Overall, it was found

Table 7.1   Hypothesized relationship between profitability and internationalization

Foreign vs. domestic profitability	Relationship between total profitability and internationalization	Support for
1. $p_F > p_H$	$p_T = f(\overset{+}{w})$	Positive internationalization effects. Resource based asset seeking, or seeking new clients/markets. Geographic diversification advantages might apply.
2. $p_F > p_H$	$p_T = f(\bar{w})$	While foreign activities are more profitable, managerial and overhead costs of integrating them in the organization outweigh internationalization benefits.
3. $p_F < p_H$	$p_T = f(\overset{+}{w})$	Support strategy. Foreign activities are loss making, but support total profitability. Resource based asset seeking, or seeking new clients/markets. Geographic diversification advantages might apply.
4. $p_F < p_H$	$p_T = f(\bar{w})$	Other motives to internationalize: gaining market share fast, having a long term acquisition horizon.

that banks tend to overinvest domestically, leading to suboptimal risk/return diversification advantages.

7.3.   Why internationalization should improve shareholder return

Shareholder value serves as an incentive to internationalize. In a stylized world shareholders provide the funding for the bank's capital and are as stakeholders interested in propositions to internationalize if this leads to an increase of the bank's capital and reserves, and an appreciation of the shareholder return during the process. The share price of a bank is forward looking, its price daily determined by a large group of buyers and sellers, and presents a consensus in the financial market about what the bank is worth. On the other hand, it is a dangerous criterion because it is unstable. Table 3.2 presents a possible relationship between factors driving shareholder return and how internationalization strategies might influence these factors. For example, if cash flow generation is a driver that management can influence to increase shareholder return, and higher cash flow generation cannot be achieved at home, then it might be a driver to internationalize. By setting up or acquiring foreign activities, a higher expected cash flow might be achieved.

Is there a DOI which optimizes shareholder return? Suppose that the equity price is determined by the reduced form of the dividend discount model:[2]

$$p = \frac{d}{k-g} \tag{3}$$

Where p is the equity price, d the payout ratio, k the required rate of return by shareholders and g dividend growth. The required rate of return by shareholders, k, is determined by a number of factors:[3]

$$k = r_f + r_1\beta_1 + \ldots + r_N\beta_N \tag{4}$$

Where r_f is the risk free rate of return, $r_{1\ldots N}$ the risk premium factors and $\beta_{1\ldots N}$ denote the sensitivity of required rate of return to factor N. The determinants of the required rate of return can be based on factors such as industrial growth, change in yield curve, changes in short term and long term inflation rate, and changes in the credit risk by the bank itself (Behm, 1994). Other relevant factors might be earnings variability, earnings surprises in the past and general sector characteristics. International activities of banks make sense from a shareholder perspective if one or more of the following assumptions are expected to materialize:

- Dividend payout *(d)* will be higher as a result of internationalization. The bank generates more cash flow or more income with the same resources (higher efficiency, tax advantages).
- Dividend growth *(g)* will be higher as a result of internationalization. The bank generates more income and growth opportunities in foreign banking markets than domestically.
- The required rate of return *(k)* will be lower as a result of internationalization. Earnings are more diversified, decreasing variability of earnings and possibility earnings surprises. The lower sensitivities to these factors also lower the required rate of return.

If internationalization creates higher earnings growth with the same amount of capital, this could be translated in an increase in dividend growth. This represents another angle for risk/return benefits as an incentive to internationalize. Internationalization can lower the required rate of return if it on average lowers the sensitivity to one or more factors. If the correlation between return on bank activities in the home country and outside the home country is less than one, higher earnings can be achieved through internationalization activities with the same or lower risk. Internationalization then would reduce the bank's sensitivity to market developments, lowering the required rate of return.

7.4.   Testing the relationships

In theory, either profitability growth or reduction of the risk premium through geographical diversification should improve shareholder return. Therefore, we test the following relationships:

- We first examine whether foreign profitability is higher than domestic profitability (7.4.1).
- Next, we analyze in 7.4.2 the relationship between total profitability and the DOI, and identify a possible shape.
- Geographical diversification advantages are analyzed in 7.4.3.
- Internationalization and shareholder performance are examined in 7.4.4. Five types of realized internationalization strategies were identified based on the case study analyzed. Is a difference in realized shareholder return detectable?

7.4.1.   Is foreign profitability higher than domestic?

To test whether $p_F > p_H$, the following analyses focus on differences in profitability based on reported data by banks (actual figures for a smaller number of banks). Banks have published this information to a limited degree. In 1980, 15 out of 44 banks reported such information, increasing to 20 out of 44 in 2004. Incidental reporting by for example Deutsche Bank has been left out, as have incidental reporting for Rabobank, NMB Bank and Tokyo Bank. A second analysis is then set up to analyze differences in performance for the whole sample with estimated figures for the whole sample. An alternative measure is developed here for foreign and domestic profitability, using benchmark profitability data and asset weightings.

The best disclosed performance measure for the banks in the sample with a geographic dimension is profit before tax as a share of total assets. Table 7.2 presents the banks that have reported longer series of foreign and domestic profitability. Information before 1990 leans strongly on the information provided by British and American banks, and to a lesser extent on French banks. It cannot be stated that when

Table 7.2 Data availability of domestic and foreign profitability

Country	Bank, period of data availability
France	Crédit Agricole (1992–2004), BNP (1982–2004), Crédit Lyonnais (1983–2000), Société Générale (1983, 1987–2000)
Germany	Commerzbank (1995–2004), Deutsche Bank (2001–04), Bayerische Hypobank (na), Dresdner Bank (1997–2004), Hypovereinsbank (1998–2004), Vereinsbank (1992–97), Westdeutsche Landesbank (2001–04)
Spain	Argentaria (na), BBV (na), BBVA (na), BCH (na), Santander (na), BSCH (na)
Switzerland	Credit Suisse (1995–2004), UBS (na), SBC (na)
United Kingdom	Barclays (1980–2004), HSBC (1992–2004), Lloyds TSB (1980–2004), Midland (1980–91), National Westminster (1980–2000), Standard Chartered (1980–2004), Royal Bank of Scotland (1996–2004)
Netherlands	ABN (1980–89), ABN AMRO (1990–2000), AMRO (na), Fortis (1996–2004), ING Bank (1992–2000, 2003–04), NMB (na), Rabobank (na)
United States	Bank of America (1980–97, 2001–04), Chase Manhattan (1980–2004), Chemical Banking (1984–95), Citicorp (1980–2004), JPMorgan (1980–99), Manufacturers Hanover (1980–90)
Japan	Dai Ichi Kangyo (1994–2000), IBJ (1994–2000), Mitsubishi Bank (1987–95), Sumitomo Bank (1997–2003), Tokyo Mitsubishi (1996–2004), Tokyo Bank (na), Mizuho (2001–04)

na: not available

internationalization became more important for banks, they started to report more internationalization-related information in their financial reports. Banks like SBC, UBS or Deutsche Bank did not report this information although they progressed significantly with their internationalization activities. A general remark is usually found in the financial report stating something like "due to the integrated nature of our activities worldwide a geographical breakdown does not provide additional information"; the information provided by British and American banks in the 1980s proves otherwise. Difference in profitability between foreign and home activities (p_D) is calculated as:

$$p_D = p_F - p_H \tag{5}$$

The relative size of foreign activities does not influence the value of p_D; the difference in profitability does not change if the bank has 1% or 10% foreign assets.

In total 30 out of 44 banks have reported at some time foreign and domestic profitability figures for three or more years between 1980 and 2004; 14 banks have not reported such figures. Of these 30 banks, 15 have shown a negative difference in profitability (Figure 7.1). When banks show a negative difference in profitability, is this related to a higher or lower total profitability? The scatter plot presented in Figure 7.2 shows on the vertical axis the average yearly difference between foreign and domestic profitability, the horizontal axis represents yearly total profitability. The time periods are variable, similar to Figure 7.1.

The relationship presented in Figure 7.2 is overall negatively sloped for Continental European and Japanese banks. There is one visual outlier, Fortis, reporting a relatively higher difference between foreign and domestic profitability than expected given the general relationships. An explanation for this might be the relatively favorable period of reporting for Fortis, between 1996 and 2004. The scatter plot indicates a clustering of three groups: German and Japanese banks, Continental European banks, and American and English banks. p_D is overall negative weakly related to total profitability.

A positive total profitability is not necessarily related to a relatively successful foreign profitability. It suggests that lagging domestic performance might have been an incentive for some banks to internationalize since additional performance is relatively easier to achieve outside the home country than within.[4] Japanese and German banks need foreign profitability to shore up their total performance. On the other hand, American and English banks seem to pursue the same profitable strategies at home as outside the home countries: internationalization adds to their profitability. Continental European banks hold a middle ground position between these two extremes.

The observed negative relationship between p_D and the relative domestic performance is difficult to generalize, due to differences between time periods of banks. Banks which reported on average a negative p_D did this during an average length of 13.6 years compared to 8.6 for banks reporting a positive p_D: the difference in years is a combination of not reporting the figures, and the higher number of mergers in the 1990s, limiting the maximum reporting period for some banks. A better approach would be to consider the information per year for the sample. Figure 7.3 shows the average and median difference in foreign and domestic profitability between 1980 and 2004.

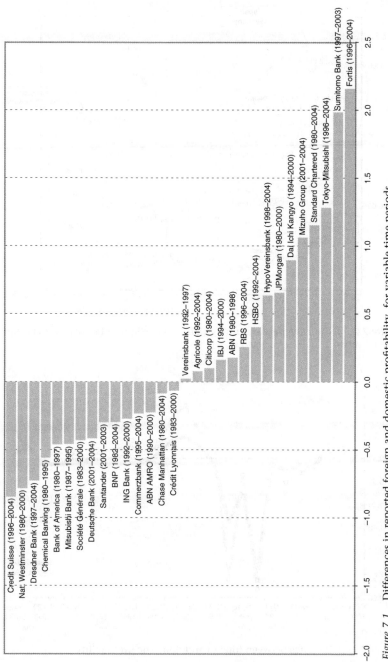

Figure 7.1 Differences in reported foreign and domestic profitability, for variable time periods
Note: Average difference foreign and domestic profit before tax, % total assets. Time period between brackets.

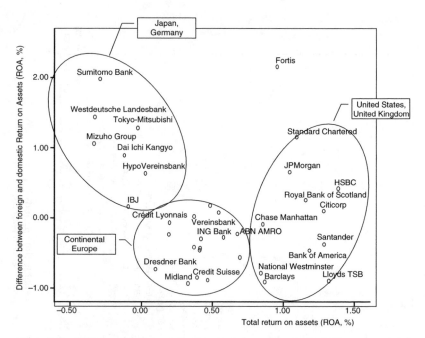

Figure 7.2 Difference between foreign and domestic profitability versus total profitability

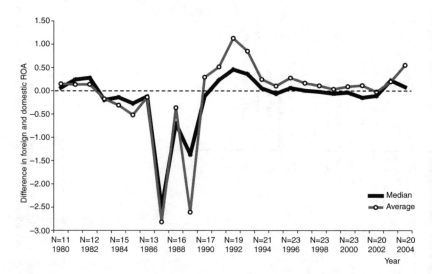

Figure 7.3 Difference between foreign and domestic profitability

Of the 25 years, the median value is negative for 14 years. The representativeness of the banks who reported foreign and domestic profitability compared to the sample increased throughout the period: before 1990 not more than 16 banks reported these figures, increasing to 22 in 2000. The highly negative values for p_D between 1987 and 1989 are followed by a short period of high p_D values between 1990 and 1994. The values from 1980 to 1987 and 1994 to 2000 remain closer to zero. p_D does not differ significantly from zero for the whole sample.

Figure 7.3 shows that p_D in 1987 or 1989 differs substantially from the other p_D values. This can be explained by the large provisions banks had to take in 1987 and 1989, since securities activities were mainly concentrated in financial centers (outside the home country for a number of banks). Another explanation is the large provisioning in 1987 banks booked to write off LDC loans, led by Citibank after six years of unresolved negotiations to reschedule LDC debts. Two years later, LDC write offs were once again large when the Baker plan led to a final agreement to end the LDC crisis for banks.

To determine in which years p_D showed values significantly different from zero, a regression model has been estimated with p_D as the dependent variable, and the year dummies as independent variables. The estimated model is $p_{Dijt} = \gamma_t T_t + \varepsilon_{ijt}$. Independent variables are the year dummies (T_t). The results are shown in Table 7.3.

Estimated coefficients with p values < 0.05 were 1987, 1989, 1992 and 1993. From 1983 to 1989, foreign activities were on average less profitable, especially since 1987. A financial recovery period was visible in the early 1990s, especially in 1992 and 1993. This suggests that timing has been important: banks that have increased their international activities significantly in the early 1990s should have enjoyed above average returns, while banks which established international activities in the 1980s would have experienced rebounding foreign profitability. On the same note, an exit from international banking in the early 1990s would have meant that "recovery advantages" were not reaped, while exiting or expanding from 1995 would not on average have changed performance for better or for worse. The conclusion is then that for the banks which have reported geographic distribution of profits:

- Performance of foreign activities was lower than domestic, but did not differ significantly from zero.

Table 7.3 Estimated dummy regression model, p_D as dependent variable

Dummy	1980	1981	1982	1983	1984	1985	1986	1987	1988
Coefficient	0.1477	0.1340	0.1373	-0.1728	-0.3079	-0.5177	-0.1385	-2.8181	-0.3641
p value	0.7138	0.7395	0.7218	0.6285	0.3723	0.1629	0.7087	0.0000**	0.2760
N	11	11	12	14	15	13	13	16	16

Dummy	1989	1990	1991	1992	1993	1994	1995	1996	1997
Coefficient	-2.6056	0.2946	0.5170	1.1290	0.8538	0.2456	0.1029	0.2786	0.1656
p value	0.0000**	0.3635	0.1222	0.0003**	0.0055**	0.3997	0.7118	0.3175	0.5438
N	16	17	16	19	19	21	23	23	24

Dummy	1998	1999	2000	2001	2002	2003	2004
Coefficient	0.1089	0.0347	0.0910	0.1140	-0.0246	0.1968	0.5524
p value	0.6960	0.8988	0.7439	0.6891	0.9344	0.4898	0.0650
N	23	24	23	22	20	22	20

$F_{(25, 428)} = 6.721$**, adjusted R Square = 0.2399

**: p value < 0.01

- The negative performance difference was concentrated around 1987 and 1989.
- Entry and exit moments matter for the total profitability of the international activities.

7.4.2. Internationalization and total profitability

The previous test focused on the relationship between foreign and domestic profitability where the relative weight of foreign or domestic activities exerted no influence. The next test determines if internationalization is positively related to a higher performance. This is tested in two steps: does such a relationship exist for the individual banks in the sample between 1980 and 2000? Next, does such a relationship exist for the whole sample? A straightforward approach is to evaluate one variable regression model per bank:

$$Y_{it} = \alpha_i + \beta_i DOI_{it} + \varepsilon_{it} \tag{1}$$

The dependent variable Y is profit before tax as a percentage of capital and reserves; DOI is the independent variable. The constant α in the model represents the level of profitability if the bank had not internationalized (DOI = 0). This test focuses on the direction of the coefficient β. If β is negative (positive), then a higher DOI is associated with lower (higher) profitability. The number of observations varies per bank, so the significance of β provides less information and is ignored here. At the most, 25 observations per bank can be found (1980–2004), while on the lower side at most three observations per bank can be observed. Table 7.4 presents the estimated coefficient β per bank, in combination with the adjusted R-Square and the p value for β.

There are 44 banks in the sample, of which 25 show a negative relationship between DOI and profit before tax as a percentage of capital and reserves. In other words, there is no tendency towards a positive or negative relationship for the whole sample. For 12 banks, the adjusted R-Square is negative indicating absence of any relationship. This is not due to the number of observations for the regression; 7 of these 12 banks have the longest possible period of data availability (21 years). Also, most of the banks showing no relationship between performance and DOI have pursued strategies increasing their DOI: *Accelerating* strategies (UBS, Dresdner bank, Credit Suisse, BBV, Argentaria) or *Moderate* strategies (Commerzbank, BCH, Hypovereinsbank).

A stronger relationship is observed for 15 banks in the sample, showing a relationship between DOI and performance with an

Table 7.4   Relationship between performance and DOI per bank

Bank	Constant		DOI		Adjusted R-Square	No. of observations
Mitsubishi Bank	−41.3403	**	1.7493	**	0.7557	16
NMB Bank	25.0459	**	−0.8618	**	0.7402	10
Lloyds TSB	40.8273	**	−0.6490	*	0.6615	25
Fortis	15.9625	**	0.0833		0.6338	15
Tokyo	38.8449	**	−0.7703	*	0.5535	13
Vereinsbank	21.0989	**	−0.7011	**	0.5343	18
HSBC	−20.0926	*	0.6838	**	0.4947	15
ABN AMRO	5.7927	**	0.1051	**	0.4671	15
Rabobank	16.1571	**	−0.2609	**	0.4467	22
Dai Ichi Kangyo	−14.3657		0.7910		0.3978	21
Tokyo Mitsubishi	115.2125	*	−3.1175	*	0.3918	9
SBC	44.1307	**	−0.8999	**	0.3229	18
Santander	31.5417	**	−0.2247	**	0.2668	21
Deutsche Bank	25.5364	**	−0.2011	**	0.2627	23
Agricole	13.4136	**	−0.1682	**	0.2572	22
ABN	25.2620	**	−0.4412		0.2520	10
UBS	2.7517		0.2360	*	0.2177	23
AMRO	17.0741	*	−0.4891		0.1840	7
Bayerin Hypobank	19.5128	**	−0.6486	*	0.1798	18
Bank of America	27.9889	**	−0.4274	*	0.1738	25
JPMorgan	−62.9405		1.7605		0.1520	20
Citicorp	−4.2473		0.5330	*	0.1382	25
Mizuho Group	125.5943		−7.1787		0.1344	4
Sumitomo Bank	−22.4163		0.9919	*	0.1325	24
BBV	26.0057	**	−0.1136		0.1259	18
Paribas	30.3045	**	−0.4571		0.1243	19
Standard Chartered	−91.7682		1.4155		0.1047	25
National Westminster	1.9009		0.4299		0.0829	21
Westdeutsche Landesbank	7.6952	**	−0.1489		0.0818	25
Credit Suisse	11.2083	*	−0.0151		0.0767	25
BNP	2.2922		0.3371		0.0663	25
ING Bank	10.9241	**	−0.0202		0.0611	12
Royal Bank of Scotland	37.9332	*	−0.7409		0.0320	9
Chemical Banking	0.0016		0.4739		0.0268	16
Manufacturers Hanover	−26.3997		0.9058		0.0091	11
Hypovereinsbank	25.2638		−0.6549	*	−0.0249	7
Société Généralé	19.0519	*	−0.0478		−0.0413	25
Barclays	21.1276	**	−0.0333		−0.0415	25
Crédit Lyonnais	36.2514	**	−0.8560	**	−0.0423	23
Commerzbank	11.1152		0.0602		−0.0427	25
Chase Manhattan	14.5893		0.0214		−0.0432	25
Dresdner Bank	20.5568	**	−0.5070	**	−0.0447	25
Midland	−0.1956		0.2294		−0.0493	12
IBJ	19.4314		−0.3583		−0.0828	21
BCH	13.1716	*	−0.1587		−0.0891	7
Argentaria	13.0206	*	0.1912		−0.1120	9

**: p value < 0.01, *: p value < 0.05

adjusted R-Square higher than 0.25. Of these banks, 10 out of 15 show a negative relationship between the level of DOI and profit before tax. In short, the estimated signs of relationship between DOI and performance for the banks are equally distributed for the positive and negative direction. For almost a quarter of the sample, there is no relationship observable. Similar results are obtained if profit before tax as a percentage of total assets is taken as a measure for performance, or if performance is corrected for domestic performance or the performance of the sample.

A limitation of the analysis is that different and overlapping time periods are covered. For example, data for Midland Bank is available from 1980 to 1991 while data for Bank of America covers the full 21 years between 1980 and 2000. The regression results for Midland might have less explanatory power than Bank of America's due to the shorter time period. On the other hand the estimation for Bank of America might yield insignificant results because over the long time period, a "V-shaped" recovery is in general poorly estimated by a single linear measure. To counter this problem, different time periods were considered by calculating average DOI and profitability for five-year periods, further grouping the DOI in steps of 20%.

In Table 7.5, the numbers represent the number of occurrences of the DOI values for full five-year periods, moving from one DOI-bracket to another. Condensing the total number of 867 yearly observations to full five-year periods produces 152 observations; the largest group has a DOI of 20–40%. Observations for DOI larger than 60% should be ignored when drawing general conclusions; the 8 observations constitute only 6% of the total number of observations (that is, Standard Chartered, Credit Suisse and UBS).

Table 7.5 Change of DOI between 20% brackets per five-year period

		Change DOI from					
		0–20	20–40	40–60	60–80	80–100	Total
	0–20	31	9				40
	20–40	10	42	12			64
To	40–60	3	16	15			34
	60–80			6	3	1	10
	80–100				2	2	4
	Total	44	67	33	5	3	152

How many banks shift from one DOI-bracket to another? Changes take place between the 20–40% DOI-bracket, and the 40–60% DOI-bracket. Few banks like Credit Suisse and Deutsche Bank moved from one bracket to a higher one while Bank of America did the opposite. The average profitability per DOI-bracket, excluding DOI higher than 60%, for the different five-year periods is shown in Figure 7.4.

For the sample as a whole this suggests that between 1980 and 1984 there was a linear and positive relationship between DOI and performance, and between 1985 and 1989 the relationship became weakly negative but still was linear. From 1990 onwards the relationship moved towards a V-shape: profitability for banks with DOI levels of 20–40% was lower than for banks with DOI levels of 0–20%, but increases again for the 40–60% level.

Summarizing, for most banks and most time periods there is a negative relationship between performance and DOI. The V-shape of the relationship suggests internationalization costs outweigh benefits for a DOI lower than 40%; from 40% upwards the benefits start to outweigh the costs. This suggests that a DOI lower than 20% would have yielded the best performance and that for most banks an increase in

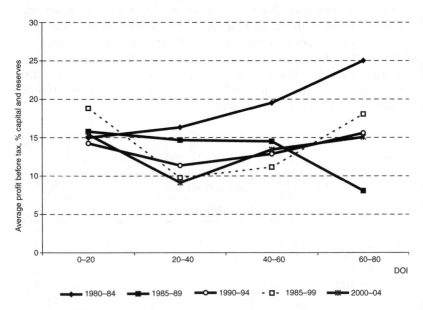

Figure 7.4   Relation between DOI and performance, five-year periods

internationalization correlates with a decrease in profitability, but this result is valid cross section and not longitudinal.

A closer look warrants the positive linear relationship between DOI and profitability in 1980–84 in Figure 7.4, changing to a slightly negative one in 1985 to 1989. The relation between total performance and DOI is determined by calculating the bivariate correlations between DOI and profit before tax per year. Figure 7.5 shows that the relationship between the two measures steadily breaks down: the correlation was almost 0.6 in 1980, steadily declining to under 0.2 in 1986. Negative correlations can be observed for 1987, 1989 and 1990; from 1991 onwards the relationship between DOI and profitability has broken down completely.[5] Correlations between DOI and profitability as a percentage of assets remain more persistent, suggesting an asset driven approach to DOI until 1985. After a restructuring period in 1987–90, similar values for the correlations indicate that both performance measures have been synchronized.

Summarizing, a positive relationship between profitability and the DOI cannot be found on a bank level. For almost a quarter of the banks in the sample no such relationship has existed between 1980 and 2000; for the other half no tendency towards a positive or negative relationship

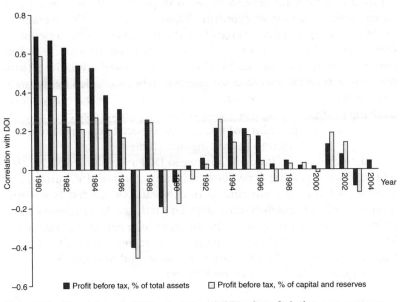

Figure 7.5 Bivariate correlations between DOI and profit before tax, per year

can be observed. For the total sample, there is only a positive relationship between 1980 and 1984. For the other periods there is a negative relationship between profitability and the DOI. The negative relationship in 1985–89 is determined by the years 1987 and 1989. After 1990 a weak form of a negative and V-shaped relationship exists. Banks with the lowest levels of DOI in the sample, 0–20%, have shown the highest performance. Banks with DOI levels of 40–60% have shown a higher performance than banks with a DOI of 20–40%, but both reported lower performance levels than banks with DOI of 0–20%. Overall the results do not support the hypothesis that a higher DOI is positively related to a higher performance of the total bank.

7.4.3. Geographical diversification advantages

So far the analyses have failed to support the hypothesis that foreign profitability is higher than domestic profitability or that banks with a higher DOI show a higher profitability. But this may not have been the bank's primary motive to internationalize: a higher DOI might stabilize profitability, or improve the return/risk profile of the bank for its profitability. Two claims are investigated in this section: a higher DOI lowers the variability of profitability, and internationalization leads to an improvement of the risk/return profile of the bank.

Risk and return are defined in terms of profitability (cf. De Nicoló, Bartholomew, Zaman & Zephirin, 2004): for return, the average of profit before tax as a percentage of capital is calculated over a period of five years, and the standard deviation for profitability over the same period is taken as a measure for risk. With these variables, the return-risk ratio is then calculated as average profitability divided by the standard deviation of profitability over the last five years. Only banks showing profitability figures for all years in a period have been used to prevent non-comparability of results when crucial years are excluded. This leaves 159 periods to be investigated (Table 7.6).

To determine the relationship between DOI and risk, a model is estimated for the separate time periods. Examination of the scatter plots suggest that the different time periods should be treated as variable intercept, variable coefficient models. This reduces the attractiveness of estimating the relationship for the different time periods in one model. Model A in Table 7.7 therefore presents the regression results of equation 6 with risk as the dependent variable, and average DOI as the independent variable, for different periods.

$$\text{RISK}_{it} = \alpha_i + \beta_{1i}\text{DOI}_{it} + \beta_{2i}(\text{PBT/CAP})_{it} + \beta_{3i}\text{ASSET}_{it} + \varepsilon_{it} \qquad (6)$$

Table 7.6   Summary statistics for profitability and risk measures

	1980–84			1985–89			1990–94		
	Average	Median	N	Average	Median	N	Average	Median	N
Profitability (average)	16.74	17.04	34	14.54	13.58	35	13.09	12.51	35
Profitability (std.dev.)	3.28	3.09	34	7.59	3.72	35	4.40	2.90	35
Return/risk ratio	6.76	6.03	34	6.97	5.01	35	7.22	3.11	35

	1995–99			2000–04		
	Average	Median	N	Average	Median	N
Profitability (average)	13.95	13.02	29	13.34	15.35	26
Profitability (std.dev.)	4.70	3.39	29	6.00	4.27	26
Return/risk ratio	5.57	4.81	29	5.79	5.38	26

Table 7.7   Risk, return regressions

Period	Constant	Profitability	Internationalization (PBT/CAP)	Assets (DOI)	Adjusted (ASSET)	R-Square F-Statistic
Model A: dependent variable standard deviation profitability						
1980–84	0.3967	0.1222	0.0076	0.0936	0.1214	F(3,28)=2.4283
1985–89	2.4266	–0.5996 **	0.2805 **	1.2087	0.4318	F(3,31)=9.6117 **
1990–94	–4.0978	–0.0473	0.1058 **	1.108	0.1476	F(3,30)=2.9047
1995–99	–5.0384	–0.1504	0.022	2.0083	0.0582	F(3,25)=1.5770
2000–04	–0.0587	–0.3249 **	–0.0477	2.1912	0.498	F(3,21)=8.9374 **
Model B: dependent variable ratio average profitability/standard deviation profitability						
1980–84	20.3732		0.018	–2.9374	–0.0467	F(2,29)=0.3080
1985–89	28.5934		–0.2291 **	–3.0342	0.1613	F(2,32)=4.2704
1990–94	58.9173		–0.3403 *	–7.8384	0.1464	F(2,31)=3.8296
1995–99	41.5198		0.0015	–6.5577	–0.0035	F(2,26)=0.9506
2000–04	15.7169		–0.0203	–1.5828	–0.085	F(2,22)=0.0594

*: p value < –0.05, **: p value < 0.01

As a control variable, profitability as proxy for return was added to account for the expected relationship between risk and return (PBT/CAP). Another control variable is the logarithm of total assets in US dollar (ASSET), hypothesizing that larger banks can spread their foreign banking activities over more countries (cf. Tschoegl, 2000) and therefore profit more from geographic diversification advantages.

As far as the direction of the coefficient is concerned, for all periods except 2000–04 the level of DOI is positively related to the level for risk. For all periods, the estimated coefficient for total assets is positive, albeit non-significant. For 1985–89 and 2000–04 a higher DOI leads to higher variability of earnings; for the other periods no relationship exists. The models have explanatory power for 1985–89 and 2000–04, periods where the standard deviation of profitability is substantially higher than in the other periods. In the periods other than 1985–89 and 2000–04 the F-Statistic for the model indicates an absence of a relationship between DOI and risk.

As a robustness check, risk and return were corrected for country averages from the OECD Bank profitability database to control for the disadvantage that the estimated model did not take structural differences in levels of return and risk between countries into account. The results are not shown here, but yielded similar outcomes.

With regard to the return-risk ratio a similar analysis as above is performed, with the return-risk ratio as the dependent variable and DOI as the independent variable (Model B in Table 7.7).

$$\text{RETRISK}_{it} = \alpha_i + \beta_{1i}\text{DOI}_{it} + \beta_{2i}\text{ASSET}_{it} + \varepsilon_{it} \tag{7}$$

Only for 1985–94 the estimated model has some explanatory power. The DOI coefficients are negative. This suggests that the assumption that internationalization improves the return-risk profile of a bank is not supported: higher levels of DOI are rather negatively but statistically non-significant related to the return-risk ratio, specifically for the 1986–95 period. Reestimating this model for country averages yields similar insignificant results and are not shown here. Overall, no relationship exists between DOI and risk. Combining the results for risk and return, internationalization in general is negatively related to the level of the return-risk ratio.

7.4.4.   Internationalization and shareholder return

The relationship between shareholder return and internationalization is examined here with two approaches. First, what can be said about the relationship between shareholder return and internationalization for individual banks? Second, if shareholders with hindsight had constructed baskets for the different strategic types and had invested in them, what would have been the result? Would the choice of strategy have mattered to shareholders?

Data

The data for the total shareholder return (and related to that market value and price-earnings ratios) was collected from the Datastream database, all in US dollar as well as local currency on a monthly basis from December 1979 until December 2004. For the equity return the total return index is used; this includes price changes as well as rein-vested dividends. Raw prices also have been collected, to check when trading ceased for acquired or merged banks. The sample of banks listed on a stock market is smaller than the total sample: Crédit Agricole, Crédit Lyonnais, Rabobank did not list shares between 1980 and 2000. ING Bank and Fortis are part of financial conglomerates, and their parent company's shares have been used. For Fortis, having two parent companies, the returns for the Belgian and the Dutch parent company were combined. Market to book value has been calculated using the total assets reported in the annual reports.

Appropriate benchmarks have been found in the Datastream indices: they are one of the few publicly available indices covering a 25-year period, providing total market value besides total return information. The indices used are the world index, covering all equities, the world bank index, covering all bank stocks, and the country bank indices. Figure 7.6 presents the total return indices for the banks in the group

■■ Total shareholder return index of sample banks

■■ Datastream total shareholder return index of world banks

Figure 7.6   Total shareholder return index for the world's largest banks
Note: Total return index, market value weighted, in US dollars. Rebased at December 1979 = 100.
Source: Datastream, own calculations

Table 7.8   Annualized total shareholder return, and standard deviation

Period	Group		World Bank Index (Datastream)		World Index (Datastream)	
	Total return	Standard deviation	Total return	Standard deviation	Total return	Standard deviation
Jan. 1980–Dec. 1984	20.82%	21.85%	19.18%	17.65%	13.28%	13.50%
Jan. 1985–Dec. 1989	39.24%	27.38%	33.80%	22.71%	29.26%	14.83%
Jan. 1990–Dec. 1994	1.25%	23.43%	2.16%	19.06%	4.35%	15.51%
Jan. 1995–Dec. 1999	12.60%	23.83%	10.59%	18.26%	19.29%	13.14%
Jan. 2000–Dec. 2004	3.97%	21.92%	5.60%	16.86%	-2.40%	15.85%
Jan. 1980–Dec. 2004	14.80%	23.86%	13.73%	19.11%	12.21%	14.79%

Note: Return and standard deviation are annualized monthly figures.
Source: Datastream, own calculations.

and the Datastream world bank index. Table 7.8 summarizes the annualized standard deviation and return per five-year periods.

The world's largest banks have shown a higher return during 1980 and 2000 than the broader world bank index (Table 7.8). The higher return is generated between 1984 and 1986, when the US dollar depreciated considerably. The higher return could therefore be explained by an overweight in the sample of banks outside the United States. For the periods after 1985, additional return is achieved through a considerable increase in risk. The returns for the sample are higher than the world bank index but the standard deviation is 4% to 5% higher, suggesting that the spread of returns around the mean is 16% to 20% higher than for the world bank index. Finally, the periods 1990–94 and 2000–2004 are the only periods where the yearly returns for the largest banks are lower than that of the world bank index.

Shareholder return per bank

To analyze the relationship between shareholder return and the DOI for the whole sample, a simple model was developed and estimated. DOI, and change in DOI were found to have a positive relationship with shareholder return in line with the hypothesis, especially between 1990 and 2000. We find that the DOI does not have a statistical relationship, but control variables for performance have. The following model is estimated:

$$TSR_{ijt} = \alpha_i + \beta_1 r_{1it} + \ldots + \beta_n r_{nit} + \varepsilon_{it} \tag{2}$$

Total shareholder return, TSR_{ijt}, is the dependent variable for bank i in year t. $\beta_{1...n}$ represents the sensitivity of total shareholder return (TSR) to the different risk premium factors r_{it}. A constant (α_i) is introduced to take account of the variables not specified. Six different measures for TSR are created as independent variables, 1...j, to examine the generality of the results (cf. Sirower, 1997):

- *TSR1: raw return.* Total return in local currency.
- *TSR2: country adjusted return.* Total return$_{it}$ -/- local stock market return in local currency.
- *TSR3: world adjusted return.* Total return$_{it}$ -/- world stock market return in local currency.
- *TSR4: raw return, US$.* Total return in US dollar.
- *TSR5: country adjusted return, US$.* Total return$_{it}$ -/- local stock market return in US dollar.
- *TSR6: world adjusted return, US$.* Total return$_{it}$ -/- world stock market return in US dollar.

The independent variables are presented in Table 7.9, together with their definitions and expected signs. Goldberg and Saunders (1981) examined incentives for foreign banks to enter the United States. A low price earnings ratio (PE ratio) could be a reason to acquire banks in the foreign country. The PE ratio might be low compared to the PE ratio in the domestic country, making it attractive for the bank to acquire a bank in the foreign country: while domestic funding is relatively cheap, the contribution to earnings is immediate. An acquisition of a high PE ratio indicates that either the bank expects to improve earnings or that the acquisition is herding-inspired. The macroeconomic environment is represented by the change in *yield curve spread, change in exports* and *GDP per capita.* Increases in the yield curve spread and GDP per capita serve as an indicator of positive economic expectations, influencing banks through an increase in the net interest margin and lower loan provisions, increasing profitability.

The *change in exports* serves both as an indicator of the domestic economic growth opportunities as well as a signal for investors the potential profitability of foreign activities, supporting the DOI and DOI change variables. Finally, herding is represented by *change in asset position.* If investors are sensitive to herding, there would be a positive relationship between shareholder return and a closing of the asset gap between the bank and the world's largest bank. Finally, profitability is represented by *net income* and total *provisions.* By definition,

Table 7.9   Variable definitions for total shareholder return

Variable	Definition	Expected direction
DOI change	Change in DOI, year on year difference	+
DOI	DOI of bank	+
Fee income	Non-interest income/gross income, percentage	+
Capitalization	Capital and reserves/total assets, percentage	+
Net income	Net income/capital and reserves, percentage	+
Provisions	Total provisions/capital and reserves, percentage	−
PE ratio	Total market value/profit before tax, percentage	+
Change in yield curve spread	Difference between long term interest rate and short term interest rate, year on year difference	+
Change in asset position	Difference between total assets of bank and total assets of largest bank in sample, year on year difference	−
Change in exports	Exports/GDP, year on year percentage change	+
Change in GDP per capita	GDP/capita, US dollar, percentage change	+

Table 7.10   Model summary

	Independent Variable	Adjusted R-Square	F-Statistic		df	Durbin-Watson
1980–2004	TSR1	0.1218	8.1492	**	(11,556)	2.1933
	TSR2	0.1212	8.1120	**	(11,556)	2.1183
	TSR3	0.0898	6.0865	**	(11,556)	2.0724
	TSR4	0.1169	7.8217	**	(11,556)	2.0283
	TSR5	0.0270	2.4311	**	(11,556)	2.1931
	TSR6	0.0884	5.9962	**	(11,556)	2.1078
1980–1990	TSR1	0.1922	6.2347	**	(11,231)	2.0851
	TSR2	0.1311	4.3180	**	(11,231)	2.0736
	TSR3	0.0863	3.0767	**	(11,231)	2.0641
	TSR4	0.2517	8.4003	**	(11,231)	1.9732
	TSR5	0.0492	2.1390	*	(11,231)	2.2391
	TSR6	0.1619	5.2505	**	(11,231)	2.1269
1991–2004	TSR1	0.1740	7.2042	**	(11,313)	2.0458
	TSR2	0.1319	5.4749	**	(11,313)	2.0634
	TSR3	0.1807	7.4971	**	(11,313)	1.9132
	TSR4	0.1088	4.5966	**	(11,313)	1.9925
	TSR5	0.0157	1.4712		(11,313)	2.0312
	TSR6	0.1012	4.3176	**	(11,313)	1.9153

*: p value < 0.05, **: p value < 0.01

net income -/- provisions yields profits before tax, the measure examined in the earlier analyses.

The independent variables are available on a yearly basis. Therefore, the different measures for TSR are calculated on a yearly basis, and regressed in an unbalanced panel model. Beforehand, no country or bank specific effects are expected for TSR2, TSR3, TSR5 and TSR6. These variables are adjusted for average country or world TSR. In line with earlier analyses, the model is estimated for three different periods, 1980–90, 1991–2004 and 1980–2004. Table 7.10 presents summary statistics for the estimated models, grouped by different periods and six measures of TSR. The coefficients are displayed in Table 7.11.

For five measures of TSR the models have explanatory power; the exception is model 5 where the independent variable total return is adjusted for local stock market return in US dollar. Estimating the models for different time periods makes sense: the F-Statistics for the sub-periods are higher than for the total period, suggesting shifting relationships between the dependent and independent variables. The US dollar influences the adjusted R-Squares for the different periods: for 1980–90, the adjusted R-Square is higher for TSR4, 5, 6 (TSR in US dollar) compared to TSR1, 2, 3 (TSR in local currency) while the opposite applies for 1991–2004. Table 7.11 shows the coefficients of the different models for the three time periods.

First, DOI change shows mostly positive coefficients for the 1980–90 and 1991–2004 periods. The coefficients for DOI are mostly negative in the 1980s changing to positive in 1991–2004. DOI and DOI changes are non-significant in nearly all models. On the other hand both *net income* and *provisions* have the expected signs and also p values < 0.05. Two other variables add to the explanatory power and show the expected signs, *change in exports* and *change in GDP per capita*. This especially applies to TSR1, 2 and 3: returns calculated in local currency. *Change in yield curve spread* shows negative signs for most models and periods, contrary to what was expected. The estimated values for the *PE ratio* are positive, in line with expectation, and *capitalization* shows more positive than negative estimates (a positive relationship was hypothesized). The estimated values for the *change in asset position* showed negative values for the 1980–90 (a positive relationship was expected), while the 1991–2004 period shows mixed results. *Change in asset position, PE ratio, capitalization, change in yield curve spread* in general do not have p values < 0.05.

Summarizing, based on the adjusted R-Square for 1980–90 and 1991–2004, three measures for shareholder return of banks are best

Table 7.11 Coefficients, dependent variable total shareholder return (TSR1–6)

	TSR1		TSR2		TSR3		TSR4		TSR5		TSR6	
	coefficient	p value	coefficient	p value	coefficient	p value	coefficient	p value	coefficient	p value	coefficient	p value
1980–2004												
Constant	-2.3667	0.7670	-9.1802	0.0797	-15.1168	0.0473*	5.6447	0.4887	-2.4102	0.6275	-8.1213	0.2812
DOI change	0.5727	0.1148	0.2519	0.2894	0.7298	0.0350*	0.2999	0.4181	-0.0148	0.9477	0.4841	0.1575
DOI year end	0.0044	0.9633	0.0833	0.1802	0.0407	0.6524	-0.0493	0.6105	0.0584	0.3225	0.0004	0.9966
Fee income	-0.0697	0.5281	0.0068	0.9256	0.6309	0.1078	0.3393	-0.0411	0.5501	0.0178	0.8645	0.8645
Capitalization	-0.1533	0.8858	0.8992	0.1986	0.9058	0.3729	-0.5086	0.6405	0.7775	0.2417	0.6293	0.5318
Net income	0.9836	0.0000**	0.3027	0.0042**	0.6685	0.0000**	1.0203	0.0000**	0.3188	0.0015**	0.7008	0.0000**
Provisions	-0.6845	0.0000**	-0.3082	0.0011**	-0.6542	0.0000**	-0.7430	0.0000**	-0.3463	0.0000**	-0.7101	0.0000**
PE ratio	0.0600	0.1147	0.0175	0.4810	0.0419	0.2470	0.0539	0.1646	0.0117	0.6207	0.0360	0.3148
Change in yield curve spread	-3.2320	0.0123*	-0.2617	0.7563	-0.6701	0.5848	-3.3964	0.0000**	-0.1988	0.8039	-0.6788	0.5763
Change in asset position	-0.2325	0.2281	-0.3803	0.0027**	0.1830	0.3191	-0.0188	0.9237	-0.1438	0.2309	0.3850	0.0346*
Change in exports	1.2526	0.1054	2.7805	0.0000**	1.1399	0.1218	-3.2725	0.0000**	-0.7635	0.1125	-2.6105	0.0004**
Change in GPD per capita	1.0084	0.0006**	0.5951	0.0021**	0.7985	0.0044**	0.3923	0.1905	-0.1262	0.4894	0.1522	0.5825
1980–1990												
Constant	0.2589	0.9872	-18.9640	0.0897	-8.9864	0.5860	-0.4202	0.9802	-19.5139	0.0702	-11.5372	0.4853
DOI change	1.3195	0.0596	0.6095	0.2069	1.5452	0.0312*	1.1437	0.1195	0.3047	0.5122	1.3705	0.0563
DOI year	-0.0617	0.7173	0.0292	0.8043	-0.0915	0.5998	-0.1693	0.3447	-0.0404	0.7219	-0.1759	0.3148
Fee income	-0.0675	0.7560	-0.0628	0.6753	-0.1391	0.5312	0.0643	0.7780	0.0063	0.9651	-0.1759	0.3248
Capitalization	-2.5876	0.2408	3.6186	0.0181*	-1.0604	0.6380	-2.8871	0.2126	3.6726	0.0129*	-1.3258	0.5571
Net income	0.9450	0.0040**	0.4167	0.0646	0.5287	0.1129	1.1887	0.0006**	0.5847	0.0074**	0.7702	0.0216*
Provisions	-0.8697	0.0002**	-0.5050	0.0019**	-0.6687	0.0053**	-0.9284	0.0002**	-0.5150	0.0010**	-0.7381	0.0022**
PE ratio	0.2318	0.1716	0.1162	0.3208	0.2416	0.1638	0.2577	0.1497	0.1156	0.3057	0.2406	0.1663
Change in yield curve spread	-3.5381	0.0705	-0.6132	0.6489	-0.4042	0.8393	-3.8798	0.0589	-1.1423	0.3792	-0.9011	0.6520
Change in asset position	-2.3791	0.0000**	-0.8528	0.0102*	-0.4032	0.4087	-1.9813	0.0000**	-0.3798	0.2324	0.0064	0.9895
Change in exports	-2.4986	0.0363*	2.5617	0.0020**	-2.2087	0.0700	-8.2943	0.0000**	-1.4182	0.0739	-6.5032	0.0000**
Change in GPD per capita	1.9772	0.0077**	0.5194	0.3074	2.1246	0.0051**	1.2464	0.1076	-0.1494	0.7604	1.5874	0.0361*
1991–2004												
Constant	-7.1219	0.4523	-4.5470	0.4655	-15.1646	0.0703	-0.5591	0.9507	2.7609	0.6361	-8.3339	0.3009
DOI change	0.5014	0.2072	0.1082	0.6787	0.1659	0.6359	0.1975	0.6024	-0.1334	0.5856	-0.1034	0.7592
DOI year end	0.0412	0.7040	0.1034	0.1470	0.0980	0.3057	0.0599	0.5625	0.1279	0.0560	0.1142	0.2152
Fee income	-0.1111	0.3829	-0.0297	0.7226	-0.0111	0.9211	-0.1797	0.1397	-0.1020	0.1937	-0.0737	0.4956
Capitalization	0.8943	0.4712	-0.5248	0.5201	1.0622	0.3321	1.2023	0.3102	-0.3048	0.6900	1.3404	0.2042
Net income	0.9576	0.0000**	0.3981	0.0009**	0.7871	0.0000**	0.8458	0.0000**	0.3030	0.0066**	0.6806	0.0000**
Provisions	-0.4459	0.0192	-0.1527	0.2211	-0.4514	0.0073**	-0.5616	0.0021**	-0.2883	0.0140*	-0.5692	0.0005**
PR ratio	0.0399	0.2486	0.0077	0.7366	0.0197	0.5188	0.0359	0.2776	0.0030	0.8875	0.0158	0.5905
Change in yield curve spread	-1.4750	0.3745	-0.3501	0.7484	-0.9317	0.5248	-0.2388	0.8802	1.0878	0.2878	0.3516	0.8032
Change in asset position	0.2657	0.1661	-0.2558	0.0430*	0.1847	0.2751	0.4561	0.0131*	-0.0446	0.7054	0.3681	0.0243*
Change in exports	4.0384	0.0001**	2.5993	0.0001**	3.8412	0.0000**	1.4317	0.1328	0.0153	0.9802	1.1589	0.1717
Change in GPD per capita	0.6819	0.0243*	0.7166	0.0003**	0.7251	0.0067	-0.0954	0.7403	-0.1422	0.4442	-0.1044	0.6839

explained by the model: total return in local currency (TSR1), country adjusted total return in local currency (TSR2), and total return in US dollar (TSR4). The model provided the least explanatory power for TSR5, adjusting the total return for country market indices in US dollar. *DOI*, and *DOI change* have a positive relationship with shareholder return as expected, especially between 1991–2004. However, variables with significance levels of $p < 0.05$ and expected signs were *net income* (positive relationship with TSR measures) and *provisions* (negative relationship with TSR measures).

In other words, profitability emerges as the main driver for shareholder return in this model, not the DOI; an interesting finding because earlier analyses indicated that there is a negative relationship between internationalization and performance. This suggests that shareholders do not value the effect of internationalization directly (hence the non-significant effect of DOI and DOI change) but value the effect of internationalization indirectly (through its effects on profitability).

Shareholder return and internationalization strategy

If shareholders with hindsight had made baskets for the different strategic types, what would have been the result? Figure 7.7 presents the cumulative return in US dollar per strategic type rebased at 100 in 1979. The presented yearly returns are equally weighted to control for banks with relatively large market values. (The results essentially do not change when the returns are market value weighted with the exception of *Moderate* Banks, where Royal Bank of Scotland's market value dominates the results from 1996 onwards). A substantial difference over time emerges between two groups: *Established* (19.1% yearly return) and *Retreating* (18.9%) internationalization on the one hand and *Accelerating* (11.8%) on the other hand. Banks with *Moderate* (14.8%) internationalization hold a middle position. An investment in banks with *Established* internationalization compared to banks with *Accelerating* internationalization over a period of 20 years would have resulted in a total return five times as large, or an additional 7.3% per year.

The large differences in total return urge a closer examination of the underlying data. The differences might simply be caused by a country bias: most banks classified as *Retreating* and *Established* are American or British; banks in these countries have in general shown higher shareholder returns than other countries. Another point of examination is the Japanese banks. Since 1990, their equity prices have been steadily falling,

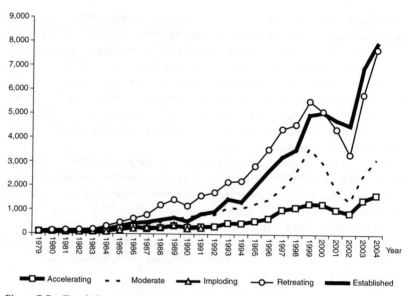

Figure 7.7   Total shareholder return per strategic type
Note: Total return in US dollars, rebased at 31 December 1979 = 100, return equally weighted in US dollar.
Source: Datastream, own calculations

and classifying them all into one category might give biased results. Table 7.12 presents the bank per strategic type, and shows the number of banks that are American/British, Continental European, and Japanese. Most of the Japanese banks fall either in the *Retreating* or *Established* category, more likely dampening the results for the *Accelerating* and *Moderate* type banks which were already substantially higher.

As a robustness test, the cumulative shareholder return adjusted for the country's bank index was calculated and shareholder return indices constructed. The substantial differences in returns per strategy are mitigated to some extent. Overall, the division in returns between *Accelerating* and *Moderate* banks on the one hand and *Retreating* and *Established* banks on the other hand is upheld.

In short, if indices are created for the different strategy types, then *Established* and *Retreating* banks would have generated the highest return between 1980 and 2004, if this is measured in absolute returns, or adjusted for country averages. *Moderate* and *Accelerating* banks would have generated the least returns, in spite of *Accelerating* banks having attracted relatively large amounts of capital to fund their activities.

Table 7.12 Classification of banks per region and strategic type

Type	United States, United Kingdom	Continental Europe	Japan	Banks
Accelerating	0	9	0	ABN AMRO, BBV, Credit Suisse, Deutsche Bank, Dresdner Bank, Hypovereinsbank, Paribas, Santander, UBS
Moderate	1	7	1	AMRO, Argentaria, Bayerische Vereinsbank, Bayerische Hypobank, Commerzbank, Fortis, IBJ, Vereinsbank, Royal Bank of Scotland
Imploding	1	1	0	Crédit Lyonnais, Midland
Retreating	7	0	3	Bank of America, Barclays, Chase Manhattan, Chemical Banking, Dai Ichi Kangyo, Lloyds TSB, Manufacturers Hanover, Mitsubishi Bank, National Westminster, Sumitomo Bank
Established	4	3	2	ABN, BNP, Citicorp, HSBC, JPMorgan, Société Générale, Standard Chartered, Tokyo Mitsubishi, Bank of Tokyo

British and American banks embraced *Established* and *Retreating* internationalization strategies that have generated 5 times more investment return than *Accelerating* and *Moderate* strategies. The obvious explanation is that this difference can be traced back to performance differentials. The analyses in this chapter point to a) an overall negative difference between foreign and domestic profitability, and b) a positive relationship between profitability and shareholder return. Combining these findings suggest the following reasoning: banks with *Accelerating* (and *Moderate*) internationalization have strongly increased their foreign activities, thereby dragging down profitability which was consequently rewarded by shareholders into a lower investment return. *Retreating* banks on the other hand divested and/or shifted their focus to domestic activities. Foreign divestments increased profitability and freed up capital to further invest in more profitable domestic activities, strategic decisions that were rewarded by shareholders.

The negative difference between foreign and domestic performance notwithstanding, banks with *Established* strategies demonstrate that internationalization can evolve into a profitable proposition for banks and shareholders. HSBC, Citicorp, BNP and Standard Chartered apparently have created the right organizational fit between foreign and domestic activities. Although these banks have taken up their share of restructuring, they are banks with a long term commitment to bank internationalization; retail banks make up a major share of their foreign activities.

Foreign activities for banks with *Moderate* strategies tend to result in a modest reduction of profitability, which is reflected in the middle position for investment returns in Figure 7.7. For *Moderate* banks internationalization is essentially a support strategy: foreign wholesale banking activities to support domestic clients, sometimes combined with foreign activities that extend domestic competitive advantages or create a regional sphere. For example Rabobank focuses on foreign agricultural banking in line with its domestic banking roots. Other *Moderate* banks combine their foreign wholesale activities with a regional extension of their home market. Fortis and HVB (and its acquirer UniCredito) extend their definition of a home market by encompassing neighboring countries, similar to regional banks in the United States. Fortis seems to have been inspired by Generale Bank's foreign strategy which it acquired in 1998: Generale Bank pictured a circle with a 500 kilometer radius around Brussels and defined this as its market.

Finally, the difference in investment returns between *Established* and *Retreating* strategies on the one hand, and *Retreating* banks on the other hand can to a large degree be attributed to different corporate strategies: "One of the key strategic issues for banks is the extent to which they adopt a shareholder-value approach by seeking to maximize the rate of return on equity (ROE) and economic value added (EVA), or whether other business criteria predominate". (Llewellyn, 2005). Llewellyn distinguishes between the Shareholder Value (SHV) strategy applied by English and American banks and the Stakeholder Value (STV) strategy which Continental European banks adhere to. Banks with a SHV focus have strong incentives to maximize efficiency, and produce interests that are aligned with shareholder interests. On the other hand, SHV provides no guidance to a long term strategy. After more than a decade of SHV focus, Lloyds TSB's domestic growth opportunities are limited but the bank has not yet formulated an adequate strategic response for further growth.

STV banks' strategy satisfies more stakeholders whose interests need to be served than only shareholders reducing the focus on efficiency.

The STV model might be better equipped to resist pressure for short term SHV strategies to maximize short term interest even though this might not be in the bank's long term interest.

A benign explanation of the lagging investment returns of banks with *Accelerating* strategies is that they have a long term SHV goal in mind with STV consequences. They aim to become *Established* banks with the right organizational fit between foreign and domestic activities, rewarded by a future premium in valuation. Shareholders with a short term view are unable to rightly assess this strategy, depressing investment returns in the short term. Is this reasoning behind Deutsche Bank's or Credit Suisse's strategy? Probably not; similar to other sectors bank managers tend to stay on for limited periods, disputing the durability of such a long term plan. Also, this strategy would be further flawed because the short term depressed valuation makes the bank vulnerable to the market of corporate control and eventual take-over.

8
The Competitive Future of Internationalization Strategies

So where is internationalization heading? Is it a second-best strategy for bank management until their home markets are deregulated; or is it a strategy with its own merits? International growth drags down performance; performance is the main driver for shareholder return. Banks that strongly increased their internationalization activities posted low shareholder returns while banks who did the opposite posted high shareholder returns. It seems no coincidence that in 2001–04 the profitability difference of foreign relative to domestic activities picked up when international M&A showed low volumes. It is not likely that all banks that substantially expanded their foreign bank activities (*Accelerating*) in the 1980s and 1990s, will maintain their high degree of internationalization in the near future. Future domestic deregulation and absence of stable sources of foreign income will probably prompt a reorientation of foreign bank activities for at least half of the number of *Accelerating* banks. There seems to be a tacit understanding between banks that the end goal is a merger end game: a highly concentrated international banking market, perhaps resembling the automobile industry or the airlines. Given our findings, this strategy can backfire. More foreign asset accumulation does not automatically equate to a higher market value. National Westminster exhausted its resources in a flawed internationalization strategy, its turnaround strategy came too late and the bank was acquired by Royal Bank of Scotland. Also, there are plentiful examples around of local banks that are highly profitable and do not seem to have the ambition to go abroad. This chapter explores viable future patterns for success:

- Strategies: which internationalization strategies are best positioned for future success? Which banks are most likely to gain in the near future from internationalization?

- Financial systems: which banks are best equipped for the increasing role of capital markets and Anglo-Saxon governance?
- Regionalization and European integration: which banks are strategically placed for the European integration wave?

8.1. Summary of findings

- *Degree of internationalization increases since 1995*
  The world's largest banks have increased their international activities dramatically in dollar terms. If upon closer inspection the growth of international activities is compared to domestic activities a more subtle pattern emerges. The relative DOI has only risen substantially since 1995. For individual banks, more dramatic patterns emerge. Several American and English banks have substantially decreased their internationalization activities, while Continental European banks expanded dramatically.
- *Foreign profitability lower than domestic*
  The different analyses support the conclusion that foreign profitability on average has been lower than domestic profitability for banks in the sample between 1980 and 2000. An objection usually raised by banks in their annual reports is that for reported figures, the allocation of foreign and domestic profitability is to some extent arbitrary because some financial services generated are consumed in more than one place. Examining the relation between the DOI and total profitability took this objection into consideration, but here too an overall negative relationship between the DOI and total profitability was found.
- *V-Shaped relationship between profitability and internationalization*
  The V-Shape of the relationship between profitability and internationalization is reminiscent of the research debate in the international business literature, where organizations might show learning effects when their commitment and involvement in foreign activities increase, resulting in different benefit-cost payoffs for the organization. Our findings come close to a "J-curve", assuming that over time banks can learn to minimize the additional costs associated with foreign expansion. This means that internationalization costs outweigh benefits until banks gain experience and learn to deal with them. Consequently, banks will reach an inflexion point along the expansion path at which incremental benefits start to outweigh incremental costs. This scenario implies that banks undergo a period of performance deterioration before experiental knowledge can lead

to higher performance levels. However, we find that a) the period of performance deterioration is considerable and b) banks have to substantially increase their international commitments before the inflexion point is reached.

- *Internationalization activities need time to prosper*
  Furthermore, internationalization patterns change over time. Internationalization should not be looked at as a single process, but as a chain of separate but linked processes. The end of one chain represents the point of departure for the next. Internationalization can be described as a "sedimentation" process, where different phases are stratified upon each other (Nilsson, Dicken & Peck, 1996). Since a large number of banks have substantially increased their international activities over time, this sedimentation process may hide the positive effects of individual foreign banking activities that should emerge after a period when banks show few foreign acquisitions. This agrees with the recent upsurge in foreign versus domestic profitability in 2001–04, a period when M&A activities were subdued.

- *Shareholders gain by established or retreating internationalization strategies*
  Shareholders clearly attached different valuations for different realized internationalization strategies. *Retreating* and *Established* banks generated the highest total shareholder return, whether this is measured in absolute returns or adjusted for country averages. These groups include relatively many American and British banks. *Moderate* and *Accelerating* banks generated the least shareholder return, in spite of *Accelerating* banks having attracted relatively large amounts of capital to fund their (foreign) activities. The high TSR for *Retreating* banks supports research that for example shareholders in the United States experienced negative abnormal returns when foreign acquisitions were announced; with this type of realized internationalization strategy on average more foreign divestments than acquisitions have been announced. Additional analyses considered the relationship between risk, return and the degree of internationalization. No support was found that the level of internationalization is a predictor for out- or underperformance in the consecutive periods. In general, a higher degree of internationalization is negatively related to additional shareholder return, albeit non-significant. On the other hand, profitability had significant explanatory power for shareholder return, a relevant result given the earlier finding that foreign profitability on average has been lower than domestic profitability.

8.2. Which internationalization strategies are best positioned for future success?

The intensity and focus of internationalization activities have changed considerably between 1980 and 2004. Internationalization experienced three consecutive "waves": in 1980 American and English banks were at the helm of internationalization, Japanese banks overtook their position in 1990. By 2004 many European banks had raised internationalization to new unprecedented heights, perhaps only matched by the internationalization of banks in the colonial system at the start of the 20th century (cf. Jones, 1993; Born, 1983). The average DOI for the sample did increase, but not dramatically though: the DOI moved around 30% in the 1980s, and increased to 40% at the end of the 1990s.

There are similarities observable between the early 1980s and the late 1990s. In the early 1980s, American and English banks had to make strategic choices with regard to their internationalization activities just as Dutch, German, Spanish and Swiss banks had to reconsider the role of their foreign banking activities at the end of the 1990s. In the early 1980s, banks were confronted with the decline of a smooth source of foreign income, the LDC loans; by the late 1990s banks were confronted with the decline of stock markets reducing both fee income and the attractiveness of the stock markets as a source of foreign acquisition financing. A large number of banks in the sample undertook some form of restructuring in 1999 and 2000, and continued this in the years after. While the decrease in stock markets from 2000 onwards might be alleviated, other triggers of strategic change are bound to follow, such as financial crises.

Overseeing 25 years, the internationalization of banks has been a mixed blessing for shareholders with a long term horizon. Banks with long established foreign bank activities (the *Established* banks) generated in the long run as a group the highest shareholder return, similar to banks who substantially decreased the role of foreign bank activities (the *Retreating* banks). On the other hand, banks which either increased their internationalization activities steadily (the *Moderate* banks) or with increasing pace (the *Accelerating* banks) have generated the lowest shareholder return.

From the shareholder point of view, which banks' internationalization strategies are best positioned for the near future? *Accelerating* banks have increased their foreign bank activities at the end of the 1990s to such an extent that these banks have become comparable in their DOI to

Established banks throughout the 1980s and 1990s. Given the relative successful (shareholder) performance of *Established* banks, what banks with *Accelerating* strategies are likely to emulate the success of *Established* banks? Possible future courses of internationalization strategies (*Moderate, Established, Accelerating, Retreating*)[1] are projected in Figure 8.1. For example, *Established* banks have a relatively high DOI; the solid line in the figure projects the current DOI into the future, assuming no funda-

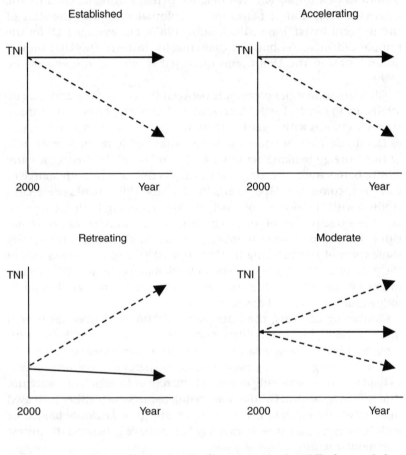

Note: 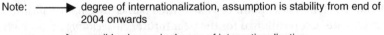 degree of internationalization, assumption is stability from end of 2004 onwards

‒ ‒ ‒ ‒▶ possible change in degree of internationalization

Figure 8.1   Future directions of internationalization

mental change in the role of foreign activities in the bank. On the other hand, the dotted arrow shows a strategic change in the DOI.

If past experience provides any guidance, then an investment in banks with realized *Established* and *Accelerating* strategies for the coming decade might be worthwhile, while investments in banks with *Retreating* and *Moderate* strategies should be considered with more caution.

Established banks (such as Citicorp, HSBC) have found a durable balance in the 1980s and 1990s between foreign and domestic bank activities. These banks have in common foreign bank activities that are broadly based, branching out in investment banking, corporate finance as well as retail banking (consumer finance) and asset management. Also, their foreign activities are geographically well diversified. *Established* banks have to maintain the right configuration to keep internationalization a relatively profitable activity, or the bank might divest activities that do not contribute to the total profitability of the bank.

Accelerating banks on the other hand present a paradox: these banks have on average delivered the least shareholder return in the past but are best positioned to generate the most shareholder return in the near future. *Accelerating* banks (such as Deutsche Bank, ABN AMRO, Credit Suisse, UBS, Santander) have increased their internationalization activities significantly during the 1990s and are at a position in the early years of the new millennium similar to *Established* and *Retreating* banks in the early 1980s. Either they have to find the right configuration to make internationalization a relatively profitable activity, or the bank will divest activities because it has not found an opportunity for sustainable foreign profitability and refocuses on domestic activities. In other words, *Accelerating* banks have to determine whether they soon will reach the stage of *Established* banks, or they have to reconsider their portfolio of foreign activities and become *Retreating* banks. In the past, both scenarios were rewarded by shareholders.

The choice banks with *Accelerating* strategies have between developing either *Established* or *Retreating* strategies leads to the question which banks with *Accelerating* strategies have characteristics more similar to banks with *Established* strategies or more similar to *Retreating* strategies. In other words, which banks with *Accelerating* strategies are likely to evolve into *Retreating* strategies and which banks are likely to develop *Established* strategies? For an answer two additional criterions need to be introduced: the scope for domestic growth opportunities and the stability of foreign income.

The case studies first indicate that when domestic growth opportunities increase, banks favor domestic growth over foreign bank growth. For most banks, the first priority is to maintain the (relative) domestic market position, as well as seizing the best opportunities to achieve profitability growth or efficiencies. Expansion of domestic banking markets (mostly triggered by regulatory changes) led to a decrease in internationalization of banks; this applied for American banks, English banks and also Japanese banks. Naturally, this criterion does not apply for banks with small and/or highly concentrated domestic banking markets, such as the Netherlands and Switzerland. Future domestic growth opportunities are however relevant for French and German banks where demutualization, and (further) abolishment of the separation between different banking types in the country might be future events.

Second, all major retreats from internationalization have been triggered by a financial crisis. While the timing of financial crises cannot be predicted as such, the banks that retreated the strongest or earliest were on average banks with large capital market/investment banking operations. Banks with more stable foreign funding bases such as foreign retail banks or banks with more stable foreign fee income base such as asset management and private banking are probably more likely to weather economic and financial adverse conditions than banks with volatile foreign activities in capital market/investment banking. This will be used as the second criterion, both criterions suggest the following categorization of future development (Figure 8.2).

In other words, German banks with *Accelerating* strategies (Dresdner Bank, Westdeutsche Landesbank and Deutsche Bank[2]) are more likely to retreat from foreign bank activities and eventually develop *Retreating* internationalization strategies. The German banking sector is considered as one of the least concentrated; owing to this fragmented structure a concentration wave might be expected (Ayadi & Pujals, 2004). The German banks' potential domestic growth opportunities are relatively large; when regulation permits these banks might prefer domestic banking growth opportunities over foreign banking growth opportunities. Also, these banks are more sensitive to external shocks such as financial crises due to their high dependency on (foreign) capital market activities. On the other hand, the Swiss, Dutch and Spanish banks have no domestic growth opportunities; the Dutch banks ING and ABN AMRO have acquired large stable funding bases (retail banking operations) outside the Netherlands. Credit Suisse and UBS have not acquired retail networks outside Switzerland; UBS has

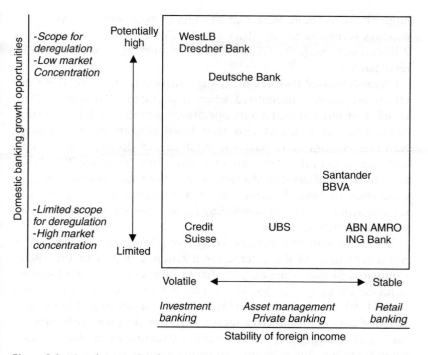

Domestic banking growth opportunities

-Scope for deregulation
-Low market Concentration

Potentially high

-Limited scope for deregulation
-High market concentration

Limited

WestLB
Dresdner Bank

Deutsche Bank

Santander
BBVA

Credit Suisse

UBS

ABN AMRO
ING Bank

Volatile ◄─────────────► Stable

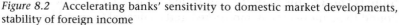

| Investment banking | Asset management Private banking | Retail banking |

Stability of foreign income

Figure 8.2   Accelerating banks' sensitivity to domestic market developments, stability of foreign income

created a relatively stable source of foreign income through asset management and private banking while Credit Suisse is more focused on expanding in investment banking. In other words, ING, ABN AMRO, UBS, Santander and BBVA may be the banks which have developed and expanded internationalization activities closest to banks with *Established* internationalization strategies.

Similar to *Accelerating* banks, banks with *Retreating* internationalization have two strategic alternatives: either to maintain or further decrease internationalization activities, or to increase them again: *reinternationalization*. Lloyds TSB, Barclays and JPMorgan Chase have reinternationalized or plan to do so. Lloyds TSB has publicly contemplated increasing their internationalization activities in 2000, while Barclays has reinternationalized in Spain but on a more subdued scale than its European and American expansion activities in the 1980s. The bank acquired Banco de Zarazogano in 2003 for 1.14 billion euro, Barclays became the sixth largest bank in Spain by assets. In comparison, the largest bank in Spain, SCH, had 20 times as many assets.[3] A year later Barclays reentered South Africa for the first time since 1986 with a 3 billion euro majority stake purchase in Absa, the country's largest retail bank.[4]

Chase decreased its foreign bank activities since the mid-1980s but effectively reinternationalized when it acquired JPMorgan in 2000 which had more than half its operations outside the United States. Royal Bank of Scotland also (re-) internationalized by acquiring National Westminster. National Westminster decreased its foreign bank activities in the 1990s; after the acquisition in March 2000 Royal Bank of Scotland developed a specialized internationalization strategy, expanding its United States retail branch network with a series of modest acquisitions and developing foreign distribution channels for motor insurance activities.

The reinternationalization of Barclays or JPMorganChase is probably not a repetition of the internationalization activities in the 1980s. Compared to earlier periods, the banks now show a strong focus on domestic banking activities. Also, bank capital has become scarcer than in the 1980s. At the end of 2003 the proposed structure and implementation of Basle II introduced a more sophisticated regulatory framework for banks and their capital. Whichever structure or implementation route is chosen, the allocation of capital to foreign bank activities is bound to be more closely monitored and evaluated than in the 1980s. Some internationalization incentives remain the same; Lloyds TSB announced a reinternationalization strategy, in search of new growth opportunities after domestic expansion activities failed when Lloyds TSB was not allowed to acquire Abbey National in 2000. The other *Retreating* banks have not reinternationalized; Bank of America autonomously expanded investment banking operations in London but substantially reduced the relative role of its foreign operations when it acquired FleetBoston. For the retreated Japanese banks, the climate for reinternationalization has become more favorable but the banks have largely been engaged in domestic mergers to absorb the large write off of bad loans, increase profitability and regain solvency.

Finally, question marks surround the future shareholder returns of *Moderate* banks: they have the widest range of strategic options available to them, and are probably the most diverse bank group of realized strategies. Most *Moderate* banks have as yet sought to increase their DOI. Fortis for example has essentially stayed focused on the Benelux and Spain, consolidating and integrating its bank operations and striving for autonomous growth. However, Fortis announced in

Table 8.1 Possible changes in future internationalization of banks

		Change from			
		Established	Accelerating	Retreating	Moderate
Change to	Established	Tokyo Mitsubishi Financial Group HSBC Standard Chartered Citigroup BNP Paribas Société Générale	ABN AMRO ING Bank UBS Santander[1] BBVA		
	Accelerating				Royal Bank of Scotland[5] Fortis
	Retreating		Credit Suisse[2] Deutsche Bank Dresdner Bank Westdeutsche Landesbank Hypovereinsbank[6]	Bank of America Mizuho[3] Lloyds TSB[4]	
	Moderate			JPMorganChase Barclays	Rabobank Commerzbank Crédit Agricole

The banks in the sample at the end of 2004 are included in this table.
Notes:
(1) The bank has been renamed SCH.
(2) Credit Suisse could also be classified as retreating.
(3) Mizuho incorporates IBJ and Dai Ichi Kangyo.
(4) Lloyds TSB announced a reinternationalization in 2000, this has not materialized between 2000 and 2003.
(5) Royal Bank of Scotland acquired National Westminster in 2000, and continued its foreign banking activities.
(6) Acquired by Italian UniCredito.

early 2005 that it would expand further in central Europe and consider acquisitions, striving to generate 30% of its profits outside the Benelux by 2009,[5] subsequently buying the Turkish Disbank for almost 1 billion euro in April 2005. Crédit Agricole boosted its foreign activities since its acquisition of wholesale bank Indosuez in 1994 but also strengthened its domestic focus by acquiring Crédit Lyonnais in 2002.

What road leads to a sustainable and equal profitability development of foreign and domestic banking activities? Table 8.1 summarizes the hypothesized changes in realized internationalization strategies for the near future. The number of banks with *Established* strategies will increase, so will the number of banks with *Retreating* internationalization strategies.

Shifting from *Moderate* to *Accelerating* strategies will probably pose the greatest challenges. Royal Bank of Scotland successfully integrated domestic National Westminster; after two major foreign acquisitions, Charter One (the 25th American acquisition since 1988 for 10.5 billion US dollars) and a financial participation in the Bank of China in 2005 for 1.6 billion US dollars, shareholders seemed not convinced by Royal Bank of Scotland's overall strategy and foreign plans. Despite solid profits the share prices traded at 8–9 times price-to-equity, compared to for example 13.4 for HSBC in June 2005. Perhaps Royal Bank of Scotland points to a weakness in the shareholder approach similar to Lloyds TSB: it is a strategy concept poorly equipped when applied to internationalization strategies.

8.3.   Coping with changing financial systems: is it a challenge or opportunity?

On the basis of the relationship between countries and international-ization strategies of banks two country groups could be established: Continental European countries and with the largest financial centers: the United States, the United Kingdom and Japan (Table 8.2).

Table 8.2 shows that by and large, American, British and Japanese banks tend to be banks with predominantly *Retreating* and *Established* strategies. On the other hand, Continental European banks have shown predominantly *Moderate* and *Accelerating* strategies. This does not however imply that *Retreating* and *Established* strategies are specific to market oriented financial systems where banks pursue a shareholder approach (Japan is the exception here), or that *Moderate* and *Accelerating* strategies are specific to bank oriented systems where banks have shareholder based strategies (the Netherlands and Switzerland are classified as market based). What are then possible implications of this dichotomy?

If one reconsiders the future implications of internationalization strategies, a case was made that most *Accelerating* banks (who had until the late 1990s expanded their foreign activities considerably) faced a strategic choice to become either *Established* banks or *Retreating* banks. Table 8.2 would then suggest that this would coincide with banks located in financial systems with large capital markets, in other words a shift from the Continental European model to the large capital markets model. Such a shift takes place with the integration of the European banking markets and the continuous integration process in the European capital markets (cf. the concentration of European securities markets in Eurex and Euronext).

Table 8.2 Financial systems and realized internationalization strategies

	United States	United Kingdom	Japan	France	Germany	Netherlands	Spain	Switzerland
Accelerating				Paribas	Deutsche Bank Dresdner Bank Hypo-Vereinsbank Westdeutsche Landesbank	ING Bank ABN AMRO NMB Bank	BCH BBV Santander	Credit Suisse UBS
Moderate			IBJ	Agricole	Vereinsbank Commerzbank Bayerische Hypobank	Rabobank Fortis AMRO	Argentaria	
Imploding		Midland		Crédit Lyonnais				
Retreating	Chemical Banking Manufacturers Hanover Bank of America Chase Manhattan	Barclays Lloyds TSB National Westminster	Mitsubishi Bank Dai Ichi Kangyo Sumitomo Bank					
Established	JPMorgan Citicorp	Standard Chartered HSBC	Tokyo Mitsubishi Tokyo	BNP Société Générale		ABN		SBC

Continental Europe

Largest financial centers/capital markets

Two parallel developments might take place that have similar consequences and are bound to interact closely in the near future. Viewed
from top down, for most European countries the integration of the
capital markets may eventually emulate characteristics of the United
Kingdom, the United States and Japan, countries where the banks in
the sample showed *Retreating* and *Established* internationalization
strategies. Viewed from bottom up, banks which accelerated their internationalization activities are likely to enter a reorientation phase to
develop either *Established* or *Retreating* internationalization strategies.

The study has also found implications for the role of changing
financial systems, but more on an individual bank level. A (major)
example in this case is Deutsche Bank. Its expansion in the 1990s in
capital market activities in the United States and the United Kingdom
was financed by equity issues. The bank increased its dependency on
shareholders, and in the process compared itself to American and Swiss
competitors. Transparency and comparability with other banks was
improved by separating the differing characteristics of a German bank,
its industrial shareholdings were eventually moved towards a different
holding, clearly indicating that these were for sale. In other words,
internationalization might create its own momentum to change bank
based systems to market based systems.

There is also a cross over from bank oriented systems to market oriented systems though. American banks have moved from a specialized
bank model in the 1970s to a European universal banking model in the
1980s and 1990s; and started to move towards the bank assurance
model in the late 1990s, with the Travelers-Citicorp merger. If this
trend were to be followed by more banks, it might support the earlier
implication that domestic growth opportunities for American banks
are further enlarged, shifting focus further from international to
domestic activities, reducing the degree of internationalization.

8.4.   European integration: one banking market at last?

Examination of the regional internationalization patterns in Chapter 5
showed that a large degree of the foreign activities of European banks
(as well as American banks) have taken place within European banking
markets. Another implication to consider is then the consequence of
regional integration such as the European Union, representing an economic and political extension of the home market and a regional uni-
formization of the regulatory regime. The European integration process
accelerated in two periods, between 1988 and 1991 (in preparation of

the Single Market) and between 1996 and 1999 (in preparation of the Eurozone). The economic integration programs liberalized capital markets, and the introduction of the euro led to a convergence of monetary policies between the major EU countries. With European integration, will the extension of the home market imply similar high profitability as domestically, or should expansion in the Eurozone still be considered internationalization to a foreign country, with lower foreign performance than domestic as this study found?

Banks have dealt with European integration in several ways: pan-European strategies were formulated by National Westminster, Barclays, Deutsche Bank and Crédit Lyonnais in the 1980s. They built up a branch network in the major European cities, and acquired retail or private banks in European countries, mainly in Germany, France and Spain. In the 1990s, a new concept was introduced: the "second home market" in Europe. These were acquisitions of foreign banking activities with the expected benefits enjoyed domestically (such as a large depositor base). Banks which followed this strategy were ING with its 1997 acquisition of Belgian BBL, HSBC which acquired French CCF in 2000, Santander acquiring Abbey National in 2003 or ABN AMRO buying Antonveneta in 2005. If banks view Europe as an extension of their home market, then the findings of this study would suggest that this extension in general lowers overall profitability. Is this finding also valid for European banks internationalizing in the (integrated) European banking market?

Supporting the concept that European integration extends the concept of the home market are convergence of net interest margins in the Eurozone, the structural removal of regulatory barriers and reduction of fluctuations in GDP growth with converging economic cycles in the Eurozone. What these developments have in common is that differences decrease between "domestic" and "foreign" economies within the Eurozone.

Outwardly one might interpret the process of European integration for the banking markets as following the path taken by American banks since the mid-1990s, where ongoing deregulation of interstate banking has led to a natural extension of the home market. Deregulation of interstate banking has basically created new markets with similar customers, introducing opportunities for increased efficiency and higher profitability. However, European integration cannot be compared to the banking deregulation in the United States.

There are two arguments that do not support the concept of an extension of the home market within Europe. First, potential efficiency advantages may be difficult to exploit. Consolidation of the banking market moves at different paces in different countries; European labor markets are considered to be rigid implying that part of the cost-to-income ratio levels for banks in a country are structural, especially for labor intensive retail banking. In other words, efficiencies might be difficult to gain by foreign banking acquisitions in Europe.

Second, fiscal policies with regard to savings and pensions are not harmonized. They determine to a large extent the growth of the savings pool and the opportunities to be had. A scenario could be that further European banking consolidation follows along these lines: capital market activities in Europe are to a large extent consolidated; dominated by a few American and European banks for the region, with complementary dominant positions for country based banks. Consolidation in the European banking market is then directed at acquiring foreign retail banks, preferably in the immediate region. Examples are Bavarian bank HVB acquiring Austrian Bank of Austria, or Italian UniCredito buying HVB. Capital markets are less influenced by local tastes than retail banks, whether this is by a branch network or a virtual network.

Notes

Chapter 2   Banking since the 1980s: Challenges and Issues

1 A more stronger view is taken by William Seidman, former chairman of the FDIC, who summarized the disintermediation process as "banks' troubles began when they lost their big corporate customers to the commercial paper market [in the] early 1970s" in relation to the LDC debt crisis (Federal Deposit Insurance Corporation, 1997, p. 196).

2 The FDIC defines disintermediation as the "*withdrawal* of funds from interest-bearing accounts at banks [...] when rates on competing investments [...] offer the investor a higher return" (Federal Deposit Insurance Corporation, 1997, p. 214). This suggests that disintermediation a) is a funding related problem and b) per definition leads to a decline in total assets.

3 Fees and commission form the most important component of non-interest income, around 54% of total non-interest income in 1998. The second most important source is income from financial operations (the result from buying and selling on own account, ranging from 19% to 22%. The relative distribution of components differs widely on a country basis. For example, the third component, income from securities (shares, variable yield securities and other participating interests) accounted for 24% to 35% of non-interest income in 1998 in countries like Sweden, Germany, Denmark, Austria and Spain, compared to 1% in the United Kingdom, indicating different levels of diversification through subsidiaries between those countries (European Central Bank, 2000a, pp. 11–13).

4 The European Central Bank finds an inverse correlation between interest and non-interest income, but notes that this should be treated with caution since the composition of non-interest income has not been stable, and banks might actually enforce such a negative correlation, for example by offering credit with very thin margins hoping that this will be followed by a stream of non-interest income (European Central Bank, 2000a, p. 6).

5 Another supranational institution is the IMF. Its regulatory framework applied to the period before 1973, coordinating capital flows and exchange rates.

6 Short for the Basle Committee on Banking Supervision, preceded by the Standing Committee on Banking Regulations and Supervisory Practices.

7 The criticism on the capital adequacy rules of the Basle Accord is broader, for example: the risk-weights are too crude, the rule cannot vary to absorb shocks or reflect the financial structure of the country, no account is taken of covariance between risk categories penalizing widely (risk) diversified banks, funding risk is not covered, market risk arising from security positions is not accounted for (Davis, 1995, pp. 125–6). These objections are (mostly) covered in the New Capital Adequacy Framework introduced in 1999.

8   Stock market participants shared this view. Wagster (1996) measured the wealth effects of shareholders of international banks from Canada, Germany, Japan, the Netherlands, Switzerland, the United Kingdom and the United States between 1985 and 1990 on the basis of major events concerning the Basle Accord. Japanese bank shareholders seemed to interpret the events in favor of Japanese banks, showing an abnormal cumulative return of 31.6% during the period, while German and Dutch banks were unfavorably treated with abnormal cumulative returns of –7.3% and –9.1% respectively.

9   See for example Karacadag & Taylor (2000) for a review of the New Capital Adequacy Framework (Karacadag & Taylor, 2000), or the Center for the Study of Financial Innovation (2002) for critiques on the proposed framework.

10   *Source*: website BIS (www.bis.org), consulted on December 20, 2002.

11   This section is based on Kanaya & Woo (2000).

12   *Source*: Kanaya & Woo, 2000, p. 44, Table 13. Source assets foreign banks in Japan: website Bank of Japan, Principal Assets and Liabilities of Foreign Banks in Japan. http://www.boj.or.jp/en/stat/stat_f..htm, consulted on September 9, 2003.

13   UNTNC classified the banks in the three groups (* denote banks that are examined in this study):
   • Leaders: Citicorp*, Chase Manhattan*, BankAmerica Corp*, JPMorgan*, Manufacturers Hanover*
   • Challengers: Lloyds*, Bank of Montreal, Bank of Tokyo*, Bankers Trust, Chemical Bank*, Canadian Imperial Bank of Commerce, Toronto Dominion Bank, Commerzbank*, Bank of Nova Scotia, Long Term Credit Bank of Japan
   • Followers: National Westminster*, Deutsche Bank*, Royal Bank of Canada, Westdeutsche Landesbank*, Dresdner Bank*, Barclays Bank*, Midland Bank*, Crédit Lyonnais*, Industrial Bank of Japan*, BNP*

14   A failure in risk estimations or creditworthiness evaluation that is converted into a systematic tendency (United Nations Center on Transnational Corporations, 1991, p. 2).

15   Virtually all costs associated with the international debt crisis were transferred to the debtors, at least during the first phase from 1982 to 1984 (United Nations Center on Transnational Corporations, 1991, p. 4).

16   See Bongini (2003) for analysis of the relevancy of EU financial liberalization for multilateral liberalization within the WTO framework.

17   The predecessor of ING, NMB joined the InterAlpha group in the 1970s. ING acquired Belgian InterAlpha partner BBL, unsuccessfully bid for CCF, and acquired BHF bank.

18   For securities, the Securities Industry Association, a self-regulatory body of the securities industry, has over the year steadily decreased the settlement risk by reducing the time between the transaction, and the actual payment. Eventually the standard moved to T+3 (Trade-date-plus-three-days settlement periods), and goals were set for T+1 in 2004. These however were postponed after September 11, 2001. Other financial protocols and requirements are Fix (financial information messaging) and ISO 15022 (as international messaging standard). For foreign exchange transactions, instantaneous

settlement was introduced in 2002 when Continuous Linked Settlement (CLS) was created by a consortium of banks.

19 For example Mastercard, VISA for credit cards, Euroclear for settlements, and Depository Trust Company for funds transfer.

Chapter 3   International Banking, a Theoretical Framework

1 Main features are: the informal regulatory framework of the Bank of England, a universally accepted language, good location well placed in the time zone to communicate with other major financial markets during working hours. In addition to this, London enjoyed a concentration of financial information services, some of the world's leading money publications, specialist printers, and a substantial skilled labor force. For American bankers, the use of English Law and English language was particularly attractive.

2 For example, Morgan Stanley Dean Witter published a report in 2000 finding that banks in the United Kingdom never managed more than two financial products each per client, out of an average number of six to seven financial products held by customers (UK Banks, Turbulence Ahead. (May 9, 2000). Morgan Stanley Dean Witter: Equity Research Europe).

3 Pretzlik, C. (October 23, 2000). Survey – German banking and finance: Foreign institutions gobble up the goodies. *Financial Times.*

4 The organizational form of international banking has been extensively researched, focusing on explaining and/or predicting (modulation between establishing) organizational forms. cf. Ursacki & Vertinsky (1992), Ter Wengel (1995), Heinkel & Levi (1992), Blandon (1998).

5 ING Direct finalizes the acquisition of Egg France savings activities, November 25, 2004, http://www.ing.com/group/showdoc.jsp?docid=092758_NL&menopt=

Chapter 4   The World's Largest Banks

1 Rabobank, September 21, 2005, Eureko and Rabobank sign merger agreement, Press release.

2 Cf. Demirgüç-Kunt & Levine (2001). This ratio can be interpreted as a combination of two ratios; 1) the ratio of banking assets in the sample to total financial assets in that country and 2) the ratio of total financial assets to the GDP of that country. The first ratio signifies the relative market power of the banks in the country, whereas the second ratio represents the relative financial development of the country, analogous to Goldsmith (1969).

3 That is, net interest income in local currency as a ratio of the average of beginning of year assets and end of year assets in local currency.

4 The rationale of looking at the CI ratio is the use of the ratio as a key measure of bank efficiency (Van Dijcke, 2001, p. 299). A change in the CI ratio heavily determines the change in profit before tax. A problem with the CI ratio is that it does not account for the fact that some product mixes cost more to produce than others (Van Dijcke, 2001, p. 324). Changes in the CI ratio should be related to either gross income and/or the composition of gross income, as noted earlier.

5   Using ANOVA comparing CI ratios for five-year periods per country. Between 1986–90, the CI ratio of Japanese and Swiss banks was significantly lower than other banks, the main differences were found between the United Kingdom, Japan, the United States and other European countries. A decade later, between 1996–2000, Japanese banks still showed lower CI ratios with p values < 0.05 compared to other banks, as did banks in the United Kingdom. Although the banks in the United States also reported lower CI ratios compared to most countries, the mean only differed significantly from Dutch and Japanese banks.

6   See VanDijcke (2001, pp. 300–6) for an overview of bank efficiency research.

7   All things being equal, the year after the provisioning would show a strong profitability rebound: not only are provisions lower the year after, but the capital basis is probably also reduced, lowering the denominator in the ratio.

8   Larsen, P.T., Wightono, D. & Swann, C. November 15, 2005, Banks warn over Basel delay, *Financial Times*, p. 2.

Chapter 5   International Patterns

1   See Van den Berghe (2004) for a review of research on the use of these internationalization indicators.

2   Country averages have shown structural differences. For example, for DOI data from 1990 to 2000 the variability of the country means is tested with ANOVA, and the Bonferroni procedure has been applied to determine which country means are different. The average DOI from banks in Germany differ significantly (with p values < 0.05) from all other countries in the sample. Average DOI in the United Kingdom differs significantly from French, German, American and Japanese average DOI, but not from Dutch and Swiss. Finally, Japanese average DOI differs significantly from average DOI in the United Kingdom. Although the sample is small and these statistics should thus be treated with caution, it is an indication that country of origin matters in internationalization.

3   For example, the 40% DOI level could be interpreted as a threshold below which stakeholders in the bank find the risks of internationalization manageable or the returns satisfying.

4   In earlier analyses, it was observed that banks have not always fully disclosed geographical information. In recent years, disclosure of geographical information has substantially improved. De Nicoló et al. (2004, p. 17) investigated internationalization patterns of banks between 1995 and 2000; the recent time period of their study (five years compared to 20 years in this study) allows a more detailed analysis of changes in foreign ownership per country. This is also valid for the regional breakdown of assets.

5   From that period onwards, banks started to report the European region as "EMEA": Europe, Middle East and Africa. Since for most banks their assets in the Middle East and Africa had become small (usually below 5% of total assets), the contribution to the European growth rate must have been limited also.

Chapter 6   Internationalization Strategies

1 One of the path-breaking management studies in the 1980s by Peters and Waterman, "In Search of Excellence", examined American (non-financial) companies between 1961 and 1980 (1982, pp. 22–3). Another example is Collinas & Porras (1994), who in 1989 studied a sample of American companies founded before 1945 to analyze their long term performance.

2 Simonian, H. (November 25, 1993). International Company News: Deutsche Bank offshoot in L470bn Italian deal. *Financial Times*, p. 27.

3 Burns, T. (March 30, 1993). International Company News: Banks look for warmer climates – Deutsche Bank's latest foray into Spain. *Financial Times*, p. 29.

4 Barber, T., Harros, C. & Iskander, S. (December 3, 1998). Companies & Finance: Europe: Deutsche Bank in Belgian buy. *Financial Times*, p. 28.

5 Harnischfeger, U. (July 5, 1999). Deutsche Bank treads gently in Europe. *Financial Times*, p. 22.

6 For example, besides EBIC bank EAB, where Deutsche Bank participated, the bank set up a New York based joint venture with UBS, which in ended in 1978 with Deutsche Bank taking full control (Gall et al., 1995, p. 768).

7 Which was below mandatory approval limit (Gall et al., 1995, p. 770).

8 Waters, R. (July 22, 1992). International Capital Markets: Deutsche Bank to merge businesses. *Financial Times*, p. 25.

9 Fisher, A. & Cohen, N. (October 29, 1994). Deutsche Bank puts its money on London. *Financial Times*, p. 24.

10 Friedman, A. (May 6, 1995). Deutsche Bank to expand in US. *Financial Times*, p. 21.

11 Corrigan, T. (December 2, 1998). Comment & Analysis: Shrinking middle ground: Now that Deutsche Bank has taken over Bankers Trust. *Financial Times*, p. 20.

12 Fisher, A. (September 2, 1992). International Company News: Deutsche Bank purchase. *Financial Times*, p. 14.

13 Fisher, A. (September 6, 1996). Comment & Analysis: Cat set among the pigeons. *Financial Times*, p. 15.

14 Fisher, A. (November 18, 1997). Survey – German banking: Shake-up sharpens focus. *Financial Times*.

15 Grant, J. (September 1, 1999). No merger for Deutsche Bank, *Financial Times*.

16 Fisher, A. (March 30, 1995). International Company News: Deutsche Bank sets up 24-hour operation. *Financial Times*, p. 26.

17 Harnischfeger, U. (October 23, 2000). Survey – German banking and finance: Life still tough for private sector. *Financial Times*.

18 *The Economist* (August 28, 2004) Deutsche Bank: A giant hedge fund, pp. 61–2.

19 Edmondson, G. & Fairlamb, D. (April 23, 2001). The Super Banks of Spain. *Business Week Online*. Retrieved November 3, 2003, from http://www.businessweek.com:/print/magazine/content/01_17/b3729023.htm?mz.

20 The share stake became an issue in 1999 with the acquisition of National Westminster. The share swap was not unique in European banking, cf. BNP-Dresdner.

21 History of Santander (n.d.). Retrieved April 27, 2003, from www.hoovers.com.
22 Banesto kept its separate brand name.
23 This changed into an 11% equity stake in First Union in 1995, when First Union acquired First Fidelity.
24 And a smaller bank operating in cities in the country.
25 Hoovers online, history of Santander, consulted on April 27, 2003, www.hoovers.com.
26 Horwood, C., 2005, Getting back to the Abbey Habit, *Euromoney*, July 2005, pp. 57–8.
27 Horwood, C., 2005, The Masters of Retail Banking, *Euromoney*, July 2005, pp. 52–5.
28 Cooperative banks have a preference for alliances and consortium banks. A reason might be that with cooperative banks, the control of capital is allocated to the local banks, leaving the central offices little financial maneuvering space to engage in (high risk) international activities.
29 North and South America, Europe, Asia and Australia (De Boer & Graafsma, 2002, p. 114).
30 Gunther, R., 2005, Rabo gaat steeds meer wereldwijd, Bank- en Effectenbedrijf, October 2005, pp. 4–11.
31 The Dai Ichi Kangyo Bank Ltd. (1988). In Grant, E.T. (ed.), *International Directory of Company Histories* (1988), vol 2, p. 273.
32 *History of Dai Ichi Kangyo Bank*. Retrieved April 27, 2003, from www.hoovers.com.
33 DKB first started its banking activities in Taipei in 1959. *Source*: Terazono, E. (March 3, 1993). Bank of Tokyo to set up Taiwan branch. *Financial Times*, p. 26.
34 The Dai Ichi Kangyo Bank Ltd. (1988). In Grant, E.T. (ed.), *International Directory of Company Histories* (1988), vol 2, p. 274.
35 The Dai Ichi Kangyo Bank Ltd. (1988). In Grant, E.T. (ed.), *International Directory of Company Histories* (1988), vol 2, p. 274.
36 The Dai Ichi Kangyo Bank Ltd. (1988). In Grant, E. T. (ed.), *International Directory of Company Histories* (1988), vol 2, p. 274.
37 Murthy, R. (January 12, 1993). International Capital Markets: Dai Ichi shuts Bombay office. *Financial Times*, p. 25.
38 McDougall, R. & Fringle, M. (January 1988). Dai Ichi Kangyo: Tough at the Top. *The Banker*, p. 41.
39 *History of Dai Ichi Kangyo Bank*. Retrieved April 27, 2003, from www.hoovers.com.
40 Eventually, six DKB executives were convicted. *Source*: *History of Dai Ichi Kangyo Bank*. Retrieved April 27, 2003, from www.hoovers.com.
41 Abrahams, P. (October 17, 1998). Companies & Finance: Dai Ichi Kangyo to sell off 30% stake in CIT. *Financial Times*, p. 23
42 Abrahams, P. (August 3, 1998). Daiwa cuts overseas operations: Jobs to be lost in London, New York and Hong Kong. *Financial Times*, p. 17.
43 Boland, V. & Harris, C. (December 8, 1998). Companies & Finance: Asia-Pacific: Fuji Bank eyes full merger. *Financial Times*, p. 32.
44 Iibison, D., March 4, 2004, Mizuho plans to pay back bail-out cash, *Financial Times*, p. 19.
45 Wels, A. (June 1981). Citicorp climbs to the top. *The Banker*, pp. 45–9.

46 The announcement was favorably received by the stock market, but the write off also forced other American and British banks with large LDC loan exposure in South America to do the same, because Citicorp's action questioned the real book value of their standing loans (Madura, 1991).
47 *The Economist* (July 27, 1991), p. 66.
48 Citicorp was also pressured by its regulators, the New York Federal Reserve Bank and the Office of the Comptroller of the Currency, to do so. For two and a half years, from November 1990 onwards, Citicorp had to consult the regulator for all its strategic decisions (Barnet & Cavanagh, 1994, p. 382).
49 In April, several others of the most expensive acquisitions were announced; the 66 billion US dollar purchase of California's BankAmerica by NationsBank of North Carolina was announced as well as the 29.5 billion US dollar takeover of First Chicago NBD by Banc One. *Source*: Authers (1998).
50 Corrigan, T. (April 9, 1998). USA: Pair looks at options on banking side – synergies. *Financial Times*.
51 Hill, A. (September 7, 2000). Associates attract mixed reception. *Financial Times*, p. 18.
52 Nakamae, N. (March 27, 2000). *Financial Times*, p. 4.
53 The following factors made the UK market attractive for Citibank: relaxations of exchange controls open the way for more sterling deposits, attractive profitability of UK banks in recent years, structurally high interest rates and the relatively "underbanked" market in the United Kingdom. *Source*: Hindle, T. (November 1980). Sizing up the retail market. *The Banker*.
54 Innovative new products were a cheque account combined with a savings facility and an automatic right to borrow up to 30 times the monthly savings payment, in effect creating the UK version of an interest bearing deposit account.
55 Portanger, E. & Beckett, P. (January 19, 2000). In Buying Schröders, Citigroup Places Bet on Europe's Future. *Wall Street Journal Europe*, p. 1.
56 One of the stakeholders was Commerzbank, holding a 10% stake after Handlowy merged with BRE where Commerzbank held a stake in. *Source*: Williamson, E. & Beckett, P. (February 11, 2000). Citigroup Wants to Purchase Majority of Bank Handlowy. *Wall Street Journal Europe*, p. 6.
57 Ibison, D. 2004, Citigroup apologizes to Japan, *Financial Times*, October 26, 2004, p. 17.
58 Lee, P. 2005, What Citigroup needs to do next, *Euromoney*, July 2005, pp. 64–70.
59 *The Economist*, February 5, 2005, Out of Life, p. 65
60 History of HSBC (n.d.). Retrieved October 12, 1999, from Hoovers Inc, Bloomberg.
61 Baker-Said, S. & Giles, T. (April 2002). HSBC: still not the champion, *Bloomberg markets*, pp. 38–45.
62 HSBC (2001). *Annual report 2000*, p. 9.
63 HSBC initially took an equity stake in Bamerindus in 1995; Midland Bank was active in Brazil and when HSBC acquired Midland the involvement was continued. *Source*: Foster, A. (August 29, 1995). International Company News: HSBC Holdings set to take stake. *Financial Times*, p. 17.

64 Baker-Said, S. & Giles, T. (April 2002). HSBC: still not the champion. *Bloomberg markets*, pp. 38–45.
65 Larsen, P.T. December 24–26, 2004, We're going through an unprecedented period of change in financial services, *Financial Times*, p. 7
66 Bergsman, S. (February 1990). BankAmerica: Shake, Rattle and On a Roll. *Bankers Monthly*, pp. 15–18.
67 Palmer, G. (October 31, 1994). Back On Top. *The Banker*, pp. 31–4. The expansion of the 1970s and subsequent restructuring are discussed in Hector (1988) and Johnston (1990).
68 Tom Clausen, who also was chairman from 1970 until 1981, engineering the growth strategy of the 1970s.
69 This was Bank of America's first foreign subsidiary with the purchase of Banca d'America e d'Italia in 1957. It had set up a London branch in 1931 (Brützel, 1981, p. 44).
70 Palmer, G. (October 31, 1994). Back On Top. *The Banker*, pp. 31–4.
71 Profile of BankAmerica Corporation (n.d.). Retrieved January 1, 2003, from www.hoovers.com.
72 Hoare Govett, after a failed management buy out.
73 Hylton, R. (March 21, 1994). BankAmerica: Go where the money is. *Fortune*, p. 70.
74 *Bank of America Corporation* (n.d.). Retrieved October 12, 1999, from Hoover's Inc, Bloomberg.
75 USA: Bank consolidation gathers pace – banking mergers. (April 14, 1998). *Financial Times*, p. 26.
76 *Bank of America Corporation* (n.d.). Retrieved October 12, 1999, from Hoover's Inc, Bloomberg.
77 ABN AMRO in Asian deal. (May 20, 1999). *Financial Times*, p. 32.
78 Bank of America to build European arm. (March 23, 1999). *Financial Times*, p. 35.
79 Which was later acquired by Barclays.
80 Lloyds Bank acquired the First State Bank in California when a change in the Bank Holding Company Act forced the owner to divest the bank, and no potential domestic buyer could pass the standards of the anti-trust law (Johnston, 1977, p. 77). Other similar cases are the purchase of the branches of Franklin National Bank by European American Bank (owned by EBIC), and the purchase of LaSalle Bank by ABN in 1979.
81 Sweet defeat (June 13, 1992). *The Economist*, p. 74.
82 Booth, T. (December 1999). Searching for the perfect partner. *Institutional Investor*, pp. 35–44.
83 Brown-Humes, C. (June 24, 1999). A marriage of convenience. *Financial Times*, p. 15.
84 Peter Ellwood, Lloyds TSB chief executive, observed in 1999 that only 4% of Lloyds TSB banking customers also bought its insurance products. Although this offered considerable room for improvement, it could also indicate that selling insurance products through bank branches remained difficult. *Source*: Graham, G. (June 24, 1999). Revenue forms the main ingredient in the Lloyds recipe. *Financial Times*, p. 24.
85 Saigol, L. & Willman, J. (December 13, 2000). Abbey rejects revised offer from Lloyds. *Financial Times*, p.19.
86 Annual report Lloyds TSB, 2003, page 7.

87 See for example an interview with Lloyds TSB CEO Peter Ellwood and chair-
    man Brian Pitman (Tanzin, B. [December 1999]. Searching for the perfect
    partner. *Institutional Investor*, pp. 35–59) or the interview with chairman van
    den Bergh (Gunther, R. & Schipper, J. [Maart 2002]. Big Blijft Beautiful.
    Bank- en Effectenbedrijf, pp. 6–11).
88 Lewis, V. (July 1980). France's nationalized banks – a whiff of reprivatization.
    The Banker, pp. 43–8.
89 Crédit Lyonnais over the years (n.d.). Retrieved on April 17, 2003, from
    www.credit-lyonnais.com.
90 Crédit Lyonnais over the years (n.d.). Retrieved April 17, 2003, from
    www.credit-lyonnais.com.
91 Equity Research: French Banks (September 28, 2000). *Credit Suisse First
    Boston*, pp. 130–1.
92 Midland (1981). *Annual Report 1980*, p. 6.
93 By the end of 1976, Barclays held 1,715 branches and offices outside the
    United Kingdom, Lloyds 501, National Westminster 27 and Midland 14,
    although the EBIC joint ventures and offices of subsidiary companies of
    Midland are not incorporated in that number. *Source*: Pringle, R. (August
    1997). The British four stake their claim. *The Banker*, pp. 113–21.
94 Midland (1981). *Annual report 1980*, p. 6.
95 The bank was sold at a 1 billion US dollar loss, but Midland also had to
    transfer 3.7 billion US dollars of Crocker's bad loans to its own balance
    sheet.
96 Midland (1989). *20-F filing 1988*, p. 5.

Chapter 7   Performance and Shareholder Wealth

1 The following paragraph about the shape of internationalization is based on
   Ruigrok & Wagner (2003).
2 Introduced by Gordon (1962), discussed in Reilly & Brown (2000,
   pp. 448–52).
3 This is the required rate of return as formulated by the Asset Pricing Theory
   (APT). It can also be determined by its predecessor, the Capital Asset Pricing
   Model (CAPM). This model is more restrictive however, allowing only the
   Beta as a firm specific factor.
4 This explanation is partly included in the small home market incentive: due
   to a small home market, growth opportunities and opportunities to exploit
   economies are limited decreasing profitability and increasing the incentive
   to internationalize.
5 For 1980–85 and 1987 significance is below a 0.05 level.

Chapter 8   The Competitive Future of Internationalization Strategies

1 The realized *Imploding* internationalization strategies are ignored here, this
   strategic type applies to only two banks and is therefore difficult to generalize.
2 Notwithstanding the statement of Breuer, CEO of Deutsche Bank, in 2002
   that Deutsche Bank would continue to expand its global mergers and acqui-

sitions activities. (cf. Breuer, R.E. (January 31, 2002). *Annual Press Conference.* Frankfurt: Deutsche Bank).

3 Levitt, J. (October 8, 2003). How to make gains in Spain. In Special Report: Banking in Europe. *Financial Times*, p. 3.
4 Croft, J. & Reed, J. 2004, Barclays in talks over taking E3bn Absa stake, *Financial Times*, September 24, 2004, p. 15
5 Laitner, S. January 31, 2005, Fortis looks to expand in Benelux and central Europa, *Financial Times*, p. 22.

References

Aliber, R.Z. 1984. "International banking". *Journal of Money, Credit and Banking*, 16(4): 661–78.

Anderson, E. & Gatignon, H. 1999. "Modes of foreign entry: a transaction cost analysis and propositions". In Buckley, P.J. & Ghauri, P.N. (eds) *The internationalization of the firm*. London: International Thomson Business Press.

Arora, D. 1995. *Japanese financial institutions in Europe*. Amsterdam: Elsevier Science.

Authers, J. (1998, May 5). USA: Big may not be so beautiful – consolidation in US banking has acquired its own momentum, but some doubt the underlying logic. *Financial Times*.

Ayadi, R. & Pujals, G. 2004. Banking Mergers and Acquisitions in the EU: Overview, Assessment and Prospects, *SUERF Studies 2005/3*. Vienna: Société Universitaire Européenne de Recherches Financières.

Bank for International Settlements. 2000. Guide to the international banking statistics.

Barnet, R.J. & Cavanagh, J. 1994. *Global dreams: imperial corporations and the new world order*. New York: Simon & Schuster.

Beck, T., Demirgüç-Kunt, A., Levine, R. & Maksimovic, V. 2001. "Bank based and Market based Financial Systems: Cross Country Comparisons". In Demirgüç-Kunt, A. & Levine, R. (eds) *Financial Structure and Economic Growth*. Cambridge, Massachusetts: The MIT Press.

Behm, U. 1994. *Shareholder-Value und Eigenkapitalkosten von Banken*. Stuttgart: Verlag Paul Haupt Bern.

Berger, A.N., DeYoung, R., Genay, H. & Udell, G.F. 2000. *Globalization of financial institutions: evidence from cross-border banking performance*. Washington: Federal Reserve Board.

Berger, A.N. & Mester, L.J. 1999. *What explains the dramatic changes in cost and profit performance of the US banking industry?* Washington, DC: Federal Reserve Board.

Bikhchandani, S. & Sharma, S. 2000. Herd Behavior in Financial Markets: A Review, IMF Working Paper WP/00/48. Washington, DC: International Monetary Fund.

Blandon, J.G. 1998. The choice of the form of representation in multinational banking: evidence from Spain, Working Paper Ref. 271. Barcelona: Universitat Pompeu Fabra, Department of Economics and Business.

Bongini, P. 2003. The EU Experience in Financial Services Liberalization: A Model for GATS Negotiations?, *SUERF Studies 2003/2*. Vienna: SUERF, Société Universitaire Européenne de Recherches Financières.

Born, K.E. 1983. *International banking in the 19th and 20th centuries [Geld und Banken im 19. und 20. Jahrhundert]*. Warwickshire: Berg Publishers Ltd.

Braithwaite, J. & Drahos, P. 2000. *Global Business Regulation*. Cambridge: Cambridge University Press.

Brützel, C. 1981. International Banking Activities in the Eighties. Paper presented at the VI. International Banking Seminar of AIESEC, Frankfurt.

Bryant, R.C. 1987. *International financial intermediation*. Washington, DC: The Brookings Institution.

Buch, C.M. & DeLong, G.L. 2001. Cross-Border Bank Mergers: What Lures the Rare Animal? Kiel Working Paper No. 1070. Kiel: Kiel Institute of World Economics.

Buch, C.M., Driscoll, J.C. & Østergaard, C. 2004. Cross-Border Diversification in Bank Asset Portfolios, Working Paper Ano 2004/11. Oslo: Norges Bank.

Burgers, I.J.J. 1991. Taxation and Supervision of Branches of International Banks: IBFD Publications.

Canals, J. 1993. *Competitive strategies in European banking*. Oxford: Clarendon Press.

Canals, J. 1997. *Universal banking*. Oxford: Oxford University Press.

Carrington, M., Langguth, P. & Steiner, T. 1997. *The banking revolution: salvation or slaughter?* London: Pitman Publishing Ltd.

Casson, M. 1990. "Evolution of multinational banks: a theoretical perspective". In Jones, G. (ed.) *Banks as multinationals*. London: Routledge.

Channon, D.F. 1977. *British banking strategy and the international challenge*. London: Macmillan Press Ltd.

Channon, D.F. 1988. *Global banking strategy*. New York: John Wiley & Sons.

Chernow, R. 1990. *The House of Morgan*. New York: Simon & Schuster.

Cho, K.R. 1985. *Multinational banks: their identities and determinants*. Ann Arbor, Michigan: UMI Research Press.

Chrystal, K.A. & Coughlin, C.C. 1992. How the 1992 Legislation Will Affect European Financial Services. *Review – Federal Reserve Bank of St. Louis*, 74(2): 62–80.

Coleman, W.D. 2001. "Governing French banking: regulatory reform and the Crédit Lyonnais fiasco". In Bovens, M., Hart, P.T., Peters, B.G. & Parsons, W. (eds) *Success and failure in public governance. New horizons in public policy*. Cheltenham: Edward Elgar.

Corrigan, T. (1998, April 9). USA: Pair looks at options on banking side – synergies. *Financial Times*.

Curry, E.A., Fung, J.G. & Harper, I.R. 2003. "Multinational banking: historical, empirical and case perspectives". In Mullineux, A.W. & Murinde, V. (eds) *Handbook of International Banking*. Cheltenham, UK: Edward Elgar.

Dalsgaard, T., Elmeskov, J. & Park, C.-Y. 2002. *Ongoing changes in the business cycle – evidence and causes*. Vienna: SUERF.

Danthine, J.-P. 2000. *Banking: Is Bigger Really Better?* Ecole des HEC, University of Lausanne, CEPR and FAME.

Davies, M., Arnold, G., Cornelius, I. & Stephen Walmsley, S. 2000. *Managing for Shareholdervalue*. London: Informa Publishing Group Ltd.

Davis, E. 1995. *Debt, Financial Fragility, and Systemic Risk*. Oxford: Oxford University Press.

Davis, E.P. & Salo, S. 1998. Indicators of potential excess capacity in EU and US banking sectors. Paper presented at SUERF conference, Frankfurt.

De Bandt, O. & Hartmann, P. 2000. Systemic risk: a survey. Working Paper Series no. 35. Frankfurt: European Central Bank.

De Boer, S. & Graafsma, C. 2002. *De andere bank*. Utrecht: Rabobank Nederland.

De Bondt, G.J. 1998. Financial structure: theories and stylized facts for six EU countries. *De Economist*, 146(2): 271–301.

De Carmoy, H. 1990. *Global banking strategy.* Cambridge: Basil Blackwell.
De Nicoló, G., Bartholomew, P., Zaman, J. & Zephirin, M. 2004. Bank Consolidation, Internationalization, and Conglomeration: Trends and Implications for Financial Risk. IMF Working Paper no. WP/03/158. Washington, DC: International Monetary Fund.
De Paula, L.F. 2002. *Banking Internationalisation and the Expansion Strategies of European Banks to Brazil during the 1990s.* Vienna: Societe Universitaire Europeenne de Recherches Financieres.
Demirgüç-Kunt, A. & Huizinga, H. 2001. Financial Structure and Bank Profitability. In Demirgüç-Kunt, A. & Levine, R. (eds) *Financial Structure and Economic Growth.* Cambridge, Massachusetts: The MIT Press.
Demirgüç-Kunt, A. & Levine, R. 2001. "Bank based and Market based Financial Systems: Cross Country Comparisons". In Demirgüç-Kunt, A. & Levine, R. (eds) *Financial Structure and Economic Growth.* Cambridge, Massachusetts: The MIT Press.
Dicken, P. 1998. *Global Shift,* 2nd edn. London: Paul Chapman Publishing Ltd.
Dietsch, M. & Weill, L. 1998. Banking efficiency and European integration: productivity, cost and profit approaches. Paper presented at SUERF Conference, Frankfurt.
Dunning, J.H. 1992. *Multinational enterprises and the global economy.* Wokingham, England: Addison-Wesley Publishers Ltd.
Ediz, T., Michael, I. & Perraudin, W. 1998. The Impact of Capital Requirements on U.K. Bank Behaviour. *FRBNY Economic Policy Review* (October 1998): 15–21.
Eichengreen, B. 1996. *Globalizing capital.* Leuven (Belgium): Leuven University Press.
European Central Bank. 2000a. *EU Banks' income structure.* Frankfurt: European Central Bank.
European Central Bank. 2000b. Mergers and acquisitions involving the EU banking industry – Facts and implications, *ECB Monthly Bulletin,* April. Frankfurt.
Federal Deposit Insurance Corporation. 1997. An examination of the banking crises of the 1980s and early 1990s.
Fleming, S. 1999. *Disarming bank credit risk.* Institutional Investor, August, 29–34.
Fujita, M. & Ishigaki, K. 1986. "Internationalisation of Japanese commercial banking". In Taylor, M. & Thrift, N. (eds) *Multinationals and the restructuring of the world economy.* London: Croom Helm.
Gall, L., Feldman, G.D., James, H., Holtfrerich, C.-L. & Büschgen, H.E. 1995. *The Deutsche Bank 1870–1995.* London: Weidenfeld & Nicolson.
Goldberg, L.S. 2001. *When is U.S. bank lending to emerging markets volatile?* New York: Federal Reserve Bank of New York.
Goldberg, L.G. & Saunders, A. 1981. The determinants of foreign banking activity in the United States. *Journal of Banking and Finance,* 5: 17–32.
Goldsmith, R.W. 1969. *Financial structure and development.* New Haven: Yale University Press.
Gordon, M. J. 1962. The Investment, Financing, and Valuation of the Corporation. Homewood, Illinois: Irwin.
Gray, J.M. & Gray, H.P. 1981. The multinational bank: a financial MNC? *Journal of Banking and Finance,* 5: 33–63.
Group of Ten. January 2001. *Report on Consolidation in the Financial Sector.* Basle: Bank of International Settlements.

Healy, P.M., Palepu, K.G. & Ruback, R.S. 1992. Does corporate performance improve after mergers? *Journal of Financial Economics*, 31: 135–75.

Hector, G. 1998. Breaking the Bank. Boston: Little, Brown and Company.

Heinkel, R., and Levi, M. 1992. The structure of international banking. *Journal of International Money and Finance*, 11, 251–72.

Hindle, T. 1980. Sizing up the retail market. *The Banker*, 111–19.

International Monetary Fund. 1998. *World Economic Outlook*, May 1998. Washington, DC: International Monetary Fund.

Johnston, R. A. 1977. California's competitive banking. *The Banker*, 69–78.

Johnston, M. 1990. Roller Coaster. New York: Ticknor & Fields.

Jones, G. 1993. *British multinational banking*. Oxford: Clarendon Press.

Kaminsky, G.L. & Reinhardt, C.M. 1998. *The Leading Indicators of Currency Crises. Staff Papers*. Washington, DC: International Monetary Fund.

Kanaya, A. & Woo, D. 2000. *The Japanese banking crisis of the 1990s: sources and lessons*. Washington, DC: International Monetary Fund.

Karacadag, C. & Taylor, M.W. (2000). *The New Capital Adequacy Framework*. Vienna: SUERF, Société Universitaire Européenne de Recherches Financières.

Kindleberger, C.P. 1974. *The formation of financial centers: a study in comparative economic history*. New Jersey: Princeton University Press.

Levine, R. 2002. *Bank Based or Market Based Financial Systems: Which is Better?* Minneapolis: Department of Finance, Carlson School of Management, University of Minnesota.

Lins, K. & Servaes, H. 1999. International evidence on the value of corporate diversification. *The Journal of Finance*, LIV(6): 2215–39.

Llewellyn, D.T. 1999. *The new economics of banking*. Amsterdam: Societe Universitaire Europeenne de Recherches Financieres.

Llewellyn, D.T. 2005. Competition and Profitability in European Banking: Why Are British Banks So Profitable? *Economic Notes*, 34(3): 279–311.

Marois, B. 1997. French Banks and European Strategy. *European Management Journal*, 15(2): 183–9.

McDonald, O. & Keasey, K. 2002. *The Future of Retail Banking in Europe*. Chichester: John Wiley & Sons Ltd.

McQuerry, E. 2001. *Banking on it: increased foreign bank entry into Brazil*. Federal Reserve Bank of Atlanta.

Merrett, D.T. 2002. The internationalization of Australian banks. *Journal of International Financial Markets*, 12: 377–97.

Mintzberg, H., Quinn, J.B. & Ghoshal, S. 1995. *The strategy process*, European edn. Hemel Hempstead: Prentice Hall International (UK) Limited.

Molyneux, P. 2003. "Determinants of Cross-Border Mergers in European Banking". In Herman, H. & Lipsey, R. (eds) *Foreign Direct Investment in the Real and Financial Sector of Industrialised Countries*. Berlin: Springer Verlag.

Morgan Stanley Dean Witter (2000, May 9). *UK Banks, Turbulence Ahead*. Equity Research Europe.

Morris, J. 1987. The Internationalisation of Banking, Technological Change and Spatial Patterns: a Case Study in South Wales. *Geoforum*, 18(3): 257–67.

Mullineux, A.W. & Murinde, V. 2003. Globalization and convergence of banking systems. In Mullineux, A.W. & Murinde, V. (eds) *Handbook of International Banking*. Cheltenham, UK: Edward Elgar.

Nilsson, J.E., Dicken, P. & Peck, J. 1996. *The internationalization process: European firms in global competition*. London: Paul Chapman Publishing Ltd.

Nolle, D.E. 1995. "Foreign bank operations in the United States: cause for concern?" In Gray, H.P. & Richard, S.C. (eds) *International finance in the new world order*. Oxford: Elsevier Science Ltd.

OECD. 1998. *OECD Economic Surveys 1997–1998 Japan*. Paris: OECD.

Pecchioli, R.M. 1983. *The internationalisation of banking*. Paris: OECD.

Peek, J., Rosengren, E.S. & Kasirye, F. 1999. The poor performance of foreign bank subsidiaries: were the problems acquired or created? *Journal of Banking and Finance*, 23: 579–604.

Pilloff, S.J. & Santomero, A.M. 1998. "The value effects of bank mergers and acquisitions". In Amihud, Y. & Miller, G. (eds) *Bank mergers & acquisitions. The New York University Salomon Series on Financial Markets and Institutions*. Dordrecht: Kluwer Academic Publishers.

Pohl, M. & Freitag, S. 1994. *Handbook on the history of European banks*. Aldershot: Edward Elgar Publishing Ltd.

Porter, M.E. 1985. *Competitive advantage*. New York: The Free Press.

Pyle, D.H. 1971. On The Theory of Financial Intermediation. *Journal of Finance*, Vol. 26, No. 3, 737–47.

Reilly, F.K. & Brown, K.C. 2000. *Investment Analysis and Portfolio Management*, 6th edn. Fort Worth: The Dryden Press, Harcourt College Publishers.

Roberts, R. & Arnander, C. 2001. *Take your partners*. Houndmills: Palgrave.

Robinson, S.W. 1972. *Multinational banking*. Leiden: A.W. Sijthoff.

Rogers, D. 1993. *The Future of American Banking*. New York: McGraw-Hill, Inc.

Rogers, D. 1999. *The big four British banks*. London: Macmillan Press Ltd.

Rugman, A.M. 1976. Risk reduction by international diversification. *Journal of International Business Studies*, 7(2): 75–80.

Ruigrok, W. & van Tulder, R. 1995. *The logic of international restructuring*. London: Routledge.

Ruigrok, W. & Wagner, H. 2003. Internationalization and firm performance: Meta-analytic review and future research directions. Presented at the External Seminar Series Tjalling C. Koopmans Institute, December 2, 2003. St. Gallen: Research Institute for International Management, University of St. Gallen.

Schmidt, R.H., Hackethal, A. & Marcel Tyrell, M. 1998. *Disintermediation and the role of banks in Europe: an international comparison*. Frankfurt: Johann Wolfgang Goethe-Universität.

Scholtens, L.J.R. 1991. *Towards a theory of international financial intermediation*. Amsterdam: University of Amsterdam.

Scholtens, L.J.R. 1996. Ontwikkeling en structuur van financiële systemen. *Financiële en monetaire studies*, 15(2): 7–74.

Sebastian, M. & Hernansanz, C. 2000. *The Spanish Banks' Strategy in Latin America*. Vienna: Societe Universitaire Europeenne de Recherches Financieres.

Shapiro, A.C. 1985. Currency risk and country risk in international banking. *The Journal of Finance*, XL(3): 881–93.

Shaw, R. 1979. London as a Financial Center. In Frowen, Stephen F. (ed.) *A Framework of International Banking*. Guildford: Guildford Educational Press.

Silverman, G. 2000. Citigroup in $31bn deal for US finance company, *Financial Times*.

Sirower, M.L. 1997. *The Synergy Trap: How Companies Lose the Acquisition Game*. New York: The Free Press.

Sluyterman, K., Dankers, J., van der Linden, J. & van Zanden, J.L. 1998. *Het coöperatieve alternatief*. Honderd jaar Rabobank 1898–1998.

Smith, R.C. & Walter, I. 1990. *Global Financial Services.* New York: Harper Business.

Smith, R.C. & Walter, I. 1997. *Global banking.* New York: Oxford University Press.

State of New York Banking Department. 1999. Foreign Banks in New York.

Stulz, R.M. 2005. The Limits of Financial Globalization, Working Paper 11070. Cambridge, MA: National Bureau of Economic Research.

Sullivan, D. 1994. Measuring the degree of internationalization of a firm. *Journal of International Business Studies,* (2): 325–42.

Swann, C. 2000. Foreign exchange banks charge into online battle, *Financial Times.*

Ter Wengel, J. 1995. International trade in banking services. *Journal of International Money and Finance,* 14(1), 47–64.

The Economist. 1992. Time to leave: a survey of world banking.

Tschoegl, A.E. 2000. *Foreign banks in the United States since World War II.* The Warton School, University of Pennsylvania.

Tschoegl, A.E. 2002. Entry and survival: the case of foreign banks in Norway. *Scandinavian Journal of Management,* 18: 131–53.

United Nations Center on Transnational Corporations. 1991. *Transnational banks and the international debt crisis.* New York: United Nations.

United Nations Conference on Trade and Development. 1998. *World Investment Report, 1998: Trends and Developments.* Geneva: United Nations.

Ursacki, T. & Vertinsky, I. 1992. Choice of entry timing and scale by foreign banks in Japan and Korea. *Journal of Banking and Finance,* 16: 405–21.

Van Dijcke, P. 2002. European financial cross-border consolidation. *Revue Bancaire et Financière* (December 2002).

Van Dijcke, P. 2001. "Impact of globalization on efficiency in the European banking industry". In Balling, M., Hochreiter, E.H. & Hennessy, E. (eds) *Adapting to financial globalisation.* London: Routledge.

Van Eerden, L.A. (forthcoming) PhD Thesis.

Van Tulder, R., van den Berghe, D. & Muller, A. 2001. *The World's Largest Firms and Internationalization.* Rotterdam: Rotterdam School of Management/ Erasmus University Rotterdam.

Wagster, J.D. 1996. Impact of the 1988 Basle accord on international banks. *The Journal of Finance,* LI(4): 1321–46.

Walter, I. & Smith, R.C. 2000. *High finance in the Euro-zone.* London: Pearson Education Limited.

Walter, I. 1988. *Global competition in financial services.* Cambridge, Massachusetts: Ballinger Publishing Company.

Walter, I. & Gray, H.P. 1983. Protectionism and international banking. *Journal of Banking and Finance,* 7: 597–609.

Wolffe, R. & Waters, R. 1998. USA: Pressure builds for change in law, *Financial Times.*

Zimmer, S.A. & McCauley, R.N. 1991. Bank Cost of Capital and International Competition. *Federal Reserve Bank of New York Quarterly Review,* 15 (Winter 1991): 33–59.

Index